STRAY

Laurie Owens
and
Milo Johnson

"The most beautiful goal was a pass."

JEAN-CLAUDE MICHÉA

Thanks to

Milo wishes to thank Stanley Johnson, Dionne Johnson, Bunny Reds, Joy Maloney and Duncan Murison for sharing their memories.

Laurie wishes to thank Lizzy Kremer for choosing to work on this story and for her precious guidance. Orli Vogt-Vincent for her kind help and her encouragement. Richard Jones for believing that this should be a book. Claudia Ascott, Laura Heyman, Charlotte Green and Cécile Brochard for their time and thoughts. My children for everything.

Milo Johnson, for trusting me with his story.

Thanks to Robert Del Naja for permission to reproduce lyrics.

Tangent Books

First published 2024 by Tangent Books

Tangent Books
Unit 5.16 Paintworks, Bristol BS4 3EH
www.tangentbooks.co.uk
richard@tangentbooks.co.uk

ISBN 978-1-914345-33-3

Authors: Laurie Owens and Milo Johnson

Design: Joe Burt, Wildspark Design

Cover Design: Talita Owens Heshiimu

Cover Photograph: Shintoki Hiko. Fukuoka, Japan, 1986

Production: Jonathan Wright, Richard Jones

Copyright: Tangent Books

Laurie Owens and Milo Johnson have asserted their right under the Copyright, Designs and Patents Act of 1988 to be identified as the authors of this work. This book may not be reproduced or transmitted in any form or by any means without the prior written consent of the publisher, except by a reviewer who wishes to quote brief passages in connection with a review written in a newspaper or magazine or broadcast on television, radio or on the internet.

A CIP record of this book is available at the British Library.

Printed by Gomer in Wales on paper from a sustainable source

Contents

Chapter One: Long Time Gone — 11

Chapter Two: The Nature of Things — 17

Chapter Three: Can We Pretend? — 25

Chapter Four: Light On The Path — 31

Chapter Five: Free As The Morning Sun — 37

Chapter Six: The Rain Before It Falls — 43

Chapter Seven: Throw Back The Little Ones — 51

Chapter Eight: Giving In Gently — 57

Chapter Nine: Across The Tracks — 63

Chapter Ten: Everyone's Gone to the Movies — 71

Chapter Eleven: Let Your Learning Be Your Eyes — 77

Chapter Twelve: Are You All The Things — 85

Chapter Thirteen: No Easy Way Down — 93

Chapter Fourteen: Haven't Got Time For Pain — 99

Chapter Fifteen: If I Find The Way — 105

Chapter Sixteen: Sailing Ships — 113

Chapter Seventeen: As The World Turns — 117

Chapter Eighteen: Stolen Moments — 123

CHAPTER NINETEEN: Time Out Of Mind	131
CHAPTER TWENTY: How Many Broken Wings	137
CHAPTER TWENTY-ONE: There's A World	143
CHAPTER TWENTY-TWO: Gold In My Ear	153
CHAPTER TWENTY-THREE: Nothing Will Be As It Was	159
CHAPTER TWENTY-FOUR: Rivers Of My Fathers	167
CHAPTER TWENTY-FIVE: Feet First	173
CHAPTER TWENTY-SIX: Something's Wrong	181
CHAPTER TWENTY-SEVEN: Little Green	187
CHAPTER TWENTY-EIGHT: Searching For The Right Door	195
CHAPTER TWENTY-NINE: Forest Of Feelings	199
CHAPTER THIRTY: Them Changes	207
CHAPTER THIRTY-ONE: Don't Stop To Watch The Wheels	213
CHAPTER THIRTY-TWO: Till Loves Touches Your Life	219
CHAPTER THIRTY-THREE: Too Real To Live A Lie	223
CHAPTER THIRTY-FOUR: The Silence That You Keep	233
CHAPTER THIRTY-FIVE: Nature Boy	241

FIRST WORD

This book started as a letter to you, my children.

I love you all very much, but the things I experienced early in my life have been an obstacle to my growth and my fathering. As I reached my fifties it became a priority to explain who I am to you. Not just the hard times, but the positives of my past too – including the things that I did not understand the significance of when I was in the moment and which I took for granted.

The idea of reconnecting with the past is a constant theme throughout the lectures and writings of the Black historians I have studied. The importance of faith and family in America was something that was foreign to me before moving to New York, but over time I better understood why the church and the family unit have such meaning within the Black community in America. Figuring out that my detachment from any familial ties is not just abnormal, but detrimental to you my children who continue along that blood line, is something I finally came to see and that's when I started to write down my memories in this letter to you.

It was a difficult story to piece together. There are hardly any photographs of my youth, no objects and no childhood home. I tried to remember as much as I could and when I couldn't remember, I'd speak with my sister, my stepdad or old friends of my mother who were still around. It was a great relief to open all the windows and let light reveal what was in the dark corners of my past.

What helped me too were the friendships I made with veterans of the Black music industry, the long talks with them over three decades. What at first looked like coincidences and mere similarities, I now see to be patterns in our collective experience as Black people outside of Africa. The number of things that I heard that linked to my own experience were just too numerous to ignore.

By my early fifties, I was making music and I was writing down page upon page of random memories. I was living in Harlem and I could see changes in the New York City I had fallen in love with coming. Then, when I was quite contentedly single, a woman from my past showed up in the city. What seemed just a happy reconnection with an old girlfriend would turn into a second romance and marriage. Having so many similarities and experiences gave us a simple, natural understanding of each other. It turned out that she could write. She said one day, "Okay, give me what you've written, I'll help you if I can." Neither of us knew then exactly what we were getting ourselves into. But Laurie, my wife, has been a gift to me. I know she quietly understood that my peace of my mind was hanging on you, my children, being able to fathom me. She carried on writing, even when it was painful to do, which it sometimes was – for both us.

When I started writing notes seven years ago, I had only you in mind as my readers. As my story began to unfold, page after page, it seemed as if there might be something in these writings that could be beneficial to people other than you, one that was beyond me, about life's struggle and what can get you through.

My backstory marked me for failure. But something made me turn my life around and thrive, even if I lost things along the way. And mine is a story with a fascinating cast. There are the famous people I made my journey with, but just as important are the friends of misfortune: the children from the ghetto, the children in care, the punks and football hooligans, the inmates and then the everyday folk of America and, more especially, Harlem. My nomadic life led me from Bristol and London to Japan and then the heart of African America. On this journey, I have redeemed my mixed-heritage identity.

This is my thank-you letter to those like me I met along the way and to music, which has served as a set of wings to me and many Black men like me, here and gone.

I hope that you might find your piece of our puzzle here, but I also hope that any child, any outcast, any stray, might find a little help in my experience.

Milo Johnson, 2024

Chapter One

LONG TIME GONE

Bristol, 2019

It's an October day of quiet constant rain and a dimmed-down sun. It's a Tuesday. Milo is at Bunny Reds'. He has come with his sister Juliette, bringing her as a facilitator. Although they were both close to Bunny as children, only Juliette has stayed in Bristol, keeping the paths back to the remaining people from their childhood clear. What's coming, the reason for their visit, will be dropped informally, but is charged with meaning. Milo and Juliette have the same mother, Betty. They don't have the same father. Bunny knew Betty, he knew Milo's father, he knew Juliette's father too. He has this knowledge over Milo and this is what Milo wants – to shake the tree of memory. Milo has an oblique line struck through the box on his birth certificate that should carry a father's name. He needs to find his father. If he and Juliette wait in the right way, are ready in the right way, then perhaps Bunny will speak freely – the lapsed time, the fifties, the beginnings – might come into this room. Milo hopes to catch a clue about his father, a man named Charlie Mackenzie. He hopes for a sketch of him as if drawn on tracing paper that he can place over his own partial picture of Charlie, so that the two might square and form a more complete outline of this man.

Bunny hasn't changed except that the heavy dreads he lifts over his forearm and throws back behind his shoulder are now almost entirely woven with pale silver. Bunny rests on the sofa surrounded by his things. His things belong to music, rather than belonging to him. As a dread – a dub poet and musician – he has gone through his life immersed in reggae music. He owns mostly music and the tools to make music. An imposing keyboard stands ready as an ironing board and everywhere you look there are stacks of reggae vinyls and boxes of CDs. He lies on the sofa in his now frail body, guarded on all sides by a fortress of songs. So many spliffs have been smoked within these walls that the permeating smell of weed, that instant musky hit and lingering pine needle scent, is as much a part of the rooms as is their colour.

What Milo knows about Charlie amounts to very little: that he was tall, bald and probably gay. That maybe he could dance. That he was Jamaican. He knows that Charlie was his mother's first love. He believes he was Charlie's only child. He thinks Charlie came out some time in the eighties and had a lover, a cab driver, with whom he lived until he died. It's mostly hearsay. Or fragments of adult conversation, words that have stayed with Milo, to the left and to the right of that important name, Charlie.

He and Juliette have pieced together their own idea of Charlie: that he left their ghetto and moved on, moved upwards. They think he was a quiet man, who was a discreet part of the community before disappearing. Milo remembers that Charlie was elegant, that he was dressed for a different life, a genteel one. He thinks that being gay must have been impossible to live out, in the ghetto. That this was maybe why he left. They imagine Charlie as working in a post office, diligent, or maybe in a bank, but definitely in an office, hidden, wearing a quiet, dark suit, his head bowed. This is what Milo has about his father, this small envelope of facts and then these stretches of imagination. He wants to find the cabbie. He wants to find out something more, anything more, about Charlie.

He watches Juliette and Bunny, they are both laughing. Bunny has his own music on, his dub poetry. He is an easy man to listen to, unhurried, careful with his words. Milo knows how much of the Black Bristol community Bunny carries inside, he is a living repository of the ghetto's past. He could draw a sequence diagram catching most of the present-day Black families in Bristol and interconnect them all, before bringing all the family threads back to the seedling Black populace of the 1950s. Also, crucially, there is the fact that Bunny knew both Milo's mother and his father and there are not so many elders around anymore who carry such a precious sesame. Milo sits very still, very upright. He respects Bunny's intellect and, perhaps even more so, Bunny's integrity. Bunny has been in Milo's life as far back as he can recall. The questions about his father have been forming in Milo's mind for years, but making that move, coming right out and asking about Charlie was something that he had never been quite ready to do. Juliette says, "Shall I make you something to eat, Bunny?"

"No, I'm all right."

"Bunny?" asks Milo, "You knew Charlie quite well, didn't you?" It's out there. Bunny looks at Milo harder, moves his head a little as if he needs to hear again.

"Milo's trying to find out about his dad, aren't you, Mi? 'Cause he doesn't know anything much, do you? You remember him, Bunny? You knew him, he was your crew, wasn't he?" asks Juliette.

"That's right. I knew Charlie." His voice is gentle. "Yeah man. I knew him good. We all used to go round his place and listen to jazz, you know?"

Milo smiles, "That makes sense. I heard he was a dancer?" It's a question, and it isn't. This, as one of just a few truths about his father that Milo carries with him, needs checking out. How this small fact being wrong might feel to him, how that might hurt, is unclear.

"He could dance all right. We called him 'Pretty Foot.'" Bunny is smiling, easy, and Milo's face breaks into a smile as well. "He loved his jazz music, knew everything, every tune. A bunch of us used to go round there all the time, to his place by West Grove. Just listen to jazz, you know. Smoke weed."

"He was really good looking, wasn't he?" asks Juliette, "The best-looking man in Bristol, it's what they said." Milo looks at his sister, a hard stare, then says, in a neutral voice, "I know he was gay."

There is a definite break in tempo, it seems to shift just as Bunny rightens himself on the sofa, turning more fully towards Milo, looking at him squarely. Milo smiles. "It's OK, man. I want to know. I only saw the dude a few times. He died, he died before I got to speak with him."

Bunny settles back down on the sofa, watching the ceiling. His hair, the locks, move with him, they fall in long lines, on to the rug. They look like brush strokes.

"Let me see. He was gay, that's right. It was a surprising thing, you know. Just all of a sudden, like that, he was with this guy. He was a Black guy."

"That was something, wasn't it, coming out in the community in the eighties? So did they move away?" asks Milo.

"They nuh move nowhere," Bunny shakes his head, he's laughing to himself, "not Charlie. They would walk through town holding hands, seen?" If Milo is shocked, he doesn't show it, he just nods his head. Bunny turns to him, "Him and his man used to dress up the same. Wear like matching outfits an' ting," Milo runs his hand over his mouth then says,

"Ain't that something? So what was his job?"

"Weed."

"What do you mean?"

"He was a dealer. Dealt weed."

After a while, Milo and Juliette leave. They get into the car in silence. They sit saying nothing, just staring into space. Then Milo looks at his sister and he's smiling. They start laughing, they can't stop, until Milo has tears trickling down his face.

"For fuck's sake, how wrong did we get that? So much for the David Niven of St Paul's."

Bunny doesn't move from the sofa. He can feel Betty's presence. She is here, this woman, this mother. His mind drifts to her, she was something else all right. Smart. Fierce. Sweet. She was damaged.

Stapleton Road, Bristol, 1960

The Bamboo Club in St Paul's was visited more regularly and with more fervour by the community than any church. It was in a basement. You went down a flight of stairs, the smell of curry goat coming from The Orange Grove where you ate, and the rumble of a bassline set the tone. On Friday nights, people let go and danced into the morning hours to reggae and to soul. It was on one of those Fridays, down on the dance floor, that a lean bodied girl was moving with lazy, sexy precision to the music. Charlie stood against a wall, watching her out the corner of his eye. On one side was an aquarium of tropical fish, that cast a ripple of light over two women with beehives and white lipstick, drinking Bacardi.

Charlie was tall, he had an athletic build. He was moving almost imperceptibly to the downbeat of the music, his eye on the dancing girl. Her skin glowed, sorrel brown. She was mixed-race and she was alone. He could see the outline of her long thigh muscles. She had a strong dancer's neck. She was moving drowsily, rocking in her own world, oblivious to the men taking her in. Charlie watched her, waiting. Waiting for her to look at him, like she had the week before. A wild, direct stare that had caught him off guard. He wanted her to look at him again. The lights were dimmed on the small dance floor. People danced, pressed up against each other. Down there, in those rooms, they came together to eat island food and whine to island music, or release their tensions dancing to soul. Down there, the weight of immigrant life was eased.

In the early hours, Charlie left the club. No one really resisted him, this man who was beautiful and strong, who had immediate charm plus the necessary, mysterious barrier between himself and others. He'd had to work hard to get this girl, though. She was an elusive one, he could sense that. He had a woman, a white woman, but she was in jail. He had men, had encounters. He wasn't a predator. His lovers came for him, and he succumbed. This girl was different. He had asked about her. She was a nurse. She was guarded. He felt himself moving in on Betty, without understanding that he had decided nothing. She had seen him first.

Betty climbed the stairs with Charlie behind her, his flat hand on the small of her back. She stopped once to look at him over her shoulder. The September night was still and mild, summer had not quite given up its ghost. Charlie took Betty's elbow and they walked away from the club, passing a stocky man.

"Hey Charlie, weh yuh a seh?" But Charlie kept his eyes straight ahead. The man turned, called after him, "Yuh nah wan fe speak wid me?" Charlie didn't answer, didn't turn. The man smiled like it was a shrug, then put his hands in his pockets and walked away too.

CHAPTER TWO

THE NATURE OF THINGS

St Paul's, Bristol, 1963

Betty's baby boy was on her lap. Her head rested to one side, on her fist. That way she could see round his head, to the television set in the corner. She was engrossed in *Coronation Street*. The baby, a year and a half, was playing with her eyelashes. They curved up, making star shapes. He pushed the upper lashes upwards, concentrating hard, then pressed the lower lashes down. All the while, Betty watched her programme although the baby's hand was in the way most of the time.

She named him Milo, despite her brother Eric telling her it was too soft for a boy. Eric baptised the boy Miles. Betty knew this had more to do with jazz than manliness, but she humoured him, letting the boy be known as Miles. When she was alone with her baby, when she looked right at him, holding his face in her hands, she called him Milo.

Six months before Miles was born, Eric had taken Betty to hear Miles Davis play at The Colston Hall in Bristol. Betty sat upright during the show, listening to the slick quintet, set in velvet light. She smiled as the musicians span their songs, releasing improbable clusters of notes. Eric sat on the edge of his seat, his feet dancing, feeling the music, feeling every language shift. He had a smile on his face.

After the show he took his sister by the arm,

"Come with me," he said, "the guy on the door is my mate, he's going to let me in. We can go and shake hands with Miles, he knows me, Miles does. I'll get his autograph for you." Eric's feet were light as he made it to the stage door.

The jazz man was there, in his dressing room. Betty hung back behind her brother in the doorway, staring openly. Here was a legend, right before her, sat at a dressing table in nifty purple trousers and a silk cravat. A cigarette was caught in the side of that wide, bowed mouth. He contemplated Betty briefly as he smoked. Then his divergent gaze returned to Eric. With a nod of recognition, he told him, "Hey brother, come in. But leave the monkey at the door."

Uncle Eric was the only stable older man in Betty's life, she admired him greatly, she wanted to please him. There was also an internalised racism at that time –1961– there were words that were swallowed, sitting in the pit of the stomach, heavy as stones. Words that it was better for her not to dwell on: she was a young, Black, single mother. She kept her mouth shut, but only for now.

Milo's fingers reached for her lashes again. This was his favourite game of all. The only light in the room, apart from the blinking TV screen, was the dark orange gleam of the street lamp caught in the drawn curtains. Then the boy, bored with the eyelash game, used his mother's wrist and then her knee to manoeuvre to the floor. He busied himself pushing Matchbox cars of poster-paint colours around. Betty's gaze never left the set, which she smiled at as if it were a faraway memory. Later, Andrea the flatmate came home. Andrea had a stiff blonde beehive and a mixed-race son. She had a John Player Special between her teeth. She elbowed the sitting room door open. Betty was in the armchair, sleeping, her long legs crossed at the ankle. Miles was sleeping too, by her stockinged feet. The room was filled with Carole King on TV singing *It Might As Well Rain Until September*.

This piece of his life happened at Oxford Place, just off Stapleton Road. At some point in his infancy, Miles and his mother moved to West Grove, in the neighbourhood of Montpelier, probably driven out because of money worries, or maybe for a man. Juliette was born. Her father was Vaughn. Then, as a family of three, they moved right back to Oxford Place again. Oxford Place was a street of lowly homes, sealed against each other and pebble-dashed grey so that they appeared to be in perpetual shadow. He and his mum lived with Auntie Andrea and Andrea's son, Shane. Andrea's man Jonesy would come round, too. That was the deal, really, his mum hung out with a lot of white women at that time, and those women, all of them, were with Black men.

That house is caught in his mind's eye, a child's eye. There are very few pictures that bear witness to those years. There is one of his mother and her girlfriends. They all have high, seventies hairdos and dresses cropped dizzyingly short. They are tilting back from the camera, the photographer is probably kneeling. There's laughter in the picture and a sense that a night of dancing down the Bamboo Club is just out of view.

That's the way it was, back then. Some of the time. His mother danced, she stood on the kitchen table and danced. People came by, their loud chat battling its way out over the songs. Miles didn't feel the hardship, though this simple life was shot through with a something sombre. As erratic as if running on an ailing heart, the pulse in the house would shift, suddenly. Men would come. He would be left alone, or alone with Juliette. She was a baby, he was four, maybe five. He had to take that baby everywhere he went, all his childhood.

****

There was one afternoon that stretched emptily into the darkening front room. His Mum was upstairs. She'd been upstairs so long. He was hungry, enough to break rules, to open cupboards, to scavenge. He could have gone upstairs, said, "Mum, me and Juliette is starving," but he knew better. She was in bed with a man.

Against the wall, a lumbering glass-fronted cabinet stood as closed as a watchman. On its top-most shelf he could make out the shape of a cereal packet. He climbed on to a dining room chair, standing on tiptoe, his fingers searching blindly until they found the edge of the box. He began knocking at it, trying to move it towards the edge. Juliette the baby girl sat on the floor, looking up at him intently. Then the cabinet lurched forwards, crashing to the floor with a thunder clap and an instant explosion of glass. It knocked Miles aside, but fell on Juliette with all the mightiness of the oak that it once was. There was a moment that felt like a blackout to him, for seconds there was absolute silence and stillness. Then his mother erupted into the room and her screaming hit every surface, its frequency so acute that Miles covered his ears with his hands. The cabinet had capsized covering Juliette so that just her baby legs stuck out, kicking hard. The cabinet must have been lifted. Moved. He has no memory of that. Thinking about it, did some man belt downstairs naked, to hoist this murderous piece of furniture aside? Miles hung back in a corner. Was he more scared for his sister, or for himself? Then he watched his mother kneeling over Juliette, checking every inch of her baby with feverish precision. Juliette lay there, quite docile. She had a cut or two, but nothing more. She was a little miracle. His mother's panic became rage and her rage seemed to swarm around the room with her, as she came and went about the business of Miles's exile, before gathering in one place and veeing down on him like a knife. She dressed him in his donkey jacket and his good trousers, packed some of his things in a small case and sat him on the front doorstep saying, "I hope someone comes to take you. I'm fed up."

These are the words that he remembers. They were probably worse. The door locked behind him. He sat there as the afternoon faded out, swallowed up by the navy night. He sat there as the cold made his hands hurt, as the rectangular lights in the neighbours' front rooms all came on, and then, one by one, vanished.

He sat there until Bunny Reds swung up the garden path, "Hey, Miles. What you doin' out in the dark?" His redeemer picked him up, held him and felt the baby face that was as cold as the night.

St Paul's, Bristol, 1965

Christmas time came. The music charts that year yielded an offering dripping with commercial diamonds. The radio was always on, this was the soundtrack to Christmas. The kitchen was a hub. The smell of cooking laced with sherry lingered, and there was laughter. A lot of laughter. Children were in and out of there, getting fed biscuits, sitting at the table drawing bright green triangular Christmas trees with presents on either side, ribboned cubes neatly coloured in. Betty moved around the kitchen, from the gas stove to the table, glittery as the tinsel, smiling and cracking jokes that had her friends screeching with joy. Men dropped by. Each of the men was somebody's lover, somebody's dad. Miles knew that other little boys had fathers. For example, Miles's cousin Scott had a father, Uncle Eric. Uncle Eric lived in Clifton and the two-mile walk to Eric's home led Miles into a foreign land. Miles was from the ghetto, from St Paul's, which was just a walk from the heart of the city. He would walk out of St Paul's, with his mum and Juliette and they would make their way to Clifton where no one left a disarticulated pram or a crate of empty beer bottles in their front yard. Uncle Eric's wife was English and together they had a son, Miles's cousin Scott, who was pale enough to pass as white. When, at Eric's behest, Miles was sent, aged seven, along with Scott to Pro-Cathedral – an all-white school – Miles's darker skin made Scott come across as positively white by comparison. Miles would say later, half-jokingly, that this was the reason that he'd been drafted in to this Catholic school: so that Scott would never be the blackest one there.

Uncle Eric's story was also Betty's story, of course. Born to an African father and an English, Jewish mother. Persecution twinning in their blood. Uncle Eric told of how his father, who came, he thought, from Free Town, in Sierra Leon, at first sweated out years of his life in a Bristol cotton mill, before opening a general store in Montpelier, Bristol. To the locals, it was only ever known as The Black Man's Shop. He had once beaten a neighbour to the ground because he had called Eric, then a child, a "dirty coon". So, Miles's grandfather, proud, nomadic – whose name wasn't Johnson, of course, whose name was Mbakwe – settled in a place where he was probably the only Black man in a thirty-mile radius. (Betty remembered this name. Mbakwe. Her father died when she was thirteen. She never heard that rhythmic succession of letters after that. She just kept the name like a strange stone you find in a garden as a child, a stone you wrap in a hanky, put in a box, and carry around from home to home for the rest of your life, without ever opening it again.) Uncle Eric lived in a white neighbourhood on a sedate street, even though he was occupying just a few rooms on the top floor with bats in the attic that sometimes shot around the landing in daylight, rooms that had a permanent draft coming through every shut window. But the view from those windows was of an essentially, all-white world.

Miles didn't feel like there was someone missing. He didn't envy Scott having a dad. He'd never known a father's love. A man, to him, was his mother's lover. Someone who sat in the kitchen and had a smoke, someone who was kind to him. A man was someone who disappeared into his mother's room before disappearing from their house. The women he knew as a child were mostly white and the men he knew were mostly Black. That's a combination which made an imprint, surely, that came with a level of warmth and an undercurrent of desire, desperation and melancholy. Much later, when Miles made music, when he first loaded a heavy black bassline beneath a white woman's voice, it came from a real place, it came from home.

****

The house on Oxford Place had two floors and a basement that lead out to the back yard, which is where he was when Precious Baxter called his name. He was pushing his cars around between stones he'd laid out and under bridges he'd made from pegs. It was right before Christmas but it was warm enough, the sunlight made the yard look golden, the sky was white.

"Come down here," he looked over his shoulder at Precious, she was a dark cut-out against the sky. She should have been in her own yard next door.

"For what?"

In the basement she lay on the floor, on a blanket, wearing a stiff jumper and a wine-red skirt. Her knickers were in her hand. She looked a bit like him, her skin was amber coloured, too. The light down there in the basement was filmy, full of dust particles, but he could see her face, her clear features and her prettiness. She was tall, she was eleven or so. She had breasts. Not insect bites, real breasts with weight. Her skirt was gathered around her waist. She took his hand and pulled him on to her. Did he see between her thighs? He wouldn't remember. He felt no surprise.

"You put your thing in here," she said and with her hand lead him in. Then she told him, "Now you got to move." It was sex, what else do you call it? He had his penis inside her. He thought about it for a couple of days, then he forgot. It was like cutting your hair for the first time, there was no emotion. He was seven.

In his memory, his infant days, intertwined, are afternoons at Eric's; his mother, uncle and aunt drinking tea and chatting. There was the afternoon when he and Scott ran into the front room after their playing got out of hand. Miles had one belter of a black eye, both Scott's eyes were bruised. They looked like a pair of baby pandas. The adults were shocked into silence, then laughed. The boys, mouths in straight lines, were seething with little boy fury, at each other, at the laughter also. He remembers going to the zoo on an August afternoon. Here they were, a mixed-race mother and her brother and their respective children, Miles and Scott, wandering around the pretty Victorian zoo, with its herbaceous borders in vampy hot pink and its lawns clipped and placed like fuzzy felt. They stared in wonder at the elephant, the giraffe and the lion king. African people, displaced, staring at African animals, imprisoned. He and Scott saw a picture sign for the aquarium and ran in. It was dark in there, and cool. The reflection from the water tanks bathed the tunnel in deep purple light. They went from one tank to another, their small hands against glass. A hundred tiny fish that looked like a disco ball had exploded zipped between lazy fern. Between a stone and a capsized Statue of Liberty, one saucer eye lurked. Behind another glass wall, a long white fish with a tail like a feather boa, flickered past them in its dark world. Then it was done, they had visited the treasure chest just like children do, flitting around, not looking really then suddenly captivated into concentration by a colour, by a shape. Scott was still staring at the slice of sea, but Miles was in front of a heavy door. He called his cousin over and yanked it open. He and Scott found themselves face to face with an upright grizzly bear. The bear was as startled as the boys, and the boys ran for their lives.

At this time, seven years old, Miles was still wetting the bed. It was a concern. Betty didn't talk about it. He had to gather his own bedclothes and wash them. Betty was mothering two children, without any example of how it should be done. Her own mother died when she was a baby, leaving her with a father overcome with grief, debt and three resentful older siblings who had somehow made a link between Betty's birth and their mother's death. When she was two, it was her father's turn to fall ill. He was too weak to raise four children, and they were taken into care. Betty was left there for at least eighteen months, until her father came back to collect her. There is a single photograph of her taken at that time. Beneath a mass of thick dark curls, is a baby face filled with sadness. Her pretty mouth is shut in a pained line and her eyes, the kind that have the upward tilt of fifties movie stars, stare away to one side with a look that seems to be done with crying, a watchful apprehension has hijacked any tiny-child joy.

There is no one who has recorded how Betty grew. She was a mixed-race girl in Bristol at a time when she would have struggled to see herself reflected anywhere. She was very bright. She listened to folk music, to Joan Baez and Janice Ian. But she didn't party in clubs with white people as a teenager. She travelled to Cardiff, two hours away, another country, and did her dancing in Tiger Bay. Tiger Bay was a cut-throat dockland, where women turned tricks and men battered each other when they spilled from pubs at night. It was also a place of amazing mixity: Somali, Irish, Caribbean and Yemeni people all melding into one community. At night, down in the clubs, the atmosphere was charged, as men and women rocked away their cares to loud, fantastic music. That was where she felt at home.

A trait in her character had begun to trace itself. No one said borderline back then, but that one word would have been fitting. She lived on the border, at the edge of her emotions. She was excessive in her reactions and in her decisions. No one expects a teenager to be in complete control of themselves, but Betty was more furiously bright, trusting and vulnerable than your average English girl. It was to prove to be a terrible assembly of attributes.

CHAPTER THREE

CAN WE PRETEND?

In the late summer of 1967, the little family moved to East Grove, St Paul's and from then onwards there was a man about the house, Donovan. The house had always been Donovan's home, which he shared with his older brother, Errol. Some homes are just a happy jostle of domesticity. Some homes have comfort folded into the laundry, mixed into the stew, year upon year. Some homes are places where profound shifts in life occur as a baby is pushed into the world of air or when the father, once as reliable as the North Star, declines into poignant infirmity, and yet the days continue to tick over, always, alike and soothing. East Grove was not that kind of home. In 1942, in the barely altered kitchen that Betty moved around in on her first day, opening Formica cupboards, scrubbing the oven, in this very kitchen, there had been a tragedy. A grim death. But this loss is part of Donovan's tale, more than Miles's, so is not Miles's to tell. It gives a third dimension to Donovan, perhaps ghosting the cloistered face-offs later on – although he probably wouldn't see it that way.

Miles was happy at this address in the beginning. It was a place where music took a hold over him that would never let up. In his bedroom was a cupboard full of seven-inch ska and bluebeat records, brought from Jamaica by Donovan's father. The first time Miles opened that cupboard, he came face to face with something plentiful. Something plentiful here in his own room, giving him an oblique sense of possession. In his life, the life of a poor child, everything material was, through necessity, stripped down to the essential. Here, this cupboard in his bedroom held abundance. The records were packed in tightly, forming columns straight up, and every interstice held yet more records. Right away, Miles was intrigued by them and fascinated by the artwork on the sleeves. He would turn them over, studying the images. The reggae seven-inch artwork was always quite vibrant: a big bird of paradise, or a name, Jackpot, or a fist punching a jagged hole, arresting his eye like a cartoon might. Don was easy about him going through the records, and playing them on his brother, Errol's, record player.

Seven-inch records had a big hole in the middle and needed an accessory, called a three-legged spider, to be placed in the centre of the turntable so that the records would fit. Miles learnt quickly how all of this worked. He spent entire evenings putting on records, trying to figure out the correlation between the pictures on the sleeves and the music inside. He noticed that the music he liked held the same essence as the music Don listened to on the record player-cum-drinks cabinet in the front room. Don listened to soul. The tunes Miles liked the best were on the label with the quietest sleeves – plain navy blue with silver lettering that spelt Pama. It seemed to Miles, aged seven, that caught in the bluebeat and ska of Pama Records was this same yearning that Don loved, a yearning called soul. All of the records had the word Jamaica on them. Miles didn't know he was Jamaican. Jamaica, to him, was a place where all of his community came from, the adults. He thought it was faraway. He didn't think it was in Africa. He didn't think there were white people there. That was all he understood.

It was a Saturday morning. Don and Betty had had a skinful the night before and were sleeping off reverberating hangovers. Upstairs in the front bedroom, Miles had spread out a selection of singles on the floor.

"Juliette! Come here!" Juliette wandered over to him, "Here." He handed her his mother's wire hairbrush. "You know this tune, right? You can sing it? Stand on this." Juliette followed her brother's instructions, climbing on to a stool before the open window. "When I play the tune, you sing out the window. That's your microphone. Ready?"

Mrs Campbell from number nine walked back from the shops, the morning sun in her eyes. *Pied Piper* by Bob and Marcia vibrated from a bedroom window, putting a bounce in the street. Squinting, she saw that the music came from upstairs at Don's. A speaker was set on the ledge facing out and a sweet little girl in a nightie was singing her head off, framed between net curtains. She put her shopping bags down and, her hands on her hips, beamed at Juliette. The song stopped and Mrs Campbell clapped as Miles, hidden from view and with a concentrated frown, switched the record. As the days became darker and gradually a world of dread closed in on the little boy, music, putting on songs for anyone who passed by in the street, stayed. He would put on a record, loud, then go to the open window and lean out of it, watching the people in his road. He wanted to see if anyone looked up, he wanted to see if their pace picked up on the beat. Some people would smile at him, or break into a little dance. He wanted to know if the people outside would like his music, if they would feel how he felt. Later, as his mother moved further from her axis, as harshness slid into abuse, he had this simple and significant line of communication with the world beyond.

It was around about that time that Miles got his first sense that the body he lived in was, for reasons beyond his control, a potential threat to him. Pro-Cathedral, his school, was white, run by nuns and on the other side of town. Most kids had their mothers waiting for them at the school gates, but Miles went to and from school alone, right away. It was a two-bus ride, and then a long walk for a child. He was meandering home one afternoon, down Park Street and round the corner, past the Hippodrome and in broad daylight, when a white man, maybe twenty years old, walked towards him and spat emphatically in his face. Miles froze, a gob of phlegm sliding down his forehead. The street carried on being a street. Teenage girls linked together at the elbow kept up their chatter, a bright green bus slowed at the traffic lights, people spilled out, walked away. Nothing dimmed in the heart of the city, nobody noticed the small Black boy stood quite still, wiping spit from his face with his jumper sleeve. Of course, back home, Don wanted to go vigilante and skin the assailant alive, but that was never a possibility. Miles says that he became Black on that day. He doesn't know how he knew, exactly as he was spat at, that it was because he was a Black boy. He just knew.

The Bomb Site, 1969

Bristol was bombarded during World War II. Hotwells, an area that scrambles up a hill, was hit hard by the bombings and was like a portrait of a lost smile with so many missing teeth thereafter – someone's home still standing here, still standing there, with collapse upon collapse of rubble in-between them. It remained that way for decades. Driving into the city, pulled up at the lights, you let your eye wander over the Hotwells' hill: a house, a house, then a great gash of fallen brick. A faded painted wall remained with the ghost-print of a staircase; there was even a bath with a tree growing through.

Down the bottom of East Grove, which was a cul-de-sac, there was a gap. Beyond the gap was the bomb site. On December 2, 1940, during the Bristol Blitz, there was an air raid and a swathe of bombs detonated across the Redland, Cotham and St Paul's areas of Bristol. One hundred and fifty-six citizens died. The fury of the blasting knocked out a hole to the back of St Paul's the size of a football pitch. For a long time, there was only debris there. Houses shaken down to rubble, risky iron armatures and ill-looking trees. Then, in the late sixties, the hippies came. Spaced out and willing. They set to, and the children of St Paul's, who had always used the bomb site as a place to hang out, would now come down after school to watch as the site got cleared, and soon enough they joined in with building.

They constructed swings and a wooden adventure playground. The wreckage was cleared. The hippies went to Airbus, in Filton. They came back triumphant, with the promise of an abandoned Concorde fuselage as a gift to the inner-city kids. It was to be grounded on this wasteland. Just as a rock which holds in its sediment strata of life, here the bomb site that had been gouged out by Second World War high explosives, then played in by children of the African diaspora, would be ornamented with a supersonic shell.

In the club house, Terry, the hippy leader who had a big chin and a gentle soul, was sat with his bare feet on his desk, and the folk tune turning on the record player gave out poignancy. A joint stuck in the corner of his mouth was all but consumed. Every now and then, he toked a bit and the tip of the spliff crackled red. He could see there was a fight going on, beyond the swings. Sometimes he would wander over there and calm things. Sometimes, like today, he'd let it play out.

"Hey Miles, what's going on?" Lola had dashed over to where Miles and his crew were having a stone fight with kids from another neighbourhood. It wasn't a friendly fight, it was a bit of a rumble, rocks shooting back and forth. Lola was a neighbour, a light-skinned girl with pale orange hair. She was mild, quiet. Just as Miles turned to answer her, a rock came hurtling her way. She shot her hand in the air as every single little boy ducked. The rock landed smack in her palm. She belted it back with such force that she scared the invaders, who scattered instantly. As the boys got up, found a football, got back in to the business of play, Miles kept his eye on Lola. Figuring her out.

When he got home, Don was in the front room. It was a weekly ritual. Don, his posse. They played LPs, old soul, or listened to the horse racing in the front room, five, six of them. They sat on the floor: Kek Up, Stone, Wheeler, Vonnie, Look Up (whose eyelids plunged so heavily that he had to tilt his head back to see) and London. Newspaper was spread over the carpet and covered with what looked like the contents of a tipped-over wheelbarrow of weed.

"Wha'ppen, Miles?" one or other of them would ask, and they'd carry on with their paper twists of stalk (not too much), seeds (a bit), and a nice bit of dried leaf and bud. One-pound, two-pound, three-pound draw.

In the kitchen, his mother was making curry. Andrea and Auntie Joy were in there, sticking coupons in a book.

"Do you have homework, Mi? Have you done your homework? Hey, Andie, listen to this. Say garage Miles. Go on." Betty was smiling, Miles laughed.

"Garage." He pronounced it to rhyme with barrage.

"You going all la-di-da on us, Miles?" asked Auntie Joy.

"It's his school," said Betty, "he'll be reading the news on telly next, won't you, Bodger?"

He went upstairs to do his homework. He took out his drawing book. He got all his coloured pencils lined up and meticulously drew a bird. Every evening, he would draw a bird.

He could hear them, later. Betty and Donovan. What woke him, often, were dull thuds. Or his mother cursing. Or sounds as if furniture was being shifted around. In those daybreak hours, the light that filled his bedroom was always grey. Miles got from his bed, sat right up against the door. Something smashed, bam bam bam, you fucker, you fucker. The name Tammy came up. She was a stripper, a white girl. She was a problem. It went quiet again. His bed was wet already. He pushed all the covers to the floor and fell back to sleep.

In the morning, Juliette chattered at the table, facing him. Her hair was braided up and caught in two puffs high on either side of her head with red glass bobbles. She was giggling and the light that caught in the bobbles was pretty. Betty was at the sink, changing the water for salt fish. She turned to Miles. Steady. Blank.

"You do the laundry when you get home tonight, you hear?"

Her left eye had disappeared, it was just a black slit in a distended, swollen orb.

Chapter Four

LIGHT ON THE PATH

It was a Tuesday, which was a good day – a very good day – at school. There was swimming, which Miles didn't enjoy, feeling weighted down in the water, feeling cold, but right after that was Tuesday lunch. It was always cheese soufflé with Heinz baked beans and chips, followed by raspberry crumble and custard. Tuesday lunch felt like heaven to him.

The morning light flooded the great sash windows of the classroom. It was a room with a high ceiling, faded green walls, a waxed wood floor. On the blackboard, chalk tapped and scratched. "God created the world. God created Adam." The children stared at the staid, italic letters, deciphering their sound. "God sent a messenger." The children learned to read as they learned about a Catholic god. Miles learned that god was a white man.

He was the only Black boy in his school bar his cousin Scott. The school held a mixture of Irish children from the area, together with the children of Catholic Clifton residents, whose professions were pointedly white collar. Up until the spitting incident in the street, Miles's skin colour was just a fact. Sometimes, in St Paul's, kids told Miles he was a half breed. That was something he had had to consider. Being Black, but not as Black as his neighbours. This breed talk was so approximate to him. Half would be one Black, one white parent. But half breed was a broad stroke, taking in anyone whose skin tone was under deep brown. In the word half, he understood that he was less than whole. Here in this classroom though, he wasn't half white, quarter white, any white. From a racist perspective, any child that had Black blood, had had every melanocytic cell invaded. Not half white, but wholly tainted.

He sat with his friends, Brendon and Tomas. They ate their lunch. They chatted. It was little boys' talk, they were nine years old, maybe ten. They wanted to dress in skinhead gear. Miles wanted brogues and Sta-Prest trousers, Brendon wanted a Brutus shirt, orange and yellow check. The other kid, Tomas Walentynowicz, wanted Onitsuka Tiger boots, they all wanted those, but he said his dad had asked him how he would feel about a kick up the arse whilst he was at it.

On his way home Miles wandered into town, to the shoe shop that sold the brogues. He stared intently at the window display. The prices were high, outside his mother's budget, but he'd already started working on her and a fluttery feeling, a hopefulness came over him. He took a route home that led him up Stokes Croft, past the Polish Club which was Tomas's father's haunt, a place that he had walked Miles into, causing a brief lull in the intense card games. It was only as he got quite near to his house that he felt a tightening inside. He wondered about his mother. Some days she was normal, funny, and happy to see him. Other days though, when he pushed the door, what he saw before him was demonic. He couldn't work out the cause and effect, it seemed to come from nowhere, though scratching at the perimeters of what a nine-year-old boy could grasp was a link between Donovan going out and his mother's hairpin mood swings. He pushed the front door. She was framed in the hallway. Taking up the light, sucking in the light, so that she appeared as the centre of a cut-out, a dark space.

She held the television cables that she hid in various places around the house.

"Get in there."

He dropped his school bag and went into the front room. His mother's arm rose, she was a tall woman. Her reach seemed to stretch to the ceiling. He turned, crouched down, his hands instinctively cradling his head. His mother belted him fiercely across his back with the cables. It was a searing pain. The cables came down on his back, again and again. He knelt on the floor as she beat him. He could feel his pulse, his heartbeat in his back. He could feel the stinging lines of blood that sucked his shirt to them. He tried not to cry, that made her angrier. He felt so fearful of his mother. He felt such a shameful little boy. "Now go to your room."

Donovan was not in. Donovan was never in when she beat him. He got on to his bed, on his knees and carefully laid down, on his stomach. He pulled a comic from under his bed. The trick was to move only an arm, and keep the welts across his back quite still. He turned the pages awhile, then fell asleep, his face resting on the open *Dandy*.

****

A couple of skinheads, Shane and Terrence, were cleaning and polishing Don's dull yellow Datsun. The skinheads used to come into St Paul's on the weekend in full regalia: braces, monkey boots and button-down check shirts. They did odd jobs for people. It had started when the community in Montpelier, which brackets the back of St Paul's and is where East and West Grove are, was mostly Irish. Shane and Terrence just carried on their two-bit trade as the neighbourhood changed from an Irish population to a Jamaican one. This was before there was an affiliation between skinheads and the National Front. Their grievance was never with Black people back then, although they hit on the Pakistani community, in ritualistic hate crimes known as Paki-bashing. There was a café called Never On A Sunday, on Fairfax Street, where skinheads and mods hung out. They were working class, full of fight, wearing bovver boots which, in the late sixties, were used sometimes for kicking bikers – who had their own place, a café called the 66. In the Never they listened to ska and reggae. They really knew their stuff. Don would hand over a seven-inch record to the skinheads from his ska collection for cleaning his car.

Don was indoors, with a cup of tea, checking the racing results in the morning paper. Miles was sat on the front yard wall, watching Shane and Terrence and talking with a kid who was on his way to the bomb site. East Grove had a lazy Saturday morning feel. A lot of curtains were still drawn, milk bottles and newspapers waiting on doorsteps. The neighbours across the way, the diligent and tired-looking Jamaican man and his shy wife, had their front door open. All the daughters from the family were out on the steps in their dressing gowns, giggling. Miles was listening as his friend explained that there was a boy who said he could go all the way over on the swings.

"I don't believe you," said Miles, "you'd drop on your head if you did that." But the other kid was adamant, that was what the boy had said, although he hadn't proved it. They went over to the swings and started swinging as high as they could, cranking it up. Miles was able to make a dangerous arc, higher than all the other kids who were having a go too, but it seemed an impossible challenge. You'd get really high, but that far up you don't come back down in a circle, there is a slackening and without the necessary momentum you crash back down.

Later that afternoon, whilst Donovan and the crew measured out ganja and his mother was off somewhere with her friends, Miles went back to the swings on his own. He swung himself up, came down, swung himself up, came down again, almost hitting the crossbar. A kid or two stopped by, watched awhile, called, "Yeah, I can go higher than that, any time," then wandered off. Miles made the swing creak with such force that the whole unit lifted slightly. He could feel it, the moment when the heavy chains changed their composition in the air. The links felt like they locked together, they went from being something fluid, to something fused and their rigidity was the key. He kept rocking, for what felt like hours. Higher and higher. Then suddenly, unbelievably, he made it over. A full circle. He saw the ground, the sky, the earth, in front, behind. He kept going, round and round, so that the chains shortened and he was ducking to get under the bar. He practiced a few more times, then went home for his tea feeling fully accomplished. In the early evening, he rushed back to the bomb site because he knew that there would be a good little group down there.

"I did it," he told them, "I can go right over."

They said, "No way, you're too small, you can't do it."

They all stood back and watched the boy pendulum pick up speed, lick backwards and forwards, higher and higher. They watched with rounded eyes, smiles, amazement, as he flew right over the top bar, making a great perfect circle and went round and round again, laughing his head off.

****

Don had other women on the go. Two of them caused real pain to Betty. One was Tammy, the stripper, a white girl who was young, rough and pretty. The other was Thelma, always called Thelma The Thief by Betty. Of the two, Thelma was the real issue because she was a proud, respected Black woman. At that time, there was an unspoken quasi-segregation in St Paul's, a self-imposed one. Mixed-race women stuck together and had white girlfriends, but mostly didn't socialise with Black women. Most mixed-race women were the daughters of a Black man and a white woman, maybe that explains it, but Black women remained distanced and Black men checked their behaviour around them and possibly showed them more respect. Don's ongoing relationship with Thelma was the source of drunken showdowns that ended with Betty bruised, and Don bruised, too. Because Betty was a victim, but she was also an assailant. She would fly into Don, beat him. It was extreme. Betty hit Don. Don broke Betty's arm. Her children saw that, saw their mother with her arm in smooth white plaster.

Miles can remember his mother stood against the kitchen counter, the radio on, a mug of tea in her hand. Don in the bedroom.

"Dolling yourself up?" she bellowed from the kitchen. They heard him come downstairs, open the front door. "Off to see your gorilla, Don?" she shouted, still standing with her back to the kitchen counter.

"Mi gaan."

And the door shut.

There were variations around this theme throughout his childhood. It never ended well.

The family had changed. Betty had two children with Don by then, little Joanie a toddler and a baby named Troy. It maybe gave Betty more status, it definitely gave Miles more chores. The washing was one of them. It meant going down to the launderette on Grosvenor Road with shopping bags stuffed rigid, but it also meant that he could get his soiled bed clothes washed and dried and back in place discreetly. He was nine, and by then his sense of shame at his bed wetting was stopping him from doing normal things like sleeping over at his cousins'. So, he didn't mind the laundry run so much. The radio played in the launderette. Local busybodies were in and out, dishing out gossip in patois. Sometimes, he'd wander off and visit the shops. His favourite shop window, without a doubt, was the bicycle shop across the alley.

He decided to leave the launderette and go to the bike shop. The night before he'd taken a beating. It wasn't an arbitrary one, this time he'd known it was coming. He'd stopped at the amusement arcade under the Locarno on the way home. He leaned against a pinball machine for an hour, watching a skinhead empty his pockets. An hour of time had been swallowed up, just like that. When he pushed the front door at East Grove, his mother had leapt out at him and nearly toppled him. She beat him with a cable and when that shot from her sweating hand, she grabbed the nearest thing, one of Don's shoes. He had his hands over his head, he was bent over trying to protect himself. She bashed him until he was cradled on the ground, crying for her to stop. She carried on, hitting him and mumbling all the while, an awful, insane incantation.

Miles climbed the stairs, pushed his bedroom door. He took off his school shirt and his vest carefully. If he did it too quickly, it would sting. Then he sat on his bed. His back was raw. His little boy arms, arms that fell from the shoulders with no breadth, were mottled. Looking down, he could see his concave chest, and the swell of his belly. His hands, nails bitten down to the quick, were resting on his knees. He saw his brown skin. He saw his unlovable self.

She had woken Miles at daybreak. Her voice was warm and she said, come downstairs Milo, for breakfast. The house was scrubbed clean, Don was nowhere in sight and it wasn't clear whether she had actually been to bed. She had been so nice to him this morning. Maybe now was a good time to ask for a bike. He stared at the one in the window. It was white, with blue lettering. He had asked for a bike every Christmas for years but he never got one, his family was too poor. The sun burned the nape of his neck. Blood dripped, black splashes on his green t-shirt . He put his hand to his face, to his nose and it was pumping out blood. He bent his head forwards, as he'd been taught. The blood splashed on the pavement between his feet.

"Milo?" His mother's voice was behind him.

"I've got a nosebleed, mum."

"Come here, Bodger." She took his face very gently in her hand and dabbed away the blood from his top lip with the sleeve of her cardigan. The kindness that was in her eyes touched him.

CHAPTER FIVE

FREE AS THE MORNING SUN

On Sundays he never did much. On this particular Sunday morning, he was lying in the front room, the TV was on, Donovan was reading the paper. A man came in, with Betty. Betty said,
"This is your father, Miles. This is Charlie. He's come to take you out for the day."
Miles got up from lying on his stomach and was a little off-balance, looking up at a towering man. He put his school anorak on, zipped it up, all the while trying to find his mother's eyes, trying to read them. They got into a car, Miles in the passenger seat. As Charlie pulled out, Miles turned to look at his mother. She was holding Troy. She just nodded her head, and turned indoors. They drove out of the city. Charlie had a nice car. Miles stole a look at him, this man who was his father. He had a powerful face, yet his eyes held a softness. Miles could see he was a handsome man. Charlie was kind to him, they drove around all afternoon, then went back to Charlie's home. He lived near Herbert's the bakery, not so far from Betty and Donovan. A woman answered the door, a white woman named Jean who had a quiet voice. She'd made tea for them. Then Charlie took him home again. Miles felt like the day had been a different one, but no more so than if a number seven bus had come down a number three route.

****

Winter drew in. Down the bomb site, the collection of records in the youth club room was ever growing. Reggae and ska. Often on Fridays nights, there would be a little party. All the kids lined up and danced their heart out. Milo couldn't dance or felt that he couldn't dance, so kept his distance. He wandered in there one evening, in his school trousers and jumper, just about ten years old and tall for his age, his features affirming themselves so that baby cheeks were giving place to a stronger jaw. His eyes were wide, their colour a mid brown that was like liquid gold in some lights. His eyebrows shot up so that head-on they made a 'V'. There was no question that he was growing up to be remarkably handsome. A fact to which he was oblivious. His face, his features, were nowhere, ever. The mixed-race of England had no calendar boy or girl. Inside the youth club they called to him to come and dance but he wouldn't budge. One of the older girls came over and pulled him by the arm to the line-dancing group just as his favourite tune, *Clean Race* by Scotty came on. The little sound system in there had a bit of a kick to it. The hippies were all dancing and laughing and the lights were down. He let go. He danced, too. Of course, he could dance, it was in him already, he was the son of Pretty Foot, after all.

East Grove, Bristol, 1970

That Christmas, he came downstairs in the morning and there in the front room was the bike. The white one with the blue lettering. He felt a rush of blood to his head, it was happiness. It had snowed. He went out anyway, cycling along the dazzling pavements on his prized possession. After no more than 15 minutes, he'd got the trick of it and he cycled all over St Paul's, Montpelier and Saint Werburgh's running a dark tyre track through the snowfall. If it had been possible to see the track from the sky, you would have seen a tyre print in the shape of joy.

A few weeks after that, Miles was sat on his bike chatting to his friend, Danteen, when Baron Anderson came over and told him, "Let me have a go on that." Baron Anderson was older, with a brutal face and a bully's mind set. Younger kids avoided him. Miles felt his hands clamp harder on the handlebars of his bike.

"No, my mum said I can't let anyone go on my bike." Baron's hands shot out, grabbed him by the shoulders and pushed him to the ground. Baron put a foot on the spinning back wheel, picked the bike up and cycled off. When Miles got in through his front door, he was almost unable to catch his breath, "Mum, Mum! Baron Anderson's taken my bike. He just went off with it." Betty cut the water from the taps and turned towards her son.

"You go back out there and you get that fucking bike back."

Out in the neighbourhood, it didn't take long before Miles saw Baron, stopped up on a pavement, the bike between his legs. Miles walked over to him, his heart tight. Baron Anderson didn't even turn towards him as he spoke, "Listen, I got to have my bike back."

"Nah, man. I ain't finished with it yet." Baron was smiling, looking away, not at Miles. His hands moved slightly on the handles like he was revving up. Miles moved closer and bit Baron Anderson's bicep so fiercely that he took out a hunk of flesh. Baron Anderson hollered in pain, cursing, casting the bike down as he yelled. Miles grabbed it and peddled off frantically. Baron Anderson's flesh had been white underneath the dark brown. Baron Anderson would have a scar for the rest of his life. Miles was more scared of his mother than anyone else who walked the earth, it was that simple.

****

Every summer, the funfair came to town. Down the bomb site, the teenage boys would make some kind of loose date to wander down there in the evening. Word would spread. Younger boys ran home, like Miles, "Hey mum, I want to go down the funfair with Danteen and Wayne after tea. Can I go? Can I have some money to ride?"

There was never any money to ride, but she'd say yes, you can go. There was a sense of shame at being poor, he was always apprehensive that some boy or other would laugh at him because his parents couldn't afford to give him pocket money. Still, that couldn't keep him from going. Towards the end of the afternoon, all the boys, maybe twenty-strong, their ages ranging from six to eighteen, would make their way out of St Paul's and walk through Saint Werburgh's up to Eastville Park. The sun was almost down, the sky a dark and quiet pink. Eastville Park shouted out its presence in a thousand coloured lights, throbbing music and the thrilled screams of teenage girls plunging down the rides. Miles and his friends would weave through the attractions and the dimming daylight heightened the senses. There was the noise, cartoonish whizzings and poppings and the shamelessly loud and gimmicky music, the bass line from one stand segueing surreally into the song on the next stand. There were the smells, sweet smells of candy floss and toffee apples, and then the burnt caramel of sausages and onions frying away. This little flashing world made of neon arrows in reds and greens and ropes of multicoloured lights that lit up the pathways. The boys, the younger ones, had no money and could never play any of the games or go on any of the rides. But they had fun. They lined the sides of the bumper car floor and picked out their driver. They yelled him on, "Gwan! Gwan! Bump him!" And they whooped and laughed when their chosen driver bashed another car with verve.

Miles had never ridden a dodgem in his life. That summer night, 1970, the crew of boys from St Paul's were hanging towards the back of the fair. The younger boys took in the view, the different rides, and then ran off together. Miles stayed back. He didn't have money, even for just one ride. Devon – aka Flint – who was Danteen's older brother, was hanging there, too. He looked down at Miles, "You not going on the ride?"

"Nah. I ain't got no money for that."

"Here," Flint gave him 50p, "go on the ride." Miles couldn't believe it. He felt a burst of happiness, he grinned at Flint, thanked him and ran to the queue at the bumper cars, the dull silver hexagon pressed into his palm. He had dreamed of this. The bumper car ride was manned by a twenty-year-old with thick legs in tight flares. He took Miles's money. There was no car. The other kids, the ones before him, had only given their money when a car came in. Miles waited. A car petered out at the side and the man waved a kid behind Miles on. Miles was confused and said,

"It's my turn. I didn't get a car." The man looked at him,

"You pay to ride. Move out the way."

"But I did pay."

"Move out the fucking way."

The moment was gone, the exhilaration in his chest, snuffed. He walked back to the fence where his friends were and slouched against it. He felt bad for Flint, too. He had given him his money and it had been taken.

"Did you ride?" asked Flint.

"No." Miles couldn't look at him. "Sorry."

"What happened?" Flint listened, then said, "Come." He was talking to Miles, but every kid, every teenager grouped round there had heard, too. They all followed Flint. He took Miles to the ride, and asked which man had taken his money.

"Give him his money back."

The stallholder raised his eyebrows and ran his tongue over his teeth, sizing Flint up.

"Fuck off."

Flint rocked back just slightly on one leg and punched the stallholder square in the face with such might that the stallholder dropped to the ground. All the boys were behind Flint, shouting. Other fairground men lumbered over, "What the fuck is going on?"

Moments later, Miles was sat inside a dodgem, 50p in his pocket, justice having prevailed. There was magic in this first time, whizzing round, bumping cars, as Flint and his crew walked slowly away. Everything fraught that had led up to this moment, the horrible stallholder, the redeemer's punch, vanished. Miles was now an ace racing driver, zooming around a make-believe track in a make-believe race. It was the fastest he had ever travelled on his own, round and round, to the thumping bass in the flickering night.

CHAPTER SIX

THE RAIN BEFORE IT FALLS

In school, there was talk of where they would be going next, which secondary school. Miles sat the Eleven Plus and he passed it, easily. He had flat out refused to go to QEH, a prestigious Bristol grammar school, based on the ridiculousness of the uniform. It was inconceivable to have to walk back through the ghetto every day wearing a floor-length Renaissance coat and long yellow socks. Miles was therefore headed for the cooler Cotham Grammar. He already knew the kind of boy he would meet there – the same middle-class white boys who went to Pro-Cathedral. He felt some anxiety at the idea of secondary school, because there would be a shift. As the only Black boy in Pro-Cathedral, the most he had had to contend with was name calling. Now, he would no longer be one of the oldest children, he would be relegated to the youngest year – the most vulnerable year – and would still, probably, be one of only a few Black boys there. What might be different, or might be worse, he wasn't sure of, but worrying the edges of his mind was that the name-calling might now turn physical. He knew that some of the white boys feared him, because they had a wariness of Black people. That in itself could cause aggression. Others didn't differentiate, but when Miles was invited to their homes he would sense in the parents' welcome at the door astonishment and fleeting panic. When you sent your upper-middle-class white son to a Catholic school in the richest part of Bristol, you did not expect him to appear on your doorstep with the only Black boy there.

In school, there was a lot of talk about football, music and fashion. Miles still hadn't got the brogues that he wanted, but his mother had promised that if he did well in his school report, he could have them. His report came in. It was something to be proud of, although Miles himself had no pride at all in what he did at school. He wasn't the best in his class, he knew that. There were boys with tin boxes in their school bags that held war medals and pressed autumn leaves and these they showed to the teacher. There were boys who had been on trains and planes, boys who could play piano and knew when to say may and not can. Miles felt that he could never match them. His school report spoke differently, the turned pages showing mostly blue ink As. His mother was happy with his report, she kept her word. She showed the grades to every person who came into her house. Don gave Miles a set of folded bank notes from his pocket, enough to fund Miles's dream of a complete skinhead get-up: the brogues, the Crombie coat, the Brutus shirt. It was the first time he would look the way he wanted to, and he had earned it. When the bell went for end of term, he tore down the avenue to shops. He stopped deliberately at the bottom of Park Street, to catch his breath and also stare at the window display of a retail temple to glam rock. The store dummy shimmered in white lurex, its eyes painted like peacock feathers. There were coats made of coloured fur that trailed over the floor and a row of glitter-struck platform boots that Miles stared at, transfixed. A couple of months before, he had been watching *Top Of The Pops*, when Gary Glitter arrested the screen, mania in his draggy eyes, wearing a full spangled space suit. In the shop window, here were Gary Glitter's clothes. He looked with intent. Everything cost so much money. It made sense. To be a star, you must also be very, very rich. Later, at the brogue shoe shop, the muted atmosphere was a world apart. Walking in, there was a sense of order and the tang of leather in the air. The classic men's shoes glowed like waxed wood. He was in the shop a long time, trying on different pairs, hesitating. Finally, he walked home in his school uniform with his rucksack on his back, but wearing his new shoes. He felt like a king.

When he walked into the front room, Betty and Don were watching TV. His mother leaned forwards, over Don, smiling, trying to see the shoes. She gripped Don's arm. Don looked over, too. His eyes widened and he had trouble holding his drink steady. Miles stood there, beaming at them, in his tired school trousers and jumper, rucksack and nappy hair, in a pair of high-heeled white platform ankle boots covered in silver stars.

"Miles! What are you wearing? Don't tell me you just bought these?" Betty's hands seemed stuck to sofa. In a moment of delusion, Miles had blown the entire skinhead-look budget on a single pair of boots. Don looked up from Miles's feet to his face,

"Wha di bumba yuh a-wear?"

"I like them," said Miles, earnestly, "I do like them." With this, all three of them looked at Miles's feet, at him flexing his boots this way and that. Don kissed his teeth, and without a doubt wondered which of his friends might have run into Miles in St Paul's on his way home,

"Yuh cyaan walk di streets like that, man," said Don, not unkindly. Betty was looking at her son, so badly wanting to laugh. Miles would have to take them off, and try to get his money back. But for a few minutes still, he had elevated himself literally a good few inches and also, from being a poor Black boy, into a boy shod like a superstar.

****

In his first weeks at Cotham Grammar, he had worked out there were boys he could and would befriend, but also that he would lock down his home life from them. He was careful that no boy should know how poor he was, and that no boy should see his naked upper body, the whip marks like a tiger's strike and the white stripes across his brown skin of healed scars, of beatings past. He made sure that he was always the last boy into the showers. On his first day, Miles arrived a minute late for morning assembly, which was enough for all the boys to turn their unsure eyes his way. He slipped over in his hurry and fell into a stack of chairs that wobbled suspensefully before crashing on the floor. Though some boys giggled as he got up, all he really noticed was a rangy Black kid with dimples, rolling his bug eyes skywards as if to say, "Flippin' heck, like we aren't noticeable enough already." The boy was Claude Williams. When they were men, they laughed about that incident, it was pinned in both of their minds.

He was eleven, life was changing. Back in his neighbourhood, he had his first girlfriend, Dolores. She was his good friend Riley's cousin. She was the most beautiful girl he had ever seen. Dolores was older than Miles, and she had made the unbelievable move on him. They used to kiss a bit, but mostly wile away afternoons together, listening to music, talking. He was in the front room one evening watching TV with Don and Betty when the doorbell went. Betty went to the door, then she was back in the room, wearing a look of disbelief.

"Miles, there's a girl at the door, tells me she's your girlfriend?" Her voice had the buoyancy of shock. Miles was instantly stood up, on guard.

"Cha man," Don tutted, " Wha di problem wid dat? Di bwoy cyaan have nuh girlfriend?"

"Donovan," she answered, "the girl's got bigger tits than me!"

This was his world, then. A segregated world, in which he navigated between two, distinctly opposite, lives. The difference wasn't only the obvious one of colour, but also of class. He was occasionally a half-caste, a breed, in St Paul's, the kind of easy shot that kids take; he was a Black boy in Clifton, that was a constant. He was posh in the ghetto, with his weekly comic books that arrived magically through the letterbox and his accent – Bristolian, not Jamaican – with an already strong lexicon and the odd insanely upper-class pronunciation of random words. He was poor in Cotham Grammar, poor and dark, because that's how they spoke then: the dark-skinned child, the coloured boy. Whichever side of the tracks, he was the lesser boy. All that was spoken in the outside world, and all that was never said, taught him this about himself. His mother had a radicality when it came to race, she was well-read and one of St Paul's' most visible activists. She only ever had one parent as a child – her father, an African man. It seems that he gave her a sense of self. He certainly passed on his refusal of injustice and his bravery. There was all of this in Betty, all that she had stored as a child, a forever Black girl in a white world with an African man as her guide. Then life dealt her a blow. Her father died. She was, in the vaguest of arrangements, put into an elder sister's care. The sister vanished, leaving Betty under the wing of a local prostitute. She was thirteen.

Betty had words of comfort for her son, when he had asked her, completely bewildered, why his friends were so mean. She sent Miles and Juliette to African studies, on Saturday mornings, in a building on the bomb site. He went to African studies with an understanding that he descended from the Kru people, Betty had taught him that. In a hut in St Paul's, he was to place his identity on the map of the world. He learned about William the Conqueror in Clifton and he learned about the Nubian monarchy in St

Paul's. His mum would say, the best of both worlds. Which is exactly what no one seemed to want him to have. It should have been: you are the best of both worlds. You are more, you are many bloods. You are more, not less. It didn't work that way. He was a half-caste boy, from a half-caste country that no one could point him to. He was holding it together, more or less.

Then life coarsened.

He remembers what happened next as the beginning of the end. The beginning of the end of everything he had held up as certain.

He was at the launderette, it was summer. He had wet the bed. It happened so frequently that he knew the cycle of the washing machine, he knew the cycle of the tumble dryer. He would dash out during the washing cycle, over to the bomb site, play football, run back to the launderette and pull the wet sheets from the machine to the dryer, set the cycle on for twenty minutes, leg it back to the bomb site and knock around there again. There was a timer in his brain that told him when the washing was dry and he would collect it, then go home. This day, a Saturday, he was at the launderette a little later than usual. He had lost track of time at the bomb site, the alert didn't come up in his brain. When he got back to the launderette it was locked, the "Closed" sign facing him like a fist.

He knew immediately that to go home without the laundry was to receive the beating from hell. His mother was now out of control with him, the thrashings coming more regularly and more arbitrarily than ever before. It had got so bad that Donovan knew there was something terribly wrong. He must have seen the cuts, the bruises, or maybe just fear in the boy's eyes. Miles once heard Don ask Betty, behind a half-closed door, with sadness in his voice, "Betty, wah mek yuh beat di bwoy suh?" Juliette was also beaten with a slipper, but never the belt. She had, however, to endure watching her brother being struck until their mother had worked the frenzy out of her system. She had to watch her beloved brother being humiliated and terrified. Miles couldn't take it anymore. He couldn't take the pain, the dread or the craziness in his mother's eyes.

He could not go home. Down the end of his street, on the corner, was an abandoned utility van. It was filthy white with a green stripe around it and had no wheels. It seemed like a good place to go. He tried the door, climbed in and fell asleep. In the morning, he stayed inside the metal shell, experiencing his street from a different angle, like being hidden inside a cupboard at home. He heard familiar voices and peeked through the window when it was a friend's. Hours went by, and hunger got the better of him. He had to go home. He slipped out and went to the launderette. His bed clothes were coolly waiting in the barrel of the dryer.

The front door of his house was open. People were shadowing up his vision of the end of the hallway. The hallway smelt of bleach, of coal and of jerk chicken. His mother rushed towards him,

"Milo, where have you been? What happened? We've been so worried. I've been out of my mind with worry."

Don, other men, his mum's friend Joy, appeared behind her. Miles didn't answer right away. He felt tired, he just wanted to sleep.

"It was locked."

His voice was quiet. He looked at his mother, his eyes were unblinking, searching, "When I got to the launderette it was locked. I couldn't get the washing back. I knew you was going to beat me really bad for that. I didn't want a beating."

He dropped the bag on the floor, turned and went up to his room.

It wasn't the same after that, she laid off him for a few weeks. Then she beat him a couple of times. Then an ultimate time. He had come home late, or done something wrong, something trivial, forgettable and forgotten now.

"Where have you been?" The ice eyes, the bottom jaw jutting just slightly forwards. He didn't answer, but he heard her walking to her bedroom, to get the belt. He listlessly opened a drawer, looking for bread. Here we go, those were his thoughts, here we go again.

She belted him from behind, across his back. He flinched, gritted his teeth. Then he turned towards her and she struck him again, clean across his chest. She stared down at him, her eyes huge. This time was different. His hand went up. He grabbed the belt and held it as hard as he could, his arm shook with the effort of keeping it still. It shocked Betty, it stunned her, What, you defy me?

He let the belt go, pushed past her and walked away. She was hitting his back, thrashing him with the belt, bang, bang, in an X shape on his blazer. He went up the stairs, tears running down his face. She was behind him. He wasn't crying because it hurt, he was crying because of her mental health. He was just a kid. She stopped, halfway up the stairs. She heard him shut his bedroom door. "Yeah and stay in there!" she screamed after him.

She never touched him again.

Then Betty disappeared.

The fighting had started around six in the morning. Something crashed against a wall. The voices of Betty and Don gunned into each other. It was a bad fight, it woke all the children. Juliette, who was nine, climbed into Troy's cot and held him. It was raining, strong driven rain. They put Joanie on a stool in front of the window so that she could watch the rain drops chasing each other across the glass. Miles crept down the stairs and looked over the banister. Betty was going for Don, he saw her punch him in the face. Miles withdrew upstairs just as Don gathered his fist to punch her back. They were both yelling, then Betty's voice went quiet and it was just Don. They heard their mother cry then, in pain, plead, "Stop. Please stop." Miles was behind the bedroom door, Joanie against his knees.

The house fell silent. The children stayed completely still. Troy fell asleep, then Joanie. Miles and Juliette waited, they waited a long time.

The front door slammed.

Miles went to the window and moved the curtain back. Day had just broken. The rain was gone, the morning sun was in the water left on the asphalt and caught in the last drops on the window pane. Down in the street, Betty was sat on her knees with her back to the house. She was wearing her electric-blue quilted dressing gown, it shimmered in the morning light. After a while, she stood up and shook her shoulders a little, then walked away.

Chapter Seven

THROW BACK THE LITTLE ONES

Without their mother, but with Don who was backed up by his sister, Laurette, ordinary life carried on. Miles and Juliette didn't miss a day of school, the babies were looked after. No one knew where Betty was.

After three weeks, she returned.

Miles came home from Cotham Grammar, pushed the door and there was Betty manically putting clothes into bags. Don was out. Everything about her was quick and scared.

"What's going on, mum?" She didn't answer, but carried on running up and down stairs, opening drawers, putting paperwork and clothes into bags and taking it out again. Suddenly she said, "Get your coats."

They left the house and began the long walk to Eric's, who now lived in Fishponds in east Bristol. Betty struggled along the streets, pushing Troy, whose stroller tipped back with the weight of the carrier bags stuffed with belongings. Miles dragged a suitcase that moved on twisted wheels, Juliette pushed Joanie's pushchair. They were quiet. Miles wanted to ask if he was going to Cotham Grammar the next day, but his mother's face was shut down. Eric and his wife, Beth, were expecting them. They had tea ready and makeshift beds made up for the kids. There was no warmth in the welcome, just worry. Betty was agitated, talking fast, not making sense.

The next part is clouded in their collective memory. Betty left Eric's, just vanished. She would be gone for days, then she would show up again without any clear explanation. Miles and Juliette were still going to their schools and keeping this life shift secret from their friends. There were arguments, between Uncle Eric and Auntie Beth.

It came to this: "Eric, you are going to have to choose between your sister and me."

One day, after her children had been at Eric's for a month or so, Betty showed up. She took Juliette and Joanie. Miles didn't know where they had gone. To a children's home. He had no understanding of that. Then Troy was taken too.

One Saturday morning, Betty came to get Miles.

"Get your things, Milo. You're moving to a place for a couple a days. Not long. We need to give Eric and Beth their space back." He followed his mother. They sat on the top deck of a bus. He looked at Bristol, at the way the streets are wide in the rich parts, the houses are built of light-coloured stone. As you go into the inner city, the brick changes, the streets are tighter, there is more colour. The bus took them out of all that he had ever really seen, in all his life, except for happy Sunday afternoons in Weston-super-Mare, riding donkeys on the sand and buying ice cream on the pier with his mum and Auntie Andrea. Miles turned his head slightly so that he could see Betty. The skin under her eye was purplish, her eyelids kept closing. Her head rested on the window. She breathed out the pattern of a dandelion puffball on the cold glass. Like her son, she was watching the changing perspective. The vanishing point was no longer of terraced houses, but of heavy oak trees. He moved his hand across the bus seat, towards her hand, and he held it.

They got off the bus in a place called Mangotsfield on the outskirts of Bristol. The houses were set back from the road, they were far apart and had front lawns, all identical, with no garden walls, no garden gates. The only noise was the hit of his mother's shoes on the pavement. There were no people anywhere. They crossed a wide street, there were more trees. Betty said, "It's just there, see? We've arrived." But Miles couldn't see any buildings, just a wide country path and woodland. They walked on, then turned. A driveway lined with matronly rhododendrons was pitched into shade by sycamore trees.

There was a tall house in the distance with dark windows. As they got nearer, he read the painted sign that was planted in the lawn, Kray House.

Inside the house, his mother had been expected. Miles started to panic.

He could hear children crying. Someone came and took his school bag, someone came to take his hand.

"Mum, I don't want to stay here." There was fear in his voice. His mother was busy, signing papers. "Please, mum," he held her arm.

She prised off his fingers, her voice was flat, firm. "It's only for a few days. Okay? I'll come and get you."

She left. There was no embrace.

He was taken down a hallway, into a gloomy dining room where there were what seemed around fifty children eating tea at trestle tables. It smelled of cabbage and tears. Some of the children stared at him, none of them spoke. Kray House was a placement centre at that time and it is now a secure unit, as if its architecture and settings were already primed to become some kind of prison. For the children left there, it was often their first experience of the British care system. They were assessed and then dispatched on, to more permanent placements. In short, every child in the room had recently been removed from their parents, or their parents had left them here and vanished. Every one of them was now facing life alone.

Miles was sobbing. He was a still a boy. His mother was sick. He had no father. His brothers and sisters had disappeared. He had absolutely no idea where he was in relation to St Paul's, nor in relation to his school. Down a hallway, a boy was having an anger fit. Miles could hear his words, echoing and hollow, resonating down the high corridor and he could hear the sounds of restraint, of grown-ups putting out the fire. The boy hollered, "Fucking cunt! fucking cunt!"

Miles pressed himself against the door that looked out. It had glass panels. He kept his back to the room. When tiredness took over, he slid down and sat there, staring into space. He refused to move, he refused to eat. A bigger kid, a Black boy, came over.

"Whatcha doin'?" Miles took a while before answering, then said,

"I'm waiting for my mum. She's coming back to get me. I'm not staying here."

The other boy answered, "She ain't coming back." And wandered off.

Miles stopped eating. He stopped speaking. He spent the day time stuck by the front door waiting for his mother and the evenings lying on his bed in the dormitory. The way he figured it, he could stave off hunger for a few days until his mum came to collect him. Eating would be participating,

participating would be an acknowledgment that this was his new life and he refused that idea with all his might.

A woman, Sylvia, came to sit on his bed. She had hennaed hair and a necklace made of wooden beads. She had the firm intention of getting him downstairs for lunch. This was her:

"I understand you're upset, Miles. That's completely normal. But look, you haven't eaten anything since Saturday. You're going to get poorly if you don't eat something. We'll have to call a doctor, do you see what I'm saying? It's a lot of fuss." Miles was lying on his side, looking away from her.

"Tell my mum." Some of Sylvia's words pricked him: normal, poorly. Sylvia stared at his back in silence. Then she said, "We don't know where your mum's gone. Okay? You can't lie here like a dying swan. You've got to go back to school."

"Can I go to school tomorrow?"

"Yes. Now, come on, buck up, get downstairs. We can't have any amateur dramatics, can you imagine? If all the children here went on hunger strike?"

Miles moved slowly, like his body was an old man's. He sat on the edge of the bed. "I'll come down then."

He had surrendered on a misunderstanding.

So began his new life.

There was school the next day, but not at Cotham Grammar, as he had thought, and despite his pleas to go there. School was now in a beige mobile home on the grounds, with twelve other children, aged seven to fourteen. The kid to his right stank of piss, the kid to his left, a pretty, pixie-like girl, had razor slashes from her wrists to her elbows. Their teacher, Mr Crow, had alopecia and sucked boiled sweets. He didn't like children but believed in a fair chance. Those were his words to them.

Kray House was an institution that felt Victorian, and this was in 1972. It was drab, it was cold. The place was run by Mr and Mrs McFarland. She sat in the kitchen at night drinking herself stupid, he meted out the punishments. Little children of three and four had pegs pinched to their ears if they cried. Other small children were sat on a chair in the middle of a huge room all alone and not allowed to get off it for an entire afternoon if they had, for instance, disobeyed a rule, even if they were too young to have understood the rule. Children were plunged into icy baths as a lesson. The smaller children, who were too small to wash their own bed clothes, were punished for bed wetting by sitting in the common room for hours with their soiled sheet on their heads. Some of the employees tried to do their job, which was scraping the souls of children off the floor, but it was within a horror house, like trying to stroke a right hand when the left hand is on fire.

Miles had a bed, and a bedside table. He had been dropped off with one school bag. He no longer owned anything. He had no contact with any adult or child from his previous life. He had no idea when it would end.

This was the system, where the victim pays, where the victim is robbed of everything, even hope. Occasionally, sprouting in the concrete of inner cities, between, say, a wall and a pavement, a plant will shoot. It is in hostile territory. It is unwanted. But it is defiantly alive. In this same way, Miles somehow got on with life and just as children will, he began to make friends. There was Beak Head Clarke, with the profile of an eagle and there was Mario. There were other kids, whose names have gone from his mind, but who were comrades in arms within those dreadful walls. There were the two white sisters, who were little and heartbreakingly sweet. They were absolutely terrified and held hands the whole time. They fought back tears when they were spoken to, the elder girl protecting the smaller one. After a couple of days of seeing them so scared, Miles tried to comfort them. The elder girl said that her dad couldn't look after them anymore because he was on his own. They missed their dad very much. Miles told them not to worry, he was sure that he would come back for them, which seemed to make the sisters feel better. They latched on to Miles for few a weeks until their father really did come back for them. These are fleeting moments, in lives that go on for decades afterwards. What happens between children who are thrown together in misery never goes away. The older sister found Miles when they were both in their fifties. She lived not far from Troy, Miles's brother, in Plymouth. One day, on a visit to Troy and his family, Miles and the little girl from Kray House arranged to meet, on a platform at the train station. He stepped from the train and in the dispersing crowd, they recognised each other. She was with her son, a young man, he was holding her elbow. As she got nearer to Miles, she stopped abruptly. She put her hands over her eyes and wept.

One Saturday morning, after a month of life at Kray House, Betty showed up. Miles was eating lunch when a carer came over to tell him that his mother was in the foyer. Miles stood up instantly, his heart raced. He was smiling so hard as he went to find her and there she was, smiling back. She put her hand on his neck. She smelt different, he didn't know the smell. Before, her clothes always smelt of lavender and her hair of coconut. Now there was a new perfume to her, strong with lemon. They walked into an empty room and she sat at a table.

"You look well, Milo. I brought you some things." Miles was still standing. She pulled a bag up onto the table and out of it came comics, a Jamaican bun and a football t-shirt.

"Can I get my things?" Miles asked his mother.

"What for?"

"To come home."

"Oh no, Milo, I don't live in Bristol anymore. I'm in Southampton now."

"Where's Juliette?" His mother didn't face him,

"With some lovely people. Mr and Mrs Fry."

"Who are they?"

"They're fostering her. You know, for now. Lovely people."

"I want to go home. I have to go home, mum. I want to go to Don's."

She stood up, "I'm sorry."

"When are you coming back?"

"Soon," her eyes couldn't meet his. She touched him again, his sleeve, then left.

This time he didn't cry. He walked straight up to his dorm. Lewisham, who was a proper bully said, "Oi, Miles, you coming for a kick around?"

"Fuck off," was all Miles answered.

"That's charming, that is," said Lewisham, but he didn't push it and left the dorm. Miles sat on his bed, shoes still on. One of the carers came up,

"You left this." He handed over Betty's carrier bag. Miles stretched out his hand without looking at him. He could hear a kid in a room somewhere throwing a fit. Through the window he could see the formal grounds and a man banging a hammer at a fence. The view was like a black-and-white photograph with a white sky and wet black trees that looked burnt. From the carrier bag, he pulled out the bun, opening the packaging and releasing his favourite smell, of spices, of molasses. He tore off a piece and chewed it, it tasted so good. He sat there on his bed and ate his way through the entire bun and read each comic until the sun closed down.

Chapter Eight

GIVING IN GENTLY

Eastville, Bristol, 1972

Jim was driving. Jim looked like he should have been retired, he looked an ex-manager, a manager of maybe a big hardware store. He always wore a suit and tie, possibly the only social worker of that era familiar with ironing, starch and the *Telegraph* crossword. He was Miles's assigned carer, and bumped in and out of his life intermittently over the next few years, with an invested and affable attitude.

"You following the footie? Did you get some telly time at Kray's?"

"No."

"No? Oh well, right you are. You'll be glad here, then. Mr and Mrs Basset have got a colour TV – be able to tell the difference between the teams that way."

He drove, he chattered. Miles sat beside him, his hands clamped between his knees. He was being fostered. He was to have foster parents. Their names were Mr and Mrs Basset. They had a son, Miles's age, and a daughter who was younger. They lived in Eastville. Miles was really worried. His bed wetting was worsening. The older he got, the greater the amount of urine, simple as that. He felt ashamed of himself, but also this was a really hard problem to live with, to deal with. He sat in silence. "Now here's the thing, dropping you off, having a cuppa, having bit of chat. Sort out some paperwork. Then you'll have a bit of time to get your bearings, that'll be good. It'll be good for you, Miles. It will be."

The car was at a stop, the indicator ticking loudly. Miles suddenly knew where he was. He was in Easton, it was a street he knew well. The Black community was going about its Saturday morning business, captured behind the glass of the car window, like a silent movie. A few men in sharp suits were hanging out in front of the betting shop. As Jim's car pulled away, one of the men laughed. His entire body creased and his hand came out, he clicked his fingers. There was a rhythm to the movement, a grace, it was like a dance move. Then the men were gone.

Mrs Basset, who had livid pink skin and a crocheted waistcoat that matched the blanket on the sofa, stood quite formally at the table, wearing a frozen smile. Her husband was busier, moving a chair for Jim. The two children were eating chocolate biscuits, Penguin bars, and the girl had chocolate on her face. None of them looked at Miles, yet he felt that he was under scrutiny. He stood awkwardly in this family's home, three carrier bags of possessions at his feet. Jim pulled out paperwork and a cup of tea was set before him. Suddenly Mr Basset addressed Miles directly, "D'you want some orange squash?" Miles sat down, a plastic beaker of orange squash and a Penguin placed before him. He hadn't seen a chocolate bar in six months.

"Now, school?" Miles looked at them. "Mr and Mrs Basset want to know where you want to go to school?" Miles felt his pulse quicken.

"Can I go where I want?"

"No, not really. You can choose between the comprehensive school here, or go back to your old school."

"To Cotham?"

"Yes, but it will mean getting up early."

"I want to go back. I would like to go to Cotham, please."

"Mrs Basset?"

"Yes, that's fine." It was actually relief, she didn't want this kid in school with her son, you never knew how it might rub off.

Nothing else touched Miles all weekend. Mrs Basset was nasty, he got that straight away. She didn't want him in her home, but her husband tried a bit harder to make him feel like less of an intruder. Miles didn't care. He was going back to Cotham Grammar, he had his eye on the prize and nothing else mattered.

In the assembly room at Cotham Grammar that Monday morning, the headmaster spoke in a calm voice of the upcoming rugby tournament and the need for the boys to walk not run down the corridors. In the gathering of boys sat crossed-legged before the Head, there was Miles. He was holding his legs down, his energy was so strong. The boys looked mostly sleepy and bored, but Miles's face was one big smile.

Cotham Grammar was a special place back then. In 1972, it was in its last year as an all-boys' school. It drew in the sons, then daughters, of liberal-minded, well-heeled white people. It is astonishing that from that one school, some years later and in a tight timeframe, the bands Rip Rig + Panic, Pigbag, Maximum Joy, The Cortinas, The Pop Group, JoBoxers – among others – all had Cotham Grammar members. It seemed normal at the time, but looking back Miles can see there were subconscious and conscious reasons why he chose to return to Cotham rather than attend a more local school. Consciously, there were things that this class of people offered in the music they listened to, the clothes that they wore and the way they spent their free time, things that he desired. Subconsciously, it was the excitement in the air that was social and was musical. It was the beginning of the punk rock era, of new slogans. It's called anarchy, arsehole.

On returning to school, Miles had primed himself to beat up the first boy to goad him about being taken into care. Nobody did, nobody mentioned it. Miles wondered, later, as a man, how much of his home life was known to his classmates. The answer is, very little. Clifton had hippy shops now, selling Afghan rugs and hand-thrown pottery. Lines were blurring. Clifton was also in a neighbourhood where ostentatious shows of wealth were not done, so very privileged kids would have worn scuffed shoes and kept their rucksacks until they fell apart. Nothing about the way Miles dressed gave away his plight and nothing that came out of his mouth gave away the truth. It wasn't that he fitted in, more that other people were beginning, slowly, to fit around him.

The first boy to befriend him at Cotham Grammar was Nick Tuchband. Nick was a Jewish kid whose main love was drag racing. He painted dragster cars onto his school rucksack and Miles was transfixed. They would sit outside against a wall with Nick turning over the pages of his *Hot Rod* magazines, his finger tapping the points of interest. When you are young, to decide that you love something is to make it yours. This one car, a Blue Max Mustang, stood apart from all the others. Miles chose it as his car. Back at the Bassets', feeling uncomfortable downstairs with them, Miles would stay in the room he shared with the son and practice drawing cars, until he was ready to draw his blue car onto his rucksack. He drew a car every night.

Nick said, "Come back to mine. I've got loads of magazines and some models." They took a bus to Stoke Bishop. Nick's house was covered in ivy. He knocked the front door, his grandfather answered. The grandfather wore brown corduroy and huge glasses that magnified the look on his face almost comically.

Miles knew that look. First, startlement. What, a negro boy here? Next, primal wariness. Then the very British power of politeness taking over, "Come, come in. Nick, get some milk and biscuits."

In the kitchen sat the grandmother who stared in open disbelief at the sight of a Black boy being served milk. Miles drank the milk down, one eye on the old lady. As he placed his glass back on the table, the grandfather gestured to his upper lip and Miles stepped backwards, uncomfortably.

"You've got milk whiskers," said Nick, walking blithely from the kitchen, oblivious to the dark, checked thoughts that formed an intangible triangular drama between the other people in the room.

Nick carried on being Miles's friend, so whatever misgivings his family had had, they kept to themselves and were tolerant enough to take what probably felt like a leap of faith to them. Miles was born in England, and the Tuchband's was one of the only white homes that Miles had ever stepped inside as a friend. He was twelve.

By then, living with the Bassets was so difficult that Miles got home late enough every evening as to be able to eat alone, and spent all day Saturday and Sunday in his room. At first, Mrs Basset had reined in her vinegar tongue, and had stifled her resentment at being so close to the breadline that she had had to take in a Black child. After a few weeks, the hissing monologue to her husband and the ice-cold exchanges with Miles kicked in. This kind of snidey, "Excuse me, Miles, Mr Basset told me he didn't touch the Ready Brek, you wouldn't know why the packet's so light?" signalling the removal of the packets of breakfast cereal from the kitchen, relocating them to the matrimonial bedroom, along with the biscuit barrel and Mrs Basset's handbag at all times.

Miles would come home to the four Bassets squashed into the sofa like a row of fat canaries, the television dazzling them. Without turning her head Mrs Basset would say, "There's a can of beans on the counter. Be sure to leave the kitchen spotless." Or, "Mr Basset has just switched the immersion tank on, so don't you go running any hot water." This was instead of, "Hello, how was your day?"

It wasn't the hell of Kray House. It was the empty angst of a temporary existence in a pimped-up council house on a scruffy road with people who didn't want him, just the money he represented, as his only shelter. Anything broken, missing or diseased in that household was immediately attributed to the foster boy, as if he had brought with him some dreadful voodoo curse.

Miles bussed in out of Cotham every day. He was able to keep up in school, and mostly to keep out of trouble. Mrs Basset derided him for going to grammar school, "Bloody ridiculous, really," she said, "I mean okay, if your father's a solicitor, it makes sense, don't it? People stay with their own, unless you're a gifted child. Our Andy, now, didn't sit the eleven plus because I don't believe in getting above your station." Miles had heard this line of analysis several times – Mrs Basset, who ironed underpants and had a Tory rosette stuck behind her dressing table mirror. Mrs Basset, who spoke like the Queen when she answered the telephone that sat on its own special table in the hallway.

Miles no longer felt loneliness, no longer felt homesick. Being with his own blood was a fast-fading memory. Being with Black people, too. In Eastville, there were no Black kids. He kept indoors most of the time round there. He went to a youth club once, with Andy Basset. All the kids were white. He felt their eyes on him, he didn't know what they were thinking. There was always the fear that he would get his head kicked in. He sat on a chair, against a wall. The kids were wearing their best clothes, running round the draughty events room to *Tiger Feet*, by Mud. They couldn't dance, they were off the beat. He stayed ten minutes, then walked back home. This was how it was: at best, being ignored; at worst, being assaulted. In between, having to stomach the words said in laughter, said in hate: jungle bunny, coon, golliwog, spade, nigger, sambo, ape. He didn't answer back. Kept his head up. Kept it in.

"Daddy!" (Mrs Basset called her husband Daddy.) "Daddy! He's only gone and wet the beggaring bed again." Miles was in his room, completely still, his eyes on the door. The Basset son snored. It was very early on Saturday morning, not even seven. He'd woken to the familiar clammy sheets and had taken them downstairs straight away, pushing them into the barrel of the washing machine. Mrs Basset was the only one allowed to press the buttons. He hadn't expected her to find the sheets so quickly. Now she was shouting and what sounded like hyperventilating. "I can't do it, I just can't. That's the mattress ruined and it was almost new when Auntie Doreen bought it. Almost new! She died, she died on it, what, a year later? She'll be turning in her grave." Mr Basset's voice was too subdued for Miles to catch. Mrs Basset continued, "The mother's completely doolally. What do you expect?" Mr Basset's voice came back again and this time Miles caught the name "Jim" quite distinctly, followed by Mrs Basset's whimpering. Miles sat up on the bed. Then went downstairs. Mrs Basset looked surprised to see him, as if it were a perpetually renewed shock to have this dark cuckoo in her nest.

"Morning, Miles," said Mr Basset, caught with an armful of piss-sodden sheets and his wife's soprano still ringing round the kitchen. "You off out?" Miles didn't answer, just took his coat from the peg.

As he closed the door she snapped, "Manners!"

Miles walked through the city as it began to wake. His feet took him from Eastville, into Saint Werburgh's, then Montpelier. The streets were more or less empty of people, just a milk float was jangling around the neighbourhood. He walked into St Paul's, to the phone box on Ashley Road. He had some coins in his pocket and he had Jim's phone number committed to memory. The lady from the grocery store walked along the other side of the street. She saw a young man, half facing her, making a call. She didn't recognise Betty's boy. It had been a while.

Chapter Nine

ACROSS THE TRACKS

Hartcliffe, Bristol, 1973

In the car, later that same week, Jim said, "It'll be all right, Miles. There are children like you here. Eight in all. This will be better for you, trust me." It was to be a children's home, in Hartcliffe. Jim drove away from the Basset's carefully, as if rough driving might shake Miles up. Miles didn't know what a children's home was. He had never known a child from somewhere like that. It sounded like a place where orphans live. They drove up a hill, the roads were wide. Jim pointed out the home, on the left at the summit. Behind the home was woodland. He parked the car and disappeared inside the house, which was ordinary, red brick with a half-frame white facade, but bigger than any other house around. The front garden was vaguely tended: exuberant shrubs, bikes that were chucked on to the grass and further away, a motorbike stripped down to its steel skeleton. Miles sat in the passenger seat, his school bag on his knees, and four carrier bags stuffed around his feet, waiting for the next chapter to begin.

The man of the home, Uncle Neil, came out to meet him. He was in his early forties, a bit of a rockabilly, his hair Brylcreemed, tattoos up his arms.

"Come inside and have a look around, mate."

In the kitchen, a girl doing her homework at the Formica table stood up in surprise when she saw Miles. She smiled, shaking her head. It was Sadie, Miles's cousin. Her father was Damian, one of Betty's brothers. It was the first familiar face he had seen outside school since the day his mother had visited him at Kray House. Other children wandered in, said hello. The sugary smell of lunchtime baked beans lingered in the kitchen. Jim chatted with the rockabilly man. There was a big ray of sunshine that hit the kitchen window, showing up words that had been traced by a finger, "Dean Wuz Ere," back to front. It was better. Kray House had been the most distressing experience in his life. The Bassets had been months of feeling ill at ease, ashamed and alone. Here, there was Sadie, for a start. He knew her, she used to come to Don and Betty's, she was family. There were other children like him, and there is safety in numbers.

He came down from his room for his supper. His room-mate had explained that you need to ask for supper. It's always bread and jam. You make it yourself. Uncle Neil and Auntie Philippa eat with their own kids at tea time, not with us. Their own kids are Suzy and Angie. Suzy's all right. Angie's a fucking brat. Keep out of her way.

Philippa took a long look at Miles, and he at her. She was older than her husband, small and taut, with a slightness that was down to nerves.

"Settled in then, have you?"

"Yes, thanks. Paul said to come down and ask for supper?"

"What, you hungry are you?"

"I didn't get any tea."

"Right." She had ash-coloured hair that fell to her waist. He discovered, living there, that her hair was an obsession. She kept a boar-bristle hairbrush in the kitchen, brushing her hair vigorously several times a day. She was doing this now, leaning forwards and giving the underside a going-over. She threw her head back and with the brush pointed to the Mother's Pride white sliced, the jam and the butter on the sideboard. She left him to it.

The days were long for Miles. He now lived further than ever from Cotham Grammar School, but he clung to attending there as if it were a life buoy. Nick Tuchband and him kept tight company. On Saturdays they hung out down-town, scouring thrift shops for car magazines. Miles turned out to have a keen eye for store windows, dark and full of clutter that screened-off untold joys for two teenage boys. He would go to Nick's in the afternoon and they spent hours flicking through magazines, cutting out pictures of the best cars and sticking them in scrapbooks.

At the home, Miles kept to his room or stayed in the front room putting records on the turntable, his own records, a little collection that had begun with the unforgettable experience of ordering a seven-inch from the record shop on Picton Street, T-Rex, *Telegram Sam*.

Hartcliffe was white, working-class and one of the roughest neighbourhoods in Bristol. Miles didn't try to form any friendship with anyone. There was always the routine racism, just beyond the shelter of the home. If he went with a white boy from the home to a playing field to join a bunch of boys playing football, it would be to the tune of, "What d'you bring a coon for?"

There was, however, a magical backdrop to the home. The woodland. Down the side lane, and out into fields and the peace of oak trees. That first year, he spent every Sunday afternoon roving the countryside with other children from the home. They would walk for hours, a tiny gang of unkept kids, watching birds that they learned the names of on their own, testing the rushing water of the stream, screaming with laughter as they dodged the bull in the cow fields. Lying in the grass in the shadows of the waterside, day dreaming.

Philippa didn't take to Miles. To be fair, she didn't like any of the wards under her care. There were gradients to her disapprobation. Sadie, for example, who was older and autonomous, she disliked far less than the others, and Miles she liked least of all. Maybe it was the bed wetting. Maybe it was his skin colour. Sadie's mother was white, and Sadie herself hardly Black-looking at all. Miles had no idea really why Philippa hated him. But he felt her eyes on him in the kitchen, tracking him, as if she expected him to slip inexistent pound notes up his sleeves, or run a pocket knife the length of fridge door. Her dislike wasn't active. She didn't hurt, or even particularly disparage him. She simply didn't speak to him.

One day he came back from school, and went straight into the front room. The transistor radio was on. A song played, *Seasons In The Sun* by Terry Jacks. He felt a tightening inside. His eyes teared over. He stood in the room, alone, and wept. These tears, he couldn't fathom.

****

One Saturday in summer he woke early. He was fourteen. The dawn sunlight broke through the crack in the bedroom curtains, making a gold line on the floor towards the door. He dressed quietly, his roommate was still asleep, and he left the house. He took a bus into Easton, then walked in to Montpelier. It was shocking how every single thing in this old neighbourhood was exactly the same, when everything in his own life was obliterated.

Then he stopped. Here was his home. East Grove.

It was still only 7am. The whole street was sleeping.

He pushed the garden gate and waited. He walked to the back of the house. He knew the trick of getting in, by pushing the small kitchen window open and reaching down to open the bigger window. He hauled himself up soundlessly and dropped on to the kitchen floor with the velvet mute of a cat. Down the hallway, he glanced into the front room. There was some weed in the process of being bagged on the coffee table. The painting of a woman called Tina was still on the wall. It was tidy, but emptier. He stopped in front of Don's bedroom, the door was ajar. He held his breath and looked inside. Don lay flat on his back, his sleeping hand on Tammy's naked breast. He stepped away and walked backwards in absolute silence, to the kitchen. Don's coat was hung on the back of the kitchen chair. He felt for the wallet in the pocket. In the wallet, on the right, was a neat set of folded ten pound notes and on the left, under see-through plastic, was a yellowing photo booth picture of Betty in which she looked startled. He took a bank note, put the wallet back exactly as he found it, then pulled himself back through the window and out.

He knew that Don wouldn't be angry with him. He didn't fear Don, whose violence had never once been directed at him. He had seen Don locked in a relationship that seemed like an ongoing pub brawl with his mother. It was hard to dismantle the good guy and the bad guy in his mind, those lines were so badly drawn. However, what Don had given Miles was what fatherless sons can sometimes feel the lack of acutely: male protection. Bigger boys than Miles mostly hadn't picked on him, or never picked on him if their parents knew that Miles was Don's son. In St Paul's, as time went by, it was assumed by a lot of people that they were biologically bound. No one in St Paul's wanted to answer to Donovan.

The house on East Grove was a headquarters for some kind of activity, nefarious or not, and a lot of men came by, every day. Some of them were big men like Don. It was easy for Miles to gauge, through the interactions the men had with Donovan, that there was a hierarchy and that Don was the boss. Donovan was a bad man in the broad sense, rather than in a moral one. The reality between the breadline – hunger, shame – and a life a little less harsh was one with few options. As late as 1963, the city of Bristol was implementing an apartheid system concerning the employment of ethnic workers. The Bristol Omnibus Company operated the colour bar, a policy preventing Black and Asian people – "coloureds" – from being employed in public transport as part of the transport crew. This wasn't a policy hatched by ultra right-wing fanatics. This was trade union based, backed also by Labour councillors. It was a pervasive prejudice, affecting the way Black people were considered for all lines of employment.

Before this time, in 1948, HMT *Empire Windrush*, a colossal German-built ship, had docked in Kingston, Jamaica. It was on a round-trip, picking up Commonwealth citizens and bringing them to the United Kingdom to help solve the desperate labour shortage. The ship sat in the Caribbean waters, grand, mysterious and half-empty. An advertising campaign in the *Daily Gleaner* designed to boost the number of passengers (since the ship had only a half-load) enticed Jamaican citizens with a cut-price fare of £28 10s. This was still a considerable sum for any Jamaican. Livestock was sold and savings released by Jamaicans who felt that they should take this opportunity, since the "mother country" had made clear the need for islanders to come and work.

By the 1970s, the Black communities of Britain were mostly made up of these people, the Windrush Generation, and their children after them. They had been a trusting people, brave enough to travel faraway to do nothing more than graft in the hope of a life with more prospects than the one they had left behind. The reality was other. England took what it needed from them, then rejected them with a great level of psychological violence. What came hand in hand with the racism levelled towards Caribbean immigrants was actual deprivation. They found themselves in a hostile land, a motherland whose milk was bitter. They formed communities that were tight. There was basic necessity, hunger, cold. There was what desperation pushes you to do.

This is how many Black men, who would otherwise have certainly been law-biding, men like Donovan, ended up working from their own front rooms. With the curtains drawn.

Don's house, this ex-place of shelter to Miles, became somewhere he only remembers breaking into, after the age of twelve. Lifting a banknote from Donovan's wallet became an occasional source of money for a long time. He remembers sometimes knocking the door, in the daytime too, asking Don for money, which he always gave him. But he has no memory of going honestly inside.

An event unwittingly funded by Don was a day out at the Santa Pod Raceway in Northants. The boys, Nick and Miles and two other kids, Jamie and Mick, had set their sights on a day of drag car racing. They had chosen the event, in fact Miles had chosen based on the participation of American racers—they were the top dogs of the sport, the originators. It was a little as if Manchester United had rocked up at a soccer game in, say, Cleveland, Ohio in the seventies. They saved money for the tickets and the train fare to Podington, which was a good three-hour journey away.

They walked from the station to the circuit. It was thrilling. There was the clamour of hundreds of cars revving and racing, and there was the hit of nitro oxide, an overpowering and wonderful smell to a fourteen-year-old boy, like the air had been bombed with almond essence. Just the outside car park would have been enough for them. The event attracted hot rod enthusiasts countrywide, peacocking around their souped-up cars. Inside, around the track, hundreds of people milled about. It was hot summer's day in England. Men in capped t-shirts with lobster pink arms, loud women drinking down cans of shandy, little kids wearing huge protective earmuffs, 99 ice creams dripping on their knees. All of this. Meandering around the pits. Leaning in and looking close up at these dream vehicles so that the hundreds of tired, thumbed magazines revved into life. Between the races, there was music, piped out and thumping, and the zany Americanish man's voice over the tannoy, calling out the cars.

They sat down near the front to watch the afternoon races. Miles was staring out in wonder when something made him turn his head, then completely swivel round. Way up behind, on the higher tiers of the stands, was a mob of bikers. One of them was looking down on Miles, who was the only Black person present. The second Miles turned, the man swiped a butcher's blade into the air, violently jabbing it skywards and roared, "Nigger!" Everyone around the man heard. They carried on drinking and mucking about. Miles turned quickly back to track. He leaned in to his friends.

"Don't turn around but there's a biker back there with a knife just called me a nigger."

"Eh?"

"I said don't turn around!"

"Nah, don't worry about it. They're just drunk," said Nick, like he was worldly. Miles was scared, he was in a minority of not even one, since he was a child facing adults. Despite a wariness, a stronger emotion took hold. It was not about to ruin his day. He forgot the pack behind. He had brilliant time. The wild screeching tyres, the whooping of the crowds. Miles and his friends crazed with excitement as the cars they had painstakingly drawn so many times burst into life before them.

He got home very late that night, with special permission. Nick's dad dropped him off. He was too excited to go indoors and sleep, so he walked a bit, taking a football into the field behind. The moon was heavy and the field caught in silver light. He kicked the ball around until he felt himself coming down, and the day that was like a firework display going off in his mind faded out.

CHAPTER TEN

EVERYONE'S GONE TO THE MOVIES

It was going to happen, sooner or later. He was fifteen. Girls had started to look at him as if they were trying to fathom him. There would be a woman, or more a girl, not like the first time when he was seven and bewildered, but this time with his full consent and understanding. It was definitely about to happen.

She was a hybrid tomboy and vixen. She spoke like a docker, effing and blinding and walked with a shove to her shoulders. She wore cut-off denims that bit into her thigh tops and her hair was a miracle of lacquered engineering, two perfects rip curls of hair as formal as a pair of curtains on either side of her tight, pale face. Her name was Tonya and she was trouble. She was friends with one of the girls who lived in the children's home, she had started hanging round in the front room more and more. She would turn her head when Miles walked in and say, "All right, sexy?" And Miles would roll his eyes. Her friend told Miles that Tonya fancied him, which in equal measures scared and excited him.

"Get out," said Miles. "She's too old for me."

"She's seventeen."

"Exactly."

It was a Sunday afternoon. It seemed the whole house was either dozing or crashed out in the living room watching Errol Flynn as Don Juan on the hulking TV set that ruled the room.

Miles was on his bed, reading a racing magazine. He had the bedroom window open just a bit. It was September and it had rained relentlessly since the morning. The rain carried the nutmeg smell of autumn. He looked up sharply, like you do when you sense you're being watched. Tonya was in the doorway. She was staring at him, her eyelids were turquoise and she was chewing gum.

"D'you wanna come with me?"

"For what?"

"To the bathroom."

His immediate, boyish, thought was, "I've already had a bath this morning," but then that thought was shunted forward by a shape of a thought, rather than anything coherent. It was an empty shape. He got up, followed her.

From the other side of the landing he heard, "When Suzy was a teenager, a teenager she was, she said 'Ooh aah, I lost my bra.'" and the piping voices of two children and the clapping of their hands seemed to march him into the bathroom. Tonya locked the bathroom door.

Her face looked different, wilder. Her cheeks, normally so white, had changed, colour infusing them like Ribena in milk. She was at his belt, at his fly, tugging and rushed. Calmly, he held her back. She turned both the bath faucets on, full throttle, so that the water pounding could be heard from the landing. He undid his trousers. She sat on the sink edge, her legs apart.

"Push it up," she said. There was the noise of the rain against the window, the noise of the water rushing from the tap. As he entered her, she snorted. He hesitated, pushed in further. She snorted again. An exact imitation of a farmyard pig. Things were colliding in his brain. He was inside her. Her head was back, her eyes misted over. He was fucking her, and at every thrust, reflexively, she snorted. A pig. He came in a state of shock. She brought him up a cup of tea later and she understood there would be no encores. He told Nick about it.

"Fuck that," he laughed. "I ain't doing that again." He spoke the truth, not having sex for a long time.

Also, Miles realised at some point after this, that his bed was dry every morning. The shameful, tyrannical weight was lifted.

He was grown.

****

Three years of his life passed as a resident of the children's home in Hartcliffe. His recollections are limited. He was neither happy nor unhappy there. He felt no connection to the building, no sense of home. He formed no emotional bond with anyone, in all that time. His past – his mother, Juliette, little Joanie, Baby Troy, Uncle Eric, St Paul's – was lost to him. Donovan still existed, in the real world, but in a context that was almost unbearable. Framed in a doorway where Miles's life had played out, but where every person that he had loved was gone. Miles was unaware that Don had sought to get him and Juliette back, to bring them home, through the courts. This had been refused to him, because Don was neither a blood relative, nor married to their mother. Why had Miles not been told? Just knowing that someone out there had cared enough, had wanted him, would maybe have made a difference, would maybe have given him some sense of worth.

****

One time, on his way to school, he met a kid from the bomb site. The kid told him that the club house was being emptied and that they were giving all the records away later that day. Miles was older and he hadn't been to the bomb site in years. He thought about it all day. He thought about one song in particular, *Clean Race* by Scotty. It was his favourite tune as a little boy. It was a song like nothing he had ever heard on English TV. It had a stepping bass, it got the kids dancing at the bomb site. The children down there danced simple steps and took their cue not from the hippies, but from their own people. Miles liked the way the singer toasted – a Jamaican term for chatting in patois over a tune, the blueprint for rap – on *Clean Race*, he liked the way Scotty rode the rhythm.

The bell rang for the end of school and he was gone. He ran all the way to St Paul's, the route once so familiar. Jay's face lit up when he saw Miles, "Hey man, how's it going? How are you, Miles?"

"I'm all right. I heard you're giving all the records away?"

"Yep. This is true," said Jay. They walked to a table. There were small stacks of records. "Here you go, take what you want."

"I just want *Clean Race*, please," said Miles.

"Oh, mate. I think that one's gone already." Miles went through the seven-inchs, turning them over one by one, putting the ones he liked to one side. But *Clean Race* had found a taker. Well, it was a good tune. Miles raised his hand, said goodbye to Jay that way, from afar, and never went back to the bomb site again.

****

Dunc loved football. He spent every free moment at Cotham in the school yard, kicking a ball around. The goal posts were rucksacks and the classroom windows indicated the sidelines. Miles, being from St Paul's, had been at the toughest football school in Bristol. As a little kid, then as an older kid, he had spent entire summers running around the bomb site trying to join older boys' matches. Black kids play hard and they don't pass the ball to a younger child to make him feel good, the kid has to work for it. Miles loved football, and he did work for it. When the games were twenty aside, which yes, is forty people on the pitch, of all ages, Miles never got a look in, but on the days where there were only eight younger kids down there, he released his frustration, trying out everything he had seen. By the time he was fourteen, he was a good player, fast and incisive. At Cotham, he spent a few breaktimes on the touchline, watching the boys play, hoping for an invitation. One afternoon, one of the teams was short of a player and he bounded into the game. His ability as a player was a surprise to his team and a lament for the other kids. Dunc and Miles met up on the playing field every day. They exchanged an, "All right, mate?" then kicked the ball around.

They set up little teams, played matches, parting company with the word "later". Their friendship was sealed with football, clothes and music, the holy trinity of these now teenage boys.

One day, a Friday in spring, when Cotham glowed golden in the afternoon light, Dunc invited Miles to his home. Miles stood back behind Dunc. Mrs Murison, Dunc's mother, opened the front door. To Miles it was like a TV advertisement come to life. Mrs Murison was womanly and motherly and seemed lit up from inside. Everything about that moment, in fact, seemed caught in light. She smiled as Dunc introduced Miles to her. She smiled right at him, her eyes shining into his. No fear, no judgement. Come in. Miles could not number the afternoons spent in that house in Redland during his teenage years. He and Dunc would play football everywhere, on Redland common and if it was raining, in Dunc's bedroom with a sheet over a homework table as a goal net and Dunc's tightly rolled football socks as a ball. The Murison family opened their life to him: Dunc's cheery, lanky father who was a painter, in fact a painter of some repute, who seemed always to be passing through. Dunc's beautiful older sister, who never left the house without heavy eye makeup whose colours and glimmer reminded Miles of beetles' backs. But mostly, there was Dunc's mother, the kind Mrs Murison who would let Miles into the house, always with warmth, whether Dunc was in or not. Mrs Murison who bought the Jaffa Cakes she knew Miles liked just for him.

He borrowed Dunc's safety, for a few hours, every week. Within those walls, in those well-loved rooms, he didn't feel like he was in the way. As a mixed-race teenager in Bristol, Miles had his antennae out, always. He could scan people in a heartbeat. He could feel their prejudice and fear, it was in their eyes, no matter how hard they tried to disguise it. Mr and Mrs Murison were free of that. Something in the way the Murisons got on with their lives with Miles in their home, each of them going about their business, helped Miles to get over his crippling shyness. After a time, Miles felt comfortable enough to wait inside, even when Dunc wasn't in. The Murisons are a faded photograph that it hurts and doesn't hurt to look at. Miles was part of their lives, he was on their shopping list. Miles would make sure he was was the last boy Mr Murison would drop off after a day of football. Miles did this so he could spend as much time with the Murisons as possible. Mr Murison didn't know that he pulled up at a curb that wasn't in front of Miles's home, or even on Miles's street. The Murisons are one of the reasons Miles could never hate white people.

CHAPTER ELEVEN

LET YOUR LEARNING BE YOUR EYES

Miles had been at Cotham a little while, seven, maybe eight, months. What was curious to him, and what was diametrically opposed to St Paul's, was that a boy was not judged by how tough he was. So, he let his guard down a little. He felt himself relax, without the worry of nebulous potential violence. Miles was in the school yard, with a couple of classmates, when a kid shoved him.

"Hey Johnson, I want a fight with you." Miles was stopped in his tracks. This boy, Klerk, was older than him by a couple of years. He was from South Africa. In the seconds it took for Miles to process what was happening, the why and the who, Klerk had Miles by the lapels and head-butted him, crack, square on the nose. The shock was total and the pain of great intensity. There was no blood for a few seconds. Miles began to walk away, dazed. All the kids followed, including the head-butting brute. Miles walked into the nearest open classroom, sat at a desk and put his head on his arms. Blood, what seemed like an open faucet, flooded the desk, began to dripping on the floor. A kid ran out of the class, and Klerk, panicking, shoved a handkerchief to Miles, "Go on, wipe your face." He sounded worried. Miles remained motionless. The kid came back into the classroom with a teacher, a geography teacher. Miles can still, to this day, hear the anger in the teacher's voice, hear the way the shouting seemed to come from the pit of the teacher's stomach,

"Klerk, get to the headmaster's office now!" Klerk was expelled. Miles's confidence in other boys was as damaged as his nose.

It was a different game now.

Another time, Miles was in his maths class. The maths teacher was Mr Crose. This man was built like an ogre, towering, carrying extra weight, podge on big bones. He wore bottle-end glasses and beneath his bushily-nostrilled nose, a severe moustache. He was tweedy, his jacket too short in the arms, and threadbare. He wore a white shirt, always grey-belted trousers and white Y-fronts pulled up way beyond his trousers' waist, to halfway up his body – a perpetual source of schoolboy laughter. Mr Crose was explaining a maths equation and wandering down the aisle. Miles was messing around, folding up a piece of paper, ready to make a tiny plane. Mr Crose, all the while calmly continuing his mathematic exposé, grabbed Miles by the hair, and began to shake him around, a vice-like grip on his head. "Johnson, if you don't sit in obedience, if you don't stop mucking around in the classroom, I will have to take some drastic measures." With this, he pulled his clenched fist away. It hurt very much. Mr Crose had clumps of Miles's hair protruding between his fingers. He proceeded down through the classroom, shaking fat tufts of hair loose from his hand, like he was shaking off dirt. Miles felt all at once humiliated, singled out, very much alone. His head stung badly. The boy in front of him caught his eye, then the boy looked at the hair, black hair damp with blood, and then more blood, splashed across the wooden floor. The boy whipped back round to face the teacher. Miles had seen the terror on his face. He knew what Miles knew: no white boy would be treated like that. Another teacher at Cotham, the squat Mr Fitch, was happy to talk about jungle bunnies and spades, "You want to get that fuzz cut Johnson, you'll be looking like a golliwog soon." He was relaxed in his racism, jocularly trying to get the whole class on team with his wisecracks.

This aside, life was diversifying. Through Dunc, he met other boys and every Saturday was spent in Cotham. He was always at Dunc's it seemed, and if not there, round at other kids' homes. There was no trade-off, no return invitation. He lived with the fear of being unmasked, as the kid who lived in a children's home. To the question, asked or imagined, "Hey, Miles, can we come back to yours?" He had an answer queued up, "You don't want to come back to mine, it's the other side of town and it's really boring." Really boring was an ultimate putdown in those innocent days. Some boys were into girls at this point. Miles was guarded. He knew that if he had a girlfriend, if he got close to her, then he would have to tell her that he was in care. No one wants somebody who is in care. This was his belief. Why would you want a boy whose own mother didn't want him?

Dunc had a little crew of friends, one of them was Claude Williams. Claude was the Black kid who had rolled his eyes when Miles went hurtling into the stacked chairs on the first day of Cotham grammar. Claude had glee, he had mischief. He was tall, like Miles, but sinewy. When he laughed, it was difficult not to be drawn in. His face, the way it dimpled, his great smile, just seemed designed for laughter. Miles and Claude started hanging out together. Miles was now fifteen, closer to sixteen. He had been removed from St Paul's for nearly four years. Claude lived in Redland, a completely white, quite staid, area. One day, Claude brought him back to his house. He pushed his front door, "Mum, I'm back!" Claude slung his school bag down. In the kitchen, out of view, was Mrs Williams, cooking, answering her son (the Jamaican phrasing, the smile Miles could hear in her voice). Claude's sister, in her room, yelling something and then laughter. From another room, Derrick's room (he was Claude's older brother), came music.

Miles had just re-entered a pocket of life that had once been intimate to him, from which he had been exiled. He has never really thought about how deprived he was of Black culture all those years, nor of the significance of the Williams household. Being at the Williams' was like being at the Murisons', in the sense that this was a place he felt able to relax in, and to be himself, only with a difference. These were Black people and some things were therefore just understood. Also, Derrick had a collection of funk albums. Derrick would hear music at the Guildhall Tavern, fall in love with a song and buy it the next week, or order it on import from HMV. Music to dance to. Derrick let Miles in with open friendship from day one, and they listened to funk together all the time, back then. All the time. In this way, and others, music was back in his life. Music was to be a forever love affair.

It was some time around then that Miles went to his first concert, Doctor Feelgood, at Bristol University. All the boys who were somebody seemed to be going. These older boys, the ones in bands, got Miles's attention – they played instruments, that was new to him. Among them, for instance, were boys from The Cortinas, a Bristol punk band who would be playing the Roxy in London not so very long after. The lines between watching and creating were blurring. He can't recall the concert itself, there was no great epiphany, but he does remember how cool it was to be hanging out in a big hall on a Friday night with all these interesting kids from school.

It was now 1976, kick-off for UK punk, and the kids with their ears to the ground at Cotham Grammar were part of it. A lot of bands were formed there that made music that has stood the test of time. Miles had an ever-open ear, punk resonated with him, but he was going deeper into all music: soul, reggae, funk, folk. Music was all-consuming. He started going to the underage disco, by Bridewell Police Station in Broadmead in the centre of Bristol. It was a big deal for a certain type of kid. To wander into the dark space with its thumping bass and infinity mirrors was a taste, an electric buzz of a taste, of what was yet to come.

There were girls down there, from all over town. Their fathers would form a queue of suburban cars at 10pm. "Come on, Mandy, get in," the father would say, the passenger door open. But he would have his eye on the club door, at the youths there in their best clothes, standing up against the wall with sixteen-year-old awkwardness and beauty.

One week, Miles was standing back watching the dance floor when a girl stared at him, unequivocally.

"Hey, mate. That girl's giving you the eye." Claude said.

"No she ain't."

"She fuckin' is." Miles left it where it was. He could not begin to contemplate it, she was very pretty. The following week, she was there again. This time she got her nerve up and asked Miles to dance. That is all it took, really, to start a teenage romance. They were now going out, this white girl called Michelle and him.

In the disco, there were faces from the bomb site days that had once been familiar to him, and friendly. They were not as friendly anymore. A few times, a gang of boys from the bomb site tried to press him in the club toilets. He can remember being cornered. He recognised the boy who was glowering at him. "All right, Wyatt?" But Wyatt answered with a word, a weird slang word that Miles didn't understand, seyfan, something like that. There were maybe ten other kids with Wyatt, kids with dirty looks on their faces. Miles asked,

"What?"

Another kid answered, shoving him.

"He wants to fight you."

Ten to one, those are not good odds. Miles pushed his way past them, back to the dancefloor. He felt confusion. Why would these kids, kids that he had known for years throughout his childhood, now come at him with such aggressive energy? He thought that it had something to do with being taken away. That it had altered him. It had removed him from his community, and his community had removed themselves from him. He could not dwell on this: the chasm of rejection and loss.

*****

Dunc was into football. In Bristol, you chose your camp. You were a City man, or a Rovers man. Dunc supported Bristol City and was already, at the age of fifteen, an adept of Saturday afternoon matches. The first match Miles had been to, on a winter night in 1972, was with Donovan. A cup draw pitched small-town Bristol Rovers against Manchester United, just about the biggest team in England at that time. Donovan, whose favourite player was Man U's Bobby Charlton, took little Miles down to the stadium, to watch this David against Goliath of matches.

The second game of Miles's life would be with Dunc. The pair of them were in the dining hall and Dunc told Miles, "I think Chelsea's gonna try and take the Tote on Saturday." Miles did not, at that point, have the argot of football but whatever it was, it sounded good. Dunc explained. Rovers had got a draw, with Chelsea. Chelsea were major players and they had a set of hooligans. The Tote was the end of the Rovers stadium where the most fervent, and violent, supporters were. One set of football fans trying to take over the hooligan section of another club was an emasculation. No club's hooligans would allow that to happen without a hard fight. Miles was in.

That Saturday afternoon of the match, Miles got his first taste of football hooliganism. Of a massive, male crowd. He and Dunc were in the Tote, standing. They were 15 years old and surrounded by young men, most of them five or six years older. It was rough. All these men looked big to him. Their noses were pinched pink with the fresh air and alcohol. It smelt of spilt beer and sweat. The men were laughing, jostling each other. Miles could feel their elation at being together, and something else, something tribal, threatening the air. Dunc and Miles wore no colours, not then. But they were down among the men. They tried to shout something to each other, but they were drowned out by the singing of thousands of fans. Then, out of nowhere, a furore: "The Chel-Sea! The Chel-Sea!" Three hollow syllables, chanted.

They had been infiltrated. Five hundred or so Chelsea hooligans raged into the Tote and the Rovers fans either scattered or rose to the fight. Miles and Dunc shifted backwards, out of the way. Hundreds of men were in front of them, battering each other. The police were soon involved, swamping the lot of them. They annexed the Chelsea fans, who were removed to a penned-off part of the stadium. Then the match began. It was secondary. Miles had got the bug. He was surrounded by these ultra-hard men, bleeding, singing, roaring. He felt his heart soar. It was the most exhilarating afternoon of his life so far.

The next match Miles went to, with Dunc, City were playing. It was against West Ham United. Again, a team with a set of hooligans – Dunc told Miles that the West Ham fans were the worst, the most savage of the English Football League. Miles counted down the days to the Saturday. He met Dunc down town and they walked to the stadium together. On their way there, they went into a general store, for sweets. There was a rail, and on the rail, gleaming silver, was a butcher's hook. It was in Miles's pocket as they walked back out. Miles hadn't stolen a butcher's hook rather than a packet of batteries, or a magazine, just for kicks. He had hidden it in his pocket because it was like a steel finger beckoning him, reminding him that he and Dunc were walking into uncharted land. He and his friend would not be facing the same set of problems. He kept the hook from Dunc, in the same way that he hid his life as a ward in a children's home. He would only show as much of himself as he felt other people could understand.

At the city stadium, the topography was different. There were two ends. The East End, where all the singing occurred and the Open End, where the hardest fighters were. Many, many hours of Miles's life would be spent in the Open End as he grew older. But on this Saturday, he was down in the East End, with Dunc. The stadium was filling, the East End was already tight with City fans. Then it happened, just like before, "The West Ham! The West Ham!" This in-your-face chant, a thudding tempo, like it was being beaten out on hollow chests. Where, a moment before, there had been only a wash of red and white, City's colours, were now knots of rampant West Ham fans, who had been lurking all along among the City crowd. Like insane magicians, they whipped out lengths of claret and blue scarves from thin air and they were now everywhere you looked. Within seconds, the two clubs were locked together in violence. Bigger kids than Miles and Dunc started running in. Miles charged forwards, too, the meat hook in his hand. A man saw Miles and lunged at him. Miles ducked, then as he went to swing the meat hook into his opponent's body, he felt the hook pierce the skin of his own hand and lodge there. Police were among them, upright, hitting truncheons around like they were swatting wasps. Miles heard a man shout, "That nigger kid's got a knife." A policeman grabbed Miles by the arm, but the other arm, the one that was behind his back, was pumping blood to the ground. Miles struggled to break free of the policeman, shaking his hidden hand frantically until he felt the hook drop. The cop shouted, "Where is it?"

And Miles answered, "I ain't got nothing." The cop scanned the ground briefly, then released his grip.

Miles's hand bore the stigmata of his new life as a football hooligan.

Chapter Twelve

ARE YOU ALL THE THINGS

Hartcliffe, Bristol, 1976

At the home, there was a slow-ticking countdown to his sixteenth birthday. Sixteen was the endgame. It would cross his mind, "One day." One day, he would be out of the hands of strangers. One day he would be like other people his age. One day, he would have nothing to feel ashamed of. One day. His life had been one of exploration up until now. When he was small, seven years old, walking right across the city on his own, through roads where everyone you pass is white, and you are a Black boy – that shapes you. Having doors opened, thinking, "This is my life," then being pushed out, pushed away – that shapes you. Spending every day with white boys who have mothers and homes, when you are Black and you have no mother and no home, that puts something in your soul that, if you are lucky, and strong, will be your touchstone. That and Uncle Eric's single, defining contribution, which was making sure that Miles went to a good school. The education he received at Pro-Cathedral, then Cotham Grammar collared him and held him back from what was the irreversible destiny of so many ghetto kids, of so many kids in care. An example, 'By 2001, the children who were in residential care in 1971 were three times more likely than other children to have died.' – *Scottish Journal of Residential Child Care, March, 2008*. Education gave him language, and taught him how to structure his thoughts. Quite possibly, being around older Cotham boys, the ones who were in bands, also showed him that everything that you are, your own personal chaos, could be transfigured.

Still, right now, he was in the thick of growing up. He was falling into football, hard. It was not without danger, it was also not without comedy. It was a Saturday, it was always a Saturday. It was after a match. He and Dunc were in with a City mob, for the first time. There had been a bit of scuffle in the stadium between rival fans, and the police had dispersed the confrontational men, sending the City fans into town one way, and the Chelsea lot out towards the exits that lead out of the city. The little crew was making its way up Coronation Road, away from the stadium. "Got a few new ones?" asked Craig Morgan, referring to Miles, Dunc and another boy, Griffin. Craig Morgan was tight with Kelvin Jones, the Black City supporter who was arguably the hardest man in Bristol at that time. Miles stole a look at Dunc, Miles was smiling. Miles was also taking in information. Someone was saying, "Look out for one-armed Dray, half-caste bloke, one of the leaders of their main mob. He's a tough fucking bastard." This was a point of interest to Miles, since Chelsea were notorious for having a lot of racist fans. They were making their way up towards St Mary Redcliffe, a gothic church that stood like a cave turned inside out. It was a complete anachronism by a roundabout. Over to the side was an inner-city wasteland. A funfair had landed on it. Not so long before, Miles would have been drawn that way, but now his eyes were ahead, on the roundabout. They were thirty or forty-strong, City fans, making their way up the road, it was bedlam. A car caught Miles's eye, beyond them. He watched the car, a Triumph Herald, go whizzing round the roundabout, then a split second later, it was mowing right into his mob, catching a City fan and catapulting him above the crowd. There was the boom of the car hitting a pavement, then mayhem as the City lot legged it in every direction, running for their lives.

Miles ran into a block of flats. There was a stairwell. On every floor was a sequence of reinforced frosted glass, then concrete. Running the whole height of the stairwell was the rubbish chute. Miles raced up the stairs, stopping just once to look over a balcony. An army of Chelsea ants swarmed out of the fairground. As Miles got to the fourth floor, he was, in his own words, "Absolutely shitting myself." These were Chelsea's top boys, it was their mob. He could hear shouting, a Cockney voice, "Where's that fuckin' nigger? I saw him fuckin' come in here. Where is he?" Then he heard the sound of heavy feet banging up the stairwell. His only way out was the waste chute. He could hide in it, if he could only get in. His breathing was frantic as he opened the lid. Then a hand grabbed his shoulder and pulled him back,

"Come on, love. Come in here. I seen those boys, them's bad 'uns." An old white woman with a hair net over her rollers ushered Miles into her flat and locked the door, seconds before the Cockney thugs reached her landing.

There was pandemonium all around St Mary Redcliffe. Men were kicking the life out of each other and police cars were screaming to the scene. Miles stood at a window, contemplating all of this from a fourth-floor vantage point, with a cup of tea and hot buttered toast with jam.

He watched Chrissie James get chased around the roundabout like something out of a Buster Keaton movie, as the old woman surreally chattered and poured him another cup, "See my son-in-law's a Black boy, he's in the army," she showed Miles a framed photograph of a young man in uniform. Miles stayed in her front room hours, until he felt certain that the Chelsea fans had all been escorted to the train station by the police, and the roads had gone quiet. He thanked the woman, with feeling, for saving his life and as he left, she told him to watch himself with those football gangs, them's no good, she said. No good.

He felt he had to go to Don's. Don's notoriety was the tree Miles had sheltered beneath as a child amongst other children, children more aggressive than him. So, he walked towards St Paul's, down the side streets which were empty and darkening. He heard a motor behind him, tailing him.

"Oi!" The one Cockney syllable like a gun shot. Miles kept walking, quickening his pace, the vehicle following, "Oi, are you Bristol?" A man was leaning from the van window. Miles shook his head. Then he went running straight into the first road, on his right, with the van behind him. The road was a dead end. He was now caught between a vehicle of Chelsea hooligans and an eight-foot wall. What got him over the wall was school high jump practice and adrenalin. He jumped, caught the top of the wall and hauled himself up and over, thudding painfully to the ground. The Chelsea boys seemed to be running up against the other side of the wall where they stayed, barking blindly. Miles can't remember what happened after that, only that he found out the next day that his mate, Griffin, who dabbled both ends of the pitch, supporting City and also Chelsea, had been in the back of the Chelsea van the whole time, drinking beers.

"Was that you they were chasing?" Griffin asked. Then, "They were all right, that lot. Good blokes."

****

Miles was now officially someone's boyfriend – Michelle's. This was new to him. He found out very quickly that she lived a ten-minute walk from the children's home. There was no point in trying to hide the truth from her, so he didn't. She took him home, to meet her family. This was in Hartcliffe, in the late '70s. Hartcliffe was basically one vast council estate. The homes there were a childlike expression of how a house might look: rows of terraced houses with flat façades, plain windows that were oddly placed, the small upstairs windows too high, the front room window oversized and low. There was no individuality in the design, just block upon block of these homes, set on treeless streets, a straight line for road, and above a lot of empty sky. Imperial Tobacco had opened Europe's largest cigarette-manufacturing plant on Hartcliffe land in 1974 and this defined the neighbourhood. It was solidly working class, there was hardship. The tobacco factory handed out jobs. There were perks to working there, among them cheap cigarettes, a reward with encrypted death for many a Hartcliffe tobacco worker.

He met Michelle's mother, Marlow. The surprise was that Marlow was dark skinned, he hadn't expected that, because Michelle looked white. The Porters were a mixed-race family. There was Marlow, her man back then was Ray Jones, who was a heavy-set Welsh man with a rugged face, Michelle, and her brother, Mark, who was known as Punky. Marlow's family was an extended one, and a racially mixed one, Black, brown and white, with the common denominator of fearlessness. Marlow, with discretion and warmth, ruled the roost.

One morning at the children's home, Miles was called into Uncle Neil's office. Jim was there.

"Take a seat, Miles." This was formal, something was up. Miles sat with his arms crossed, head to one side. Jim spoke, "Mrs Porter has asked to foster you." It was a surprise. No one had told him, not Michelle, not

Marlow. Miles let this information sink in. There was silence. "How do you feel about that?" asked Jim.

"Good."

"Yeah?" asked Uncle Neil.

"Yeah. Good."

Miles left the office, went to his room. He was moving into his girlfriend's home, he was going to live with a family who knew him and were choosing him. He had to sit down for a while to take in how happy he felt.

He remembers a Christmas party, at Marlow's, in those early days. The whole Porter clan was there. There was Babycham and Bacardi, crisps and sausages on sticks, and Punky's reggae music. Miles sat on the sofa, working this family out: the uncles, Mike and Martin and the older kids who looked like heartthrobs from teen magazines, especially Punky and his girlfriend, Virg.

Marlow was the matriarch. This was a tough family, with men who governed rough neighbourhoods in Bristol and Manchester. When Marlow – small, straight-backed, honest – spoke, the uncles and brothers fell into line. She was warm, motherly and the rules of conduct in her home were clear.

Then there were the younger kids, and there was one younger kid who was different, Adrian. Adrian had knocked on the door a couple of weeks after Miles moved in with the Porters.

"Yeah, all right? I'm Adrian," said the small slight boy, eager to be let in. He was a livewire, looking up at Miles with childlike expectancy and excitement. He was Marlow's nephew. He was eight, maybe nine. Miles and Punky were hanging out in the front room, listening to records. Miles can remember Adrian's intensity, how bright this child was. "What's this? Who's that?" Adrian would ask, turning over album sleeves. Miles says he just dug this kid, right away. Adrian, who was Black, lived in Knowle West, which was a white Bristol ghetto. Adrian walked from Knowle West to Hartcliffe, always alone, to visit Marlow's and listen to music with Punky and Miles. He was like a young Miles, in that way. Covering ground, cutting through neighbourhoods where everyone you pass is white. It's that kid you see from the comfort of your car, the one you wonder at.

Adrian got it, he got music, he understood the way a song worked. Miles would talk to him,

"Listen to this, mate, get the bassline on this one." Adrian felt music like a soul who had been round this block before. Later, Adrian became Tricky and appeared to look out at the world through eyes at once fierce, yet heartbroken. But as a kid, despite the indisputable trauma the boy had been through, he just shone.

Marlow's house was full of people who loved each other, whose lives were fraught, often and extremely, but of whom Miles says, "They were happy with what they had." It was a chapter in his life defined by a sense of freedom. He had stopped being Michelle's boyfriend when he moved into her mother's house, it had been the understanding and it worked. They became family, or maybe it is more that he became part of Marlow's family. Whichever, he was no longer the boy in care. There was no longer a curfew. There was no longer school. Miles left Cotham Grammar and has no memory of sitting exams, no memory of anyone guiding him. He just wanted to get out into the wide world and start making some money.

With Dunc, he did a little work experience, learning painting and decorating. This was government subsidised, with token pay. Then Ray Jones stepped up, finding Miles a job with a company called Gunac, just as he done for Punky a few months before. The job was the removal of concrete cladding from the façades of high-rise buildings. A group of men, led by their manager – a spectral Welsh racist who in turn was given the sobriquet "Taffy" – spent their days suspended on gondolas two-hundred-and-fifty feet in the air, pulling leaden slabs from between the brickwork. It was a physical and risky job. There was danger money in it. Miles had birthdays and Christmases to catch up. He had an entire adolescence of watching other kids get good clothes and records, get nice shoes and presents and parties. Of having nothing at all, ever, for himself. He blew every pay packet for the first months down in Paradise Garage, the cutting-edge retailer in Bristol (until Marlow reminded him about rent). Paradise Garage was a narrow shop, in a small underpass, tucked behind the bus station. As a punk and vintage clothes shop, it fitted its surroundings, which were about as close to brutalist architecture as Bristol could manage: two compact tiers of blunt concrete walls and steps, darkness and dirty graffiti. It was run by Richard, who would one day become Miles's employer.

Come Friday night, Miles would be shattered from his week in work, but pumped up with anticipation for the weekend, when he would hook up with Woody and the football crowd, and hit The Bell, then The Wheat Sheaf. They would stop for a pizza and move on to Princess Court – this was with religious ritual.

Miles had reached his adult height, six foot two inches, and he was as handsome as his father. He was one of only a few Black men, most of the time, down with the football crowd. This would have been enough to make him stand out, but Miles was now able to release a side of himself that he had only been able to consider from a reader's perspective, flicking through magazines. He was able to establish his sense of style. Miles was overwhelmed with shyness as a child, his shyness never left him. So, you would wonder how such a reserved man could walk around in skin-tight black leather trousers, winkle pickers, ripped t-shirts with a Tom of Finland drawing emblazoned across his chest and withstand the staring? The schoolboy who fell in love with a pair of star-spangled boots was maybe not so far away.

He lived for music. His interior world of songs was ever expanding. Funk had got a hold of him, and punk. He loved Public Image Limited, there was both punk and funk in their bass-heavy sound. It was around this time that Miles became conscious of a tic he had, a compulsion that kicked in when he was about sixteen. Every time he taped a song that he liked, or bought a record, he would play it over and over. And over again. What would stick in his mind were the solos. It could be a solo played by any instrument, in any musical genre. What drew him to a song was the body of the music, especially when it was so good that it got him on the dancefloor. When he loved a song, it was often because the bass was wicked and the drums were heavy. The solo in a great tune caught him, held him, because it was an expression of what he felt inside. It was the response to the body of music that Milo would have given if he had been able to play an instrument. It was a language that he could understand. His mind housed a roving collection of solos, he could reproduce any one of them from thousands of songs, vocalizing it to the nearest semiquaver. Foreshadowing his life as a DJ, when he would curate music, was this collection of solos, audible only inside his head. Just like when he was a boy among poor boys, who could reach joy vicariously, watching other children ride the dodgems, Miles was able to join in with music, and love it, from the sidelines.

CHAPTER THIRTEEN

NO EASY WAY DOWN

Miles had spent his childhood before being put into care in a home where violence was routine. He had been beaten, week in, week out, for years. Miles had seen his mother's face busted, his mother's bones broken. These things were an aspect, a possibility of life itself. One word could act like a sudden spark, hitting a trip wire and rushing up it, towards a domestic bomb.

Now in his teenage years, Miles was a perpetrator of violence rather than its victim. He was never the nutter baying for blood, goading his mates into warrior mode, but he didn't step down from a confrontation either and if he had to get stuck in, then he got stuck in. Bristol City had taken over Bristol's nightlife. In town, no Rovers' fans could enter any of the nightclubs or bars. Rovers' fans were forced to stay in their own areas, mostly around Kingswood and Saint George. This territorial domination had been achieved through systemic confrontation by the previous generation of young City fans. The pressure had to be kept on.

It went something like this: the City crew Miles had become part of met up in The Bell, in Redcliffe. It was an eighteenth-century pub, that stood on a street corner, solid and squat and the colour of vanilla ice cream. The lads were down there three times a week, Wednesdays, Fridays and Saturdays, sometimes ten-strong, sometimes twenty or thirty. Miles never drank alcohol, he always had a clear head. Most of the men who fought did so charged up on beer, Miles fought dry. Down the pub, he was often stuck to an arcade game, manning a slow biplane across a monochrome screen. Just nearby was a jukebox and as soon as a punter dropped in his coin, allowing him three tunes, Miles would have an eyebrow up, "Hey, put that one on for me, would ya?" He can remember a Bowie tune he liked, *Fame*. He'd bug mates for that.

It was a Wednesday night, a quiet night. Miles was on the arcade game. Four bikers, three men and a woman, were stood quite near Miles. Because the pub room was longish and narrow, they were blocking the passage from one end to the other. One of the young City boys made his way from the bar, a pint in each hand, and not being able to get through said to a short, bearded biker, "'Scuse me, mate." The biker glanced over his shoulder and snapped, "Fuck off." Loud enough for Miles and anyone at that end to hear. The boy pushed his way on through, to a few City lads sat at a table.

"That fucking biker bloke wouldn't let me pass. Told me to fuck off," he said, his voice indignant. One of the City men sat there was Kenny. His face tightened. Kenny was unpredictable. He was guarded, off-hand with most of the mob, staying tight only with the hardest men.

He considered what the kid had said, then asked, "What, them over there?" Kenny's beer was in a pint glass, a heavy dimple tankard, and was half full. He got up and strolled over to the bikers, "I heard you told my mate to fuck off?"

The bearded biker looked at him and repeated his catchphrase, "Fuck off." To Kenny now.

Kenny's arm immediately swung backwards, smashing the biker just behind him in the face with his glass with such might that the thick glass of the tankard cracked and the biker's teeth turned red. One jagged half of glass remained in Kenny's beer-drenched hand which he then swung forwards, into the face of the bearded biker, a spiked hunk of glass puncturing near his eye. Kenny was unleashed, his weaponed fist slamming into the now kneeling biker's neck, blood geysering. Bam, bam, bam, glassing the biker over and over. The other City men were already kicking the third biker's head in, he was on the ground rolling around, moaning. Miles was stood back, stupefied by the amount of blood that was now over everyone.

Someone shouted, "Shit! Shit Kenny, you got to fucking get out of here!" Three bikers were down on the pub floor, two of them unconscious and the biker girl, untouched, was screaming her head off. The City boys left, in a hurry.

The attack was covered in the *Bristol Evening Post*, but no one had died and no one was arrested. In the football crowds of Bristol, word spread about this particular faction of City hooligans. By the coming Saturday, Miles and the men were back in the pub, quietly going about their business.

Another evening at The Bell. It was mid-week and the only patrons were fifteen or so City men. Joe sauntered in. He was a kid. He had blond hair and a white van. He was under Liam's wing and Liam was the kingpin of the Bell. Someone said in passing, "There's a pub full of Gas in Kingswood." ("Gas" was shorthand for Rovers' fans, their headquarters being near the gas works.) Someone answered, "Is that right? Let's go down there then, get a round in."

Beers were finished and Miles and the men, around ten of them, piled into Joe's van. They drove east and, as they neared the Kingswood pub, the landscape changed, opened. They drove past fields, before driving slowly past the pub itself. The bloke sat upfront in the passenger seat got a glimpse inside. "Yes!" he exclaimed, rubbing his hands together and laughing, "I believe we're in business." The men in the van, including Miles, laughed too. Miles was carefully taking notes. One thing was clear, he felt this brutal education might help him understand the dynamics between men. He was looking for the map of survival. He found guidance within this group of solidly working-class fighters and, ironically, they were white. Joe parked up on the hill, round the corner from the pub. Two men scouted down first, and were back within minutes.

"There's about fifteen of them in there."

It was on. Liam went steaming down the hill, kicked the pub door in, went straight up to the nearest punter and head butted him to the floor. He was roaring. He took a pub table, the solid picnic kind, upended it and slammed it into two men who minutes before had been working their way through pie and mash. Miles was in, grabbing a Rovers' fan by the collar with one hand, punching him in the head with the other. He kicked the man's legs from under him and once he was down, continued kicking him until he was pleading, "All right! All right, I've had enough." It was raw fighting. The landlord was gone, having run for his life within the first minutes. Men grappled each other to the ground, beating each other so badly that they were all marked, eyes swollen slits, split lips drooling blood, heads slashed. One of the City boys lifted the till, and this marked their exit, leaving fifteen Gas punched out on the pub floor.

The news of this invasion and assault made its way around the Bristol football scene, and the City boys sat on it for a few weeks before deciding to go for a rematch. This time there were more of them, this time they had the van plus a couple of cars that followed them to Kingswood. They breezed up the same hill, parking round the corner, just like the last time. There were thirty of them, maybe more. At least three times the force of before. They jumped from their vehicles and bulldozed round the corner to the pub, only to stop dead. A hundred, maybe two hundred Gas, spilled from the pub, or stormed the bottom of the hill, appearing from behind bushes and cars.

"For fuck's sake!"

The City crew could only do one thing, which was back off. They all went tearing back up the hill. All of them, except Liam. He was taking his time, walking backwards, really slowly, facing the Gas, who were shouting, "Come on you fucking cunts, come down here, we're gonna fucking kill the lot of you."

Miles was just behind Liam, "We gotta get out of here, Liam, there's too many of them."

All he answered Miles was, "I ain't running from this fucking lot."

"Fuck's sakes, Liam. We're gonna get our heads kicked in." And with that, Miles grabbed Liam and yanked him back. Then they both ran. The police were screeching into the road. The City cars had gone, but the van was revving and they jumped in, slamming the doors and then banging into each other as the vehicle took a corner as if on two wheels. To this day, no one knows how the Rovers mob got wind that they were on their way that evening. Such was the game.

****

There were times when an away game became a proper outing. City were playing Bolton, which is a long drive from Bristol. The City firm decided that they would drop in to Blackpool on the way back, though Blackpool is not on the way back at all. It was a sidestep to go there. The seaside visit was because Bristol Rovers were playing Blackpool the following weekend. This is a hooligan take on scent marking, leaving a territorial trace as a reminder of who's the boss.

The boys piled out of two coaches, onto Blackpool seafront. As a backdrop, the Blackpool Tower stood shimmering with miles of filament lightbulbs, like a tarty cousin of the Eiffel Tower. At her feet were sideshows and fish 'n' chip shops, funfair rides and pubs that spilt white-vested, big-stomached punters on to the summer pavements.

The City boys made their way down the promenade. A couple of fights broke out. Glass shattered here and there. It was casual, low-grade vandalism. Miles and his friends wandered down to take a look, not bothered about joining in. Then the police arrived, cordoning them off. The football lot were swamped. The police arbitrarily cuffed Bristol men. In their nets they took Miles – *Let's have you over here and shut your mouth, Kunta Kinte* – his mate Lenny, Tony Pearson and Wayne Worthington. None of these City boys had raised a fist, or done a single illegal thing. They were arrested and piled into a van, then driven to Risley Prison to await trial with no possibility of bail.

In the van, their faces were grim. Miles says that this was the only time he ever saw any of his football mates actually look worried. Risley Prison is outside Manchester. A 1980s report from Her Majesty's Inspector of Prisons, described the detention centre as "barbarous and squalid." A rumour had spread that a few weeks before Miles pulled up to these prison gates, some Mancunians had made a rope out of ripped sheets and fashioned a ball of inflammable debris at its end. This they set fire to, then swung it down between the bars of the cell below. The cell was insalubrious, and full of the inmates' bric-a-brac. The cell went up like a torch, a miniature inferno, burning its inmates alive. The incinerated victims had been from Liverpool, not Manchester. This had been the warrant for their execution. Lenny said, "We're going to have the whole fucking prison against us. Screws an' all." They spent three weeks jailed. Perhaps the arson attack had put the prison on maximum alert, because the Bristol boys got through their time unscathed.

Miles was sent down to be judged, in Blackpool, in a great, draughty court room. Marlow came up as a character witness, the whole Porter family coming with her. It was a day out, an opportunity for Marlow to see her brother, who lived in the infamous Moss Side area of Manchester, a land of gangs and guns back then. Marlow stood at the bar. Miles had never seen her so serious, and he had absolutely never seen her behave deferentially.

"Miles is a good boy, your Honour."

He felt laughter prickling. He tried to suppress it, breathing in deeply, clamping his lips together. The judge shot him a look.

"Don't mind him your honour, he's nervous, it's just his nerves." Marlow faced the judge, her face composed and quite regal, but Miles began to shake with laughter, his head bent down. He heard Marlow's voice trying to cover him, "He's got a good job, he's very conscientious."

Later, on the courthouse steps in the afternoon air, Marlow said, "What d'you think you were doing, you great pillock? You made me look like a proper effin' fool." Miles was so sorry and so grateful to this woman for her benevolence and her motherly love.

Chapter Fourteen

HAVEN'T GOT TIME FOR PAIN

The first knife Miles owned was a Bowie knife. It was an old knife, it had been passed around. Back in his childhood, in St Paul's, men carried knives to cut their fruit. In the 1960s, in the West Indian community, the men especially were feeling the heat. The knives that had stayed in their back pockets for the slicing of a mango back in Jamaica could be pulled as weapon on this much colder island, if the need for self-protection arose. Miles carried his knife in his waistband, underneath his shirt, much like an amulet, imagining only that should he be in danger, he could pull it out to ward off evil – or at least send an assailant running. But life is not a fairy tale. The first occasion that Miles drew a knife could have changed his life forever. He almost put his freedom on the line, for a friend.

It was August. He was coming back from a match in Swindon, where the home team played West Ham. He was with his friend, Tommy O'Doyle. On the very same day, for the Anglo-Scottish cup, Bristol City had played Bristol Rovers, in their home town. It was just to back up his mate O'Doyle, that Miles went to Swindon rather than to the historic City vs Rovers game. Miles was not certain that placing themselves in the epicentre of the West Ham supporters was such a good idea. West Ham had possibly the most racist set of fans in the UK at that time. His misgivings were confirmed when the West Ham ultras arrived – massive blokes in crusty sheepskins and steel-capped boots with their wiry, feral friends. O'Doyle was casually punched in the back of the head. It was that way. They stayed for the match, an otherwise uneventful one, arriving back to Bristol in the early evening. As Tommy's car drew to the roundabout, by the Evening Post building, they saw a group of familiar City men being chased by Gas. Although this was Bristol's city centre and workers on their way home waited at bus stops or made their way to the pub for a quick one, the rival mobs chased each other with fully focused fury, and these two realities – the orderly nine-to-fivers and the tanked-up hooligans – existed in parallel and independent worlds.

Tommy pulled up abruptly. The pair of them dashed to catch the outnumbered City boys to lend a hand. They turned a corner, coming face to face with the Rovers men whose numbers had oddly swelled. It suddenly seemed a very dangerous situation. Miles and Tommy decided to beat it back to the car. Miles had good legs, he was clear, then he noticed O'Doyle wasn't with him. He turned. O'Doyle was on his back, twenty or so Rovers fans stopped over him, silent, giving him a kicking. He ran back. One man was over O'Doyle, right on him. Miles booted a man from behind, and most of the others scattered. Then Miles drew his knife. The remaining Rovers men saw the blade and there was a spontaneous backing off. Miles moved in, swiping the blade, skimming the neck of the man leaning over O'Doyle. There was a fraction of time and movement, an almost nothing, between Miles slitting a throat open and what it was: a non-death.

Just a scuffle. Move on mate, nothing to see.

Then, later, there was a second knife. Miles chose it from a shop in the Arcade in town. All that was sold in the shop was offensive: blades, knuckle dusters, nunchucks. Miles chose his knife because it had a good aesthetic. He chose it because it might come in handy. He didn't think it through, this is a blade that is illegal, this blade could take someone's life. He chose it to feel safe, especially down town at night. He was wary. The City boys held Bristol city centre, but sometimes Rovers fans came down on the sneak. Call it a sixth sense.

One night, late, Miles left a club, Princess Court, with a woman. The street was empty, except for a white estate car, parked just south of the club door. He was listening to the woman he was with, not aware of anything else when he heard, "There he is, that's fucking Miles Johnson." He looked up. All four doors of the car swung open and five white men got out. Five Rovers men. They were coming for him. The woman he was with ran straight back into the club. The club door banged behind her, locked from inside by the bouncer, who had only ever grudgingly let Miles in.

He was alone, shut outside and about to be surrounded. He had his new knife. It was small and spiky, with a thin and wicked blade. Miles decided, seconds in, that if he was to go down, he was taking some of them, at least one of them, with him. He felt adrenalin flood him, felt rage. Two men were coming at him from the left of the car, coming up behind him, and three others from the right, head on. Miles flicked the knife open, and the three coming at him saw and stopped dead.

"He's got a knife!" And they were gone. The two other men were still running towards his back. He swung round, knife pulled, and the first man coming towards him swerved and moved away, but the second man kept coming. The second man's expression was focused and cold. He charged and as their faces closed, Miles stabbed the knife into the assailant's side, in his rib cage, looking him right in the eye. Once and again. Fast and hard.

Miles knew – it was not a thought process, exactly, but more what the guy patrolling his instincts was telling him – that if this man attacking him were somehow to get him to the ground, then the others would come belting back and Miles's brain would have little chance of remaining inside his skull. The stabbed man staggered. Miles was still holding the knife, trying to free it. Because there was no blood channel on this knife, the suction kept it in the man's body. With great force, the man pushed away from Miles and the weapon stayed planted in his back, just the handle sticking out. Then, with an unexpected burst of life, the man ran, frantically, towards Park Street, the knife still in him. Miles was grounded for a few seconds, his legs locked. Then he moved, he had to. His prints were all over that knife. He chased the man down the deep slope of Park Street. The only noise was their feet on the pavement and their urgent breathing. Miles ran faster than the man, he was gaining ground. Then the knife, as if abruptly surrendering, dropped dully to the ground. Miles stopped running, stood still, slowing the breathing that burnt his lungs. He watched until the man disappeared. The knife lay on the black pavement, dark blood smearing the blade, a midnight still life. He kicked it under a car, then ran from there, back up towards Princess Court. He had reached Park Row and it was a straight line to the place of shelter, Donovan's. It was a choice made for the most pressing reason of proximity. It was a choice made, subconsciously, because it was an address in a Black neighbourhood – there was a feeling that your people would wave you indoors and ask questions later – and there was Donovan. The one person in the world to whom there was no need to explain a single thing.

He ran down Jamaica Street. He could hear police sirens. There were always police sirens late on Friday and Saturday nights, but these sirens were carrying a personal message. They were multiplying and circling him. He kept walking. He was working out which way to go, understanding that the straight walk to Donovan's would surely expose him. He took a b-route, towards Kingsdown, where the roads were badly lit. He kept going, looping back down to St Paul's through sleeping streets. Twice, a sudden blue light appeared in the distance palpitating like his heart beat and twice he jumped into a garden, crouching low in the bushes.

As he entered Ashley Road, St Paul's, the sirens flooded his ears again, high wail then low wail and three, four cars zipped past his crouched frame, hidden between two parked cars. He got home, at last. East Grove. For a few months now, he had been coming back to Donovan's, hanging with him, watching football. His old bedroom was left almost as it was in his childhood. He would sometimes stay the night. This was where he went now, to collapse on to the bed. He lay still, he tried to slow himself down. He had been resting for about twenty minutes, when there was heavy banging on the front door. He heard Donovan moving around, then his footfall on the stairs. The bedroom door opened.

"Miles? Listen, the cops are here, they want to talk to you. Come on. You got to come down."

It's slow motion. All the clichés.

You are under arrest.

Miles's hands were cuffed behind his back.

His back was the last thing Donovan saw of him, as Miles was swallowed by the open jaws of the police van.

****

He spent the next three months in Pucklechurch Remand Centre. In a way, it was no different from being put in care. Strangers, rules, no love. He was twoed-up with Swift. Swift was the son of the family who ran Princess Court, the very night club he had been leaving on the night of the stabbing.

Swift was the son of a certain Bristol syndicate of outlaws, and Miles was the stepson of Don, who was their customer. The irony of this was absolutely lost on Johnson and Swift. Their only conversations were about what they were going to do the day they got out. You might imagine this would involve sex. In fact, the conversations led by Miles mostly featured the offerings of Mr Kipling and Mr Cadbury.

Miles had had a girl in his life, vaguely, before being put on remand. She was Sherry and you could cut her Bristolian accent with a butter knife. She threw herself into being a devoted prison wife, visiting Miles every week. She brought him cakes, mindless gossip and her personal sunshine.

Then one day, he was taken down to the court. The judge listened to the lawyer pitching Miles's history, a history of abuse and removal. The judge listened, as the nature of Miles's crime was described. He listened to the argument of self defence. This, the judge accepted. Miles had fought for his life, but with a weapon that was illegal. The judge felt that there was no way around condemning him for that. Two years probation, three months' community service and the first months as a resident of Horfield Probation Centre. Goodbye, young man, and let's not be seeing you here again.

CHAPTER FIFTEEN

IF I FIND THE WAY

Once back in Bristol, Miles picked up where he had signed off, with a vengeance. Out went Sherry, undeserving of the flippancy with which he went into and came out of relationships. In came Hazel. He never made a move on a woman, he was too shy, too unsure of his appeal. The fear of rejection lived just below the surface, making him watchful and cold, giving him an impenetrable heart. At the most, he might return an insistent look. Sometimes, one of his mates might tell him that a girl liked him. Miles would answer, "Who's she been with?" He wouldn't go with a woman who had slept with other Black men. He was scared of what he thought of as a negrophile – a white woman rinsing through Black men as though they were interchangeable toys. However, he was aware of being a gateway to an experience with Black men. Bristol, which has such a laid-back racial mixture today, was not always that way. In Miles's teenage years, Black people rarely dated white people. He felt that because he was lighter and sounded Bristolian, rather than Jamaican, he was an easy-access stepping stone for women who were curious to have a Black experience. At least fifty percent of the women he was with at that time, who had never dated a Black man before, went on to become women who thereafter dated Black men exclusively. He felt that these women objectified Black men through a mixture of desperation, sexual curiosity and an inability to find love within their own community. He resented it.

Hazel was his new girl. She had her hair cut in a blunt peroxide bob that fuzzed out like she was a hieroglyph. Her fringe was low, over her eyes, as though hiding a flaw. Hazel dressed for attention. She had the body of a pin-up and wore her clothes skin-tight and always black. She had a chalk white face. What her face lacked in prettiness, she made up for with extreme makeup, full-on punk. She didn't get much attention from men, but Miles found her interesting. She was odd, intelligent and quiet. Miles was into her in the same way that he was into other women, before and after her. There was the possibility of something more, something impermeable to the outside world between them, but realistically he would not do any of things required of him to make that happen.

He was in the Wheat Sheaf, a pub in town by the magistrate's court. It was another base for City fans. It was a Sunday. He had come down with Woody. The place was full of fans who were recovering gently from the Soul All-Dayer in London that they had all bussed up to – the coach leaving from the Wheat Sheaf – the day before. Miles hadn't been able to go, he'd had to work. Woody walked over to Miles, who was sat with friends, and told him, "I heard O'Mahoney was snogging your missus on the coach, that's what's going round. I just seen him outside."

Miles got up. His group of friends, City boys mostly from Totterdown, followed. They walked out of the pub. The pavement was crowded with men drinking pints and smoking.

Miles walked over to Ryan O'Mahoney and said, matter-of-fact, "I think we'd better take a walk, mate." O'Mahoney faced him with no trace of emotion. They walked down the alleyway opposite the Wheat Sheaf, Miles's friends and Ryan's friends in their wake. Once they were hidden from the pub crowd, on a secluded path, Miles said, "So what's the fucking crack, Ryan? I heard you was all over my missus?"

"Nah, nah, it weren't like that. We was drunk. I ain't trying to take Hazel, mate."

"It ain't about Hazel. You can have her. It's about me. You taking the piss."

Miles grabbed him by the collar. Ryan, a hard nut, punched Miles square in the face. Miles took the blow without flinching. Ryan smacked him in the face a second time and again, Miles took it. Someone shouted, "Fucking hit him back."

Miles was looking Ryan right in the eye, blank. Then, abruptly, he kicked Ryan's legs from under him and Ryan hit the ground with a bang. Once he was down, Miles booted him in the head, in the body, over and over, as Ryan pleaded, "Stop, stop! I gotta go a court tomorrow, I got me fucking hearing."

But Miles only stopped when he heard, "The Old Bill's coming up!" He stepped back. From the shadows at the other end of the alley one of the coppers called, "All right, lads? What's going on?"

"Nah, nothing, officer. We was just 'aving a laugh." Miles watched Ryan get up, sort himself out, feeling over his face for swelling. Then Miles walked back into the pub outwardly calm, certainly satisfied by the kicking, yet disappointed.

He liked Ryan and he was working out that Ryan hadn't liked him. He could hear them, the people in the pub asking, "What happened, what happened?" It was the night's distraction. Miles stayed for a couple of drinks. Then he left the pub and headed for Hazel's.

In her kitchen, he watched as she made tea. She was chattering about this and that, about the All-Dayer, how good the music had been. Miles listened. He was enjoying himself. He was enjoying watching someone who was lying by omission. He was enjoying having this knowledge over her. She said something funny, he smiled, "Is that right?" He drank his tea, took his time. Then, "Shall we go upstairs?"

They sat in bed, she was still talking. He opened a magazine. They were both naked, she pressed up against him, her hand wandering across his unresponsive body. "I heard you was getting off with Ryan O'Mahoney in the back of the bus last night?" He looked at her. Her face lost its animation.

 For a nanosecond, her expression was crippled, aghast. Then it was wiped clean. A bright smile. She said, "What are you talking about? I don't know what you're talking about." His voice was low, he went back to the magazine, sounding detached from the conversation,

"I heard you was getting off with Ryan. That's what everyone on the coach saw. That's what I was told." She fell quiet, and he turned towards her. She was still smiling, but it was a smile that trembled at the edges.

"No, it wasn't that. We were drunk, you know. It was just the drink."

He let silence take over. Then said, matter-of-fact, "Well, I guess that's it." He got up to leave.

"Please, no. Don't go. You can't leave." He was pulling his jeans on. She tried to hug him, to hold him back. She burst into tears. Began to plead with him. She was between him and the door, "Stay, please stay." Sobbing,

"I love you. Stay, please. Please." He analysed the situation, from a strictly selfish point of view. The probation house in Horfield was miles away. It was easier for him to stay put and sleep. He took a pillow and a cover and pitched down between the bed and the wall. He hadn't spoken a single word throughout her meltdown. She switched off the light. The air in the room felt like it had weight. The only disturbance was sound, the thick tick of a clock and the trickle of water through pipes. Five minutes went by. He could feel she was still rigidly awake. They were both immobile. These moments are when human beings are aware that life is also a subtraction, that there is an insufferable intensity in everything that is not done and is not said. Long heavy-breathing, dry-throat-swallowing minutes went by, then she moved. She was doing something, touching something. Then leaden silence again. He was facing away from her, his open eyes staring at the wall. He felt it, suddenly, weird dark energy and he rolled over. She was on the bed, on her knees, looming over him, in the shadows. He could make out her arm, raised above her head. Then there was swift movement. Her arm came down, towards his head. He knocked it back, and losing her balance, she fell on him. He had her wrist, then he felt her hand. It was gripped around big kitchen scissors.

"What the fuck are you doing? You could have fucking killed me!" he shouted. He was up, looking for the light switch, then scrambling for his clothes. He kept glancing at her, in disbelief. He thought he was good with violence. He thought he could handle himself. He hadn't seen this one coming, this nicely spoken, quiet girl who had almost planted a blade into his skull. She was sobbing again, don't go, I love you, don't go.

He did go. He never saw Hazel, or thought of her, again.

****

Being sent to your room to think about things is a punishment standard. Miles's community service was a little like that, in the heart of St Paul's, in an infants' school between City Road and Ashley Road. He was a teacher's help. Those few months took him back through the streets of his childhood on a daily basis. It was also a remove class for him, from adult life. From nine to four, Monday to Friday, he had six-year-olds following him around. Miles, despite the football-related violence, still had a childlike quality about him. Being with infant schoolkids absorbed him. He would get down to floor level and play at building Lego castles and pushing cars around all afternoon with enthusiasm. A child will recognise the child in you, and when they do, they let you in.

Given where the school was, he was surprised that a lot of the pupils were white kids. The classroom terror though, the stand-out boy, was Black. It was a peaceful group of children, they busied themselves through their days with the odd squabble, not much more, but this little boy was demonic. Miles would watch him. Watch as the boy sized up the kids who had built the highest tower, only to stroll by and kick it down, or which kid was dozy enough for him to swipe tuck from. Miles called the boy over, time and again, "Listen man, you can't behave like that. You got to cut it out." The boy only stared at Miles, in silence. Sometimes Miles would ask him, "Do you want me to play cars with you?" and the boy would say nothing, but nod. For an hour, often, Miles played just with this angry little man. The boy would slowly settle, sometimes he would even giggle. Occasionally, he would speak in a quiet voice as they played.

On his lunch break, nearly every day, Miles walked into town, to Paradise Garage. He ate his sandwiches in the owner Richard's company and listened to music. Richard was in a pivotal position in relation to Bristol's cultural scene. Like a magnet that draws metal filings to it, at some point every cool kid in the city would walk into Paradise Garage and meet Richard. He was kind but sharp. He had a great eye for the bizarre, for beauty that was outside of the norm in music or in fashion. He was older than Miles, he was eloquent. Miles liked being around him, it was as if all the Cotham school boys, the cool ones in bands, had grown up to become this one, interesting, man.

Then one day his community service was over, his debt paid. He was glad to get his life back, but he had had a good time in the school. The bell for the end of the day rang. The teacher said, "Well, children, Miles is leaving us today, he's finished his time here. So, let's wave goodbye."

The children, sat at their dollhouse desks, looked up at the teacher, bewildered.

"Isn't he coming back?" asked a little girl.

One child burst into tears, then just behind, a second one. The naughty boy stared at Miles, fat teardrops rolling down his face. Then the whole class seemed to be crying. Caught off guard, unsure how to respond, Miles looked to the teacher. His eyes widened. She was wiping her own tears with a handkerchief.

He knew he had to get out of there. He lifted a hand, "Bye kids." And he was gone.

He couldn't shake it off. That night, down the Wheat Sheaf, the children's tears came back to him. He had only ever been himself in the classroom, he hadn't expected to feel such love from them. It touched him when not a lot in those days ever did.

****

Miles moved out of Marlow's and lived in the probation centre in Fishponds. Because of being on remand, he had lost his job at Gunac. He was signing on, hanging out in town, going to football matches, going to clubs. His relationship to Bristol was tentacular, an access-all-areas one. Miles was one of few at that time who could navigate his way between the genteel neighbourhoods of Clifton and Redland, where he had many friends, and also be welcome in hardcore football pubs, in divey punk clubs, or down in the shebeens of St Paul's. He had the freedom of the city, in his own singular way.

Some Saturday afternoons were idled away in town. Which shop doors he chose to push had a defining quality. He would stop at Paradise Garage. Miles liked being between the boxes of creepers stacked perilously to the ceiling, listening to music. It was a hangout for random and privileged people, vetted for cool, whose natural home was between racks of Seditionary clothing and Johnson's leather jackets, rather than pootling through sunshiny Marks and Sparks. Daniel Day-Lewis hung down there, laughing when Miles put on an RP English accent to exclaim at how delicious his cake was. It was a bit of a running joke between them. The amount of people who cruised in and out of Bristol at that time, cruised in and out of a scene, one scene only, a scene that fused and grew, and who would later go on to become defining actors in the worlds of music, art and performance, is staggering.

If he wasn't in Paradise Garage, then Miles was in Virgin, which had moved from being Paradise's neighbour to a larger space on Merchant

Street in town. It was painted black inside and run by Zoe, olive-skinned and sphinxy-eyed. She was a kind of queen, and this was hallowed ground. Punks from all over Bristol congregated outside the shop. Virgin dealt in independent music back then. Miles spent nearly everything he had in there. He would zone around in front of the shop, too.

It was an unlikely place for a family reunion.

For a while now, Juliette had reappeared in his life. In fact, Juliette had held on to knowing her brother with all her might. She remembers organising for him to come her foster parents' home for Sunday lunches. Miles has no recollection of this. She found out that her brother was often in town on Saturday afternoons, so she would take a bus down there to see him. She was fifteen, she was growing up, pretty and sharp. She had a loving nature. Juliette still looked up to her brother with the unchecked hero worship of the nine-year-old she was when she had lost him.

Miles was chatting with some punks, in the sunshine outside Virgin, when he saw Juliette walking towards him, her arms crossed, her expression crossed too, between a smile and the need to confess.

"Mum's down there."

It had been seven years.

Seven years without a mother.

Seven years of growing, learning, taking knocks and giving them, alone.

He looked beyond Juliette, and there she was.

Betty.

Upright. Squinting in the sun. Older, she seemed much older to him. The slightness of youth had left her. She was dressed smartly, in a fur jacket and plain skirt. He remembers thinking she looked like a school mistress.

What did she think, facing this son? She had left him, as a frightened child, with the words, "It'll only be a couple of days." She had left him not in any way equipped to face the world he was being set down in. Now here he was, taller than her, proud-looking, wearing black, all black. He looked like Charlie. Like Charlie, without the joy.

"I don't want to see her." He turned away.

"Please, Mi. She's come down specially to see you."

He felt nothing. Or nothing happy. He felt vaguely uneasy that this was being played out in the middle of a punk rock pavement convention. Juliette said, "She's got money for you. She wants to give you money."

Did that swing it? Miles doesn't know, but thinks it might have. Juliette went back to Betty, and then they walked towards him.

"How are you, Milo?" His mother smiled at him, self-conscious, searching.

"I'm all right. And you?"

"I'm well. I'm good." She was nodding her head, smiling harder, into his eyes. "In Southampton still. You can come and visit if you like. Here, this is for you, Milo."

She pressed forty pounds into his hand. He couldn't look at her. He nodded, that was his thanks, and walked away, into Virgin. He blew the entire amount, there and then. This windfall bought him, amongst others, the album *Metal Box* by Public Image Limited and the seven-inch *Faith* by Manicured Noise. He had the records, he was glad to have them. That was all, his one emotion. He felt nothing, nothing at all at having seen his mother. For him, she didn't deserve any attention. He believed that guilt had brought her there, to give him forty quid and fuck off again for another seven years. He went from Virgin into Paradise. Sitting there with his feet up, Rich on his perch, the droning voice of John Lydon and the hypnotic, creeping dirge of PiL on loud, he felt perfectly at peace.

Chapter Sixteen

SAILING SHIPS

One Saturday afternoon, they were making their way through the city centre, him and Dunc. They had a clear stretch of time before them, to hang out. Maybe they would buy some doughnuts by the bus station. Maybe they would stop at Paradise. It had rained. They passed young mothers steering huge pushchairs whose small passengers were caught beneath plastic cloches, rivulets of water in the creases, the world from the baby's perspective at once magnified and misted. He was listening to Dunc, Dunc made him laugh. Then an interruption: a teenage boy from the bomb site years, yelling at Miles. His name was Curtis. He was struggling to catch his breath, "It's Benedict," he panted, "he's getting his head kicked in."

Miles knew Benedict from his time in the halfway house, Benedict had lived nearby. He and Dunc ran with Curtis down Union Street.

"Where to?" There was no one, no fight.

"They were here." The three of them looked towards Broadmead, a shopping street of utilitarian buildings that appeared, always, washed out. Then Miles saw them. A trio of belligerent teenagers, their faces like fists. Curtis ran, Dunc tried to run, but he was wearing his leather-soled shoes and they had him running on the spot on a patch of wet grass like a cartoon character. Miles looked for something to grab, a dustbin lid, a brick, to hit them with, but there was nothing. Ten seconds later, Miles was face down on the pavement, having his head kicked in.

He had to wait, to settle that score, for an evening a few weeks later when a guy called Trent came up to him in the pub saying, "They're on the bus, those twats from Shirehampton. You got ten minutes before the bus pulls out." Miles and twenty City boys raced to the bus and stormed it. The bus driver tried to sneak a call on his walkie talkie, but was ordered to put it down, and someone stood watch over him. The Shirehampton boys were sat at the back, wearing parkas, their faces taut. The three assailants. The one in the middle was the one who had done the most damage. Miles held his friends back. This one was for him, and him alone. He walked down the aisle, grabbed the middle man whose eyes were wide with fear and battered him, fair and square.

He had taken that kicking for Benedict. He would have time to reflect on this later, because Benedict would turn out to be the most one-sided relationship of his life.

****

It was May 1980. Miles was at Trinity, a local concert venue. The Cramps, Joy Division, Echo And The Bunnymen, all played in this deconsecrated English Gothic Church. Miles was there to see Magazine, and Bauhaus. It was already busy. He was with Claude. Miles was now a young punk wearing Vivienne Westwood, George Cox creepers, silver rings up his ear.

"Are you Miles Johnson?" Two kids looked up at him. They were in full rockabilly gear, with brilliant quiffs. They were young and looked like perfect trinkets. They had absolute swag.

Miles nudged Claude, "Check these two out," he said and Claude took a look.

"Wicked." he said, laughing.

"Yeah, I'm Miles. Who are you?"

"Nellee. From Barton Hill. This is my mate, Mower."

Miles used to go to Barton Hill, sometimes. It was rough as hell. They had people in common. Miles liked the sense of humour over in Barton Hill. For example, a kid that he hung out with had stubble before the rest of them and was therefore known as "Man's Head", or they would say things like, "Oi, Miles, where d'you get your muscles, pulling blokes off your bird?" Miles looked up to some of the guys from Barton Hill, like Geoff Shellard, a man's man, and Roy Savage who didn't talk tough, but had an edge. They were the original punks, the pair of them. When punk kicked off, they were right there.

He watched the gig with this Nellee, and something must have clicked between them because Miles said, as he was leaving, "Listen, you got to come down the Wheat Sheaf."

"Nah, they won't let us in, we're fifteen." Nellee said.

"I'll get you in."

Nellee said he would definitely come to the Wheat Sheaf. They both kept their promise.

Nellee latched on to Miles, and Miles to Nellee. For such a young kid, Nellee looked really good. Miles liked that about him, that he was a sharp dresser. Also, seminally, where their worlds collided, was with music. Miles was on probation, the kind of leash that jacks your neck back. He had to give his football life a wide berth for now. Nellee's arrival was timely. He and this kid were alike in their love of music and their explorative natures. Where they differed was that already, so young, Nelllee was driven, was capable of turning loose connections into a collective. Nellee was honing the art, also, of catching the slipstream of the charismatic figures around the city, of catching their speed until, eventually, he picked up such momentum of his own that he took off altogether, into another reality. But back to the story. We are in Bristol, in Barton Hill and Fishponds, in 1980, and a band was formed with Miles and Nellee, the unlamented A Rumba Lament. Miles couldn't play an instrument, but guesses he looked the part, so he was put on the echo chamber. Nellee was on percussion, Rob Chant on guitar, Miles's cousin Paul Johnson on bass, Rob Merril on drums. Neil Dunn was the singer. They were under the influence of new wave: Gang Of Four, Joy Division. Band practice was in the boning yard, in Barton Hill. Somebody had a key to the factory. They rehearsed in a corner space, four hundred yards from the rancid flesh outside, organised like giant lasagne. The sickly reek of decaying meat oozed into the factory, so the setting for rehearsal was as punk as it gets. The band lived, then it died, leaving no trace. Still, Miles had gone through the mirror, he was on the other side, making music.

He had a blind date one evening in the back of the Curzon cinema. In fact, it was only a half-blind date, because Milo knew Nicky's older sister, Lauren, from clubbing in town. Nicky was a white girl from Lockleaze. She had cropped black hair and bright blue eyes. She was as tall as most men and shapely. It's fair to say that, when he entered the cinema on that particular evening, he had no idea what he was letting himself in for. He liked Nicky.

They had a good time. His relationship to women was basic in the sense that women came to him, he was obliging sexually, but he didn't have feelings. He hadn't felt, except for perhaps puppy love towards Michelle, the blue that is sung about or the hunger that is the bassline for romance. He felt nothing, except sometimes concern that he shouldn't hurt a woman's feelings. Some girls had wanted something from him, some emotion, that he was incapable of giving. Nicky was different, she seemed to be fine with the lack of romance. So, it worked.

His life was this: he was seeing Nicky and, socially, he was getting more involved with Nellee. He now lived in Hartcliffe, with Punky. Music was taking a greater place and this part of his life seems, retrospectively, compressed. Things which would become fundamentals thereafter, happened in a timespan that was holding in its breath, it was so quick. He was trying to keep out of trouble. He avoided the football crowd when he knew that his boys were champing at the bit for a fight. He was spending entire afternoons in Paradise Garage. He was buying music. He was hooked up with Claude Williams, and with Nellee. It was almost the end and not, as it should have been, the beginning. He was in the dark.

Chapter Seventeen

AS THE WORLD TURNS

Hartcliffe, Saturday morning. He was lazing around in bed, with Nicky. He could hear Punky clattering around in the kitchen. There was a big match that day, City against Rovers, there was no question that trouble was in store. Down the Wheat Sheaf, the night before, Miles had been clear: "I ain't going. No way, mate. You're havin' a laugh. I'm on fucking probation. You know what they're like, the old bill, if there's a fight, they just grab the first Black man they see. I ain't risking it."

So, he went home. With Nicky. Resolute.

"Where's Miles?" It was Lenny's voice, at the bottom of the stairs.

"He ain't coming," Punky answered. "He's still in bed."

"Tell him to come down."

"No way, mate. I ain't dragging him out of bed."

Lenny bounded up the stairs, two steps at a time and burst into the bedroom. Miles and his girlfriend were naked, vaguely amorous, which didn't phase Lenny.

"Come on, mate," he said, "get out the fucking bed."

"Fuck off, Lenny," Miles laughed. "I ain't coming. Listen. Mate. I get into any kind of trouble, any kind, I'll be in the slammer."

Nicky was lying flat out next to him, holding the sheet under her chin, staring at the ceiling.

"I'll look after you, Miles. C'mon. Nothing's going happen to you."

At this, Nicky sat up, suddenly shouting, "If you go to that fucking game, we're over." There was white anger in her voice, it was a loaded gun. Miles looked at her, at Lenny, then said, "Go on then, mate. I'm coming down."

He pulled his clothes on, to the soundtrack of reason, to Nicky telling him, "If anything kicks off, they're going to come for you. You're bloody mental. I tell you what, you are asking for fucking trouble, something's not right in your head. I hope you don't live to regret this."

"See you tonight," he answered.

And he didn't look back.

****

It was the usual. The City lot met in The Bell: Saturday morning, beer, and that flat hard masculine energy ready for a fight. They heard that Rovers were going to be in the Queen's Head pub by Eastville Park. They parked their cars in Saint George and walked down the hill. There were thirty of them. One of them took a look inside the pub and turned back to the group, gesturing with his head, Inside. The City boys walked over, disappearing into the pub. Miles hung back, on the other side of the street, with another guy. Seconds later, the pub door opened and a man was catapulted out, followed by a walnut-headed thug in a red Fred Perry who kicked the first man to the ground. Hooligans scuffled out of the pub, two-headed beasts, until the pavement was a fight club. From a distance, Miles watched. Nothing in him twitched. "Shall we make a move?" And he was gone.

It was a big match, all of Bristol was down in that stadium, that's how it felt. It was January, freezing. Among the thousands of spectators, Miles could see police weaving in and out. He was uneasy at being down there. The sunlight was sharp, heightening the colours of the green pitch, of the Rovers fans' bright blue and white and banners on the opposite side. A hand came down hard on his shoulder,

"Are you Miles Johnson?" It was a policeman.

"Yeah. Why?"

"You have to come with me."

"What the fuck are you talking about? I just paid for my ticket."

"We need to get some information from you, it's all right, and you can come back up when we're done."

Outside the stadium, the police had set up a makeshift headquarters, porta cabins and vans that were vacantly waiting to impound mouthy, punchy fans. Miles was shown into a mobile cell and Ali was in there, a mixed-race City fan.

"All right, Ali? What's going on?" Ali shook his head,

"Dunno, mate."

Miles heard the sound of the stadium lifting with chants, the match had begun, so he definitely wouldn't get his money's worth. He sat with his arms crossed, legs stretched out. A half hour passed. Between Ali and him was silence. Then a copper appeared. Miles was taken to a room with a table and chairs. They sat him down.

"Were you at the Queen's? Before the match?"

"No."

"There was a fight at the Queen's."

"I wasn't there."

"There was a stabbing. A man was stabbed."

"Like I said. I wasn't there."

"We were told it was you. We were told Miles Johnson stabbed the man." Miles looked across at the policeman, who was white, in his fifties. There was something about this civil servant, the studied half-smile, the insistent look, that told of vanity and of role play. Miles's voice was hard and level,

"What the fuck are you are talking about? I wasn't there. I went straight to the match."

"We have witnesses. Some Rovers fans. They all confirm that you were armed and that you stabbed the victim."

"No."

"Milo Mackenzie Johnson, you are under arrest…" and it fades out, once more, to Pucklechurch Remand Centre where Miles spent months, three, six, he can't remember, awaiting trial.

During his time on remand, he lived in a state of suspension. There wasn't a sense of resignation because he felt certain that he wouldn't be punished for something he didn't do. Very quickly, he had been given the name of the man who should have been on remand instead of him. It was Benedict. Benedict had done the stabbing, and Benedict was a mate, the one he'd taken a kicking for. There could have been no eyewitness confusion because Benedict was white. From inside, Miles learnt that Benedict was scared of doing time. Information percolated back to him: The men that ran the City firm had spoken with their Rovers' peers. A reassuring summary of this unusual summit was given to Miles. He was told that Rovers were sorting it.

He felt hopeful. Then he heard that the Rovers witnesses went to the police to recant their statements. The police, ever willing to indict the wrong man, when the wrong man is Black, told them that if they retracted their accusation, they would be done for perjury. So, they left their statements as they were. Miles's only hope after that was that Benedict's fear of facing him when he was released would be greater than his fear of going down.

Miles asked for Benedict to come to visit him. He felt calm. He had to make Benedict see sense. In the balance were good, green years of Miles's life. He had been taken out before, put away, left behind. It couldn't happen again, not for this. Eventually, because of the weight of peer pressure and not his conscience, Benedict showed up at visiting time. "You won't go to prison, Ben. It's your first offence. I spoke with my solicitors. They're really clear on that. You got a clean slate. You'll get probation." Benedict listened, he was sat away from the table, leaning forward a little, wringing his hands. He kept nodding. Not speaking, nodding. "Look, mate," said Miles, "I'll go down for this. I can't go down. I can't get locked up for a stabbing I didn't do."

Benedict understood. Miles, with Benedict's consent, gave Benedict's name to his solicitor. Everyone: the police, the City men, the Rovers men, everyone knew that Miles didn't do it. Miles had no further control, he had to wait. For months.

He was eventually judged in Bristol Crown Court. He remembers feeling intimidated by the loftiness of the room, by the thick silence, by the judge and barristers in their grave wigs and robes. He pleaded not guilty. Behind him, in the gallery, a crowd came to support him, there were no empty seats. Betty came, with Juliette. Don was there. Marlow, Punky, Michelle, Claude, his friends from Paradise Garage, his friends from the night. They were waiting for Benedict. He was the key to the lock that would let Miles walk free. At last, Benedict took the stand. The lawyer asked him, "You admit that you were at the fight? At the Queens Head public house?"

"Yes."

"Did you witness the stabbing?"

"No."

"You are saying that you had no part whatsoever in this stabbing?"

"Yes."

"Can you enlighten us, as to what took place?"

"No. I'm sorry, I don't know."

In that brief exchange of lies, Miles's life collapsed. He put one hand behind his back, his back was all that his friends and family could see of him, and showed them four fingers. He had understood. When they rose, when the judge pronounced him guilty, the audience cried out. There was a god-almighty bang against the ten-foot court doors. Lenny and other City men were charging the court room, trying to bash the doors down and set Miles free.

Miles was sentenced to four years imprisonment, immediately effective. He was nineteen.

Chapter Eighteen

STOLEN MOMENTS

Horfield Prison, Bristol, 1980

From here, he no longer owned time. He was put in a cell, waiting for transfer. It was three in the afternoon and he sat in the cell, alone, until six in the evening. Then he was handcuffed and put in a van, in the small holding space. Through the van window, which was delineated by the mesh grid of the security glass, he watched Bristol in its ungainly freedom stream by. Through Bridewell, to the Bear Pit, along Stokes Croft. Mostly, he noticed the people at the bus stops absent-mindedly waiting. Sluggardly mums with pushchairs and carrier bags, a student girl with blue hair carefully rolling a cigarette, old men resting their swollen joints, sat beneath the bus shelters. I would give anything to be one of you. This was his thought, all the way to Horfield Prison. Anything.

Within the prison walls, he was made to strip and to hand over all that he had, which wasn't much. He was kitted up with prison issue clothing and taken to his cell. There was no cellmate. The screw slammed the door and locked it. Miles stood, his back to the door. He was holding a tray. On the tray was a plastic beaker, a jug of water, toilet paper and a fun-sized packet of dry biscuits. Each article was rubber stamped, "HMP Bristol." He carefully put the tray down, on the table to the side. He stayed where he was, facing the high, barred window. He willed himself to cry. Now is when you cry. He was thinking, "Come on, get it fucking over with. Surely, this is when you break down."

It wouldn't come.

It just wouldn't come.

Prison was depressingly familiar in its routine, in its barren objectives. Just like care, where children are placed and days are ticked off until the buck is passed elsewhere, with no sense of the here and now, or of the gift of being alive. Four years imprisonment, when you are nineteen, might as well be forever. Everyone Miles knew on the outside, everyone young like him, would forge on. He was now stuck in an all-male world, in a cell, in a uniform. So, he thought for a while, then made some radical decisions. He completely cut himself off from the free world. It was unbearable to read about real life, he felt it could have broken him. He wrote to a few people and told them not to contact him. He received some visitors in the first weeks, then he cauterised this flow from the past as well, never giving out a visiting order again. Letters came, and he threw them in the bin, still in their sealed envelopes. He says the only letters he ever opened were the ones from Nellee, and purely because he was surprised that Nellee made the effort. There was a faithfulness to Nellee. He was out there making music. Whilst Miles was inside, Nellee did a stint on *Top Of The Pops*, with Pigbag, and yet in the midst of excitement and opportunity, he didn't forget Miles, he wrote, "Listen, when you get out we'll do this and we'll do that…". It was something Miles wanted to believe, but it felt dead to him.

Miles's immediate and pressing thought was how to navigate incarceration without getting in trouble. You got time added for bad behaviour, time subtracted for walking the line. The math is simple: you get four years, but if you're a model prisoner, you'll do two-and-a-half, maybe even two. How do you achieve that discount without your daily life being a living hell as the whipping boy of your wing? He was worried, worried about being pressed by other convicts. He was only just figuring out the male experience, and how to judge another man.

He lay on his cot, tucked away on the fourth-floor balcony. The screws were beginning the morning round of opening cells and releasing prisoners for breakfast. The rattle and the clunk of iron keys in iron locks, the banging doors, the screws' orders amplified by the theatrical acoustics of a jail house. It would take the prison wardens about twenty minutes to reach Miles, and so he lay, waiting and wondering who else was inside. His first line of strategy could be to hook up with a man older, and feared. He had an idea that Jimmy Slate was doing time here. He didn't know Jimmy Slate, he had only heard of him. He was a mixed-race man, much older than Miles. People said, "He's a fucking animal." Miles thought Slate's father was maybe from St Paul's. Slate might be a life raft. He would look into it.

His first week, and he was put on cleaning duty. Down on his knees, he scrubbed the endless dinner hall floor. Scrubbed all day long. "Is this it?" he thought, "Is this now my life?" The scrubbing of floors was used as a metaphor by screws, you are beneath us, you are crawling. It was taken to extremes. As a punishment, later, Miles was made to clean a hallway with a toothbrush.

A new wing to Horfield Prison was finished not long after Miles arrived. It was drawn along more considered guidelines. There was a private toilet in each cell, rather than a bucket on the floor. All the prisoners wanted to go there. Miles got lucky. There were facilities in the new wing. The screws would open the cell door, "You going to the gym, Johnson?" And he would say yes, always, just to be out of those four close walls.

In the gym, there was what Miles describes as a small brothers' section. He started to work out with these men and to associate with them. One of them, Pullman, was probably a similar mixture of Black and white as Miles. He was ex-army, handsome, hard. He would talk to Miles, explain things to him. He said, "We deal with grasses our own way. I'm out in the country, you see? We just chuck 'em in with the pigs, big fucking hogs, they'll eat anything. Yeah man, we deal with those fuckers."

Another of the brothers, by the name of Sunday, was viciously heavy-set, with a neck like a tree trunk. He was in for armed robbery. At some point, he'd stolen a car and gone through its windscreen, leaving his face savaged, with skin in raised bumps like a crocodile. He was visually gruesome, and for protection definitely a five-star. Inmates kept out of his way, there was a feral quality to him, the possibility of bottomless physical violence. Once, out on the football pitch where Miles used to tear up most of the players and show something of his personality, this guy, Sunday, this very brother, was running up behind Miles. Miles had the ball, and Sunday, unable to retrieve it, was trying to kick Miles's legs from under him. Miles stopped, suddenly, turning on him, enraged, "What the fuck are you doing? This is concrete. What's fucking wrong with you?"

Sunday was stopped in his tracks, facing Miles, his eyes wide in surprise. They stared at each other and a screw blew a whistle, and blew again, "All right, lads, enough. Pick up the game."

So they did, pick up the game, and in that non-verbal world of male domination, Miles had established in the eyes of Sunday and the other men around, that he was less of a pussy than they might otherwise have thought. Some of Sunday's aura now settled like gladiator dust on Miles.

The men Miles met were often damaged, often violent. Some carried their run-ins on their faces, some inside themselves. Once, down in the dinner hall, Miles was eating when a white man came over. He sat down and asked Miles, "So where you from, then?"

"Montpelier. Hartcliffe now. I was living in Hartcliffe before I got banged up. You?"

"I'm from Southmead. D'you go down Southmead?" Miles was studying the man's face. It was a young face, quite a good-looking face, but blasted with scars, still pink and raised.

"What the fuck happened to you, then?" asked Miles, "What's with your skin?"

"I got glassed a couple of months ago. Tell you what, when I sneeze, glass still comes out of my nose."

"Fuck off." Miles laughed. With that, the man got a paper napkin and blew his nose into it. He revealed the contents: blood, mucus, shards of glass.

Miles was twoed-up for a while with Lee, from Knowle West. He knew Lee from outside, from the Wheat Sheaf. Lee wasn't part of the football crowd, but he was a fighter with a fierce reputation. It was known that he had taken on seven men on Park Street and had beaten them all up. He was a boxer. Miles had never spoken to him, all he'd heard was, "That's Lee Worthington, check him out. A fucking nutter." Now he was in a cell with him. They were both quite silent, reflective. They actually got on well. Miles was interested in boxing, but only as a spectator.

One day Lee said, "Come on, let's do a bit of sparring." They wrapped towels round their hands and boxed. Body shots only. Miles could hold his own. Lee was really happy about that. They would fight in the cell, getting quicker, more precise. Lee said, "When you get out, I'm taking you down the club. You got it in you."

"I don't know, mate. It's a long time away for me. Three more years."

"Nah, I promise, youze coming down that club with me. I want to see you get in a ring. You got it in you. I'm telling you."

Lee got out quite quickly, and he opened a used-car salesroom. One day, a car was stolen from his lot. Soon, Lee was told who had stolen the car, and likewise, the thief was told who he had just, unwittingly, stolen from. In the time it took for the thief to go to pieces, Lee was round his house, knocking on the front door. The thief was so terrified of what Lee might do to him that he opened his front door and shot Lee dead.

"Prison is where you promise yourself the right to live," wrote Jack Kerouac in *On The Road*. But you get outside and sometimes it's freedom that does you in.

After that, Miles was twoed-up with Phil Savage, an East Ender. Phil was a small man, with a tightly packed frame, carrying the confidence of a Londoner in his body language. He'd been brought to Horfield from London. You got moved around either because you were a danger to others, or because others were a danger to you. Miles was fairly sure that Phil fell into the second category. They never spoke about themselves, but Phil turned Miles on to a philosopher, Georges Gurdjieff, and lent Miles one of his books. Miles was on his bunk, reading the loaned book, Meetings With Remarkable Men. Miles and Phil had just eaten in their cell, and further down other prisoners were bringing their food into their own cells, where they now sometimes ate.

There were two bikers sharing a cell on the landing. One was short and fat, with an arse that stuck out like a duck. The other was monumental, a lurching seven-foot grizzly. The tall one, very *One Flew Over The Cuckoo's Nest*, was always silent. The short one, and these are Miles's words, was a mouthy little tosser.

"Fucking Hell, I'm tired of this nigger food." It was Short Biker, live and loud. Miles put his book on his chest.

"D'you hear that, Phil?"

"The whole wing heard that, mate."

"Fucking prick. He's only mouthing off because the doors are locked." Miles let it slide.

Then, two days later, once more,

"Fucking nigger food. S'a fucking joke."

"I have to step to this guy, Phil." Miles was the only Black man on the wing. It wasn't just his honour, it was his safety that was at stake. If you let one prisoner ride over you, then you became a walking target, a walking dispensary, a sort of walking dead. Miles lay on his bed, staring at the ceiling which was a foot from his face. He was itching to get out. The screws were making their clanging way up through the floors, releasing convicts for them to go to their jobs, from sewing which was the lowliest job, to kitchens, which is where the star jobs were.

They heard the bikers leaving their cell. Phil said,

"Don't worry, I got your back." Phil was five foot four. Miles smiled,

"That's a big fucking man out there."

Then they were released and Miles bounded down the iron stairwell, slowing his pace once he was behind the bikers. They had left the wing, and were walking through a yard to the sewing room. Miles was up behind the small biker, he collared him and banged him against a wall. "So what's this shit about nigger food?" The ant trail of other inmates halted, they were watchful, their eyes were on Miles, and on Grizzly Biker, stood to the side.

"Leave it out, for fuck's sake. I got court tomorrow."

"You'd better keep your fucking mouth shut else I'll break your fucking legs." Miles was putting his release date on the line, he knew it. All the while, Grizzly Biker watched. Miles held the line of the short biker's eye like a laser beam of hate. He had his forearm across the biker's throat. He stayed like that, as the biker started to strain for breath. Then he released the hold. Grizzly Biker remained impassive. The next day, the small biker was taken to court and never came back to Horfield. On the days after that, when watery curry and toothy rice was served, it was to the sound of silence.

In the new wing, they had two-up cells, and four-up cells. Life began to brighten for Miles, at the expense of his mates' freedom. First of all, Liam, City's big man, got nicked and arrived in Horfield. Then another City boy, Eddy, got nicked. That was three of them. The fourth man, and the one that they would wangle a four-up cell with, was Joey Santini. His family was mobbed up and he carried quite a bit of weight inside. Miles knew him from before, from clubbing around Bristol. Joey was a rotund, cheerful bloke, completely invested in eating. He got himself a cushy job in the kitchens, and thereafter Miles was never hungry, Joey on an honour mission to see that his cellmates were the best fed in Horfield jail. Miles remembers long evenings wiled away as the four of them elaborated a spectacular plan to rob a bank once outside. It involved tunnelling and hydraulics and caused a lot of laughter.

The days were ticking over. Miles had been imprisoned now for eight months. He tried to keep his mind off his innocence. He tried to enjoy what there was to enjoy. Sometimes, the food was okay, so queueing for lunch in the canteen was a moment of hope. This is where he was, holding his metal tray, maybe five men back from the food counter, when a young bloke strolled right past him and past the next man, cutting casually into the queue. The man in front of Miles didn't react. Miles gave him a shove.

"D'you know that bloke?"

"Nah."

Miles leaned forward, "Oi. You. There's a line here. Oi! Get to the back." But the bloke ignored him superbly. Miles stepped forward, put a hand on his shoulder, "I said there's a fucking line here. Get to the back of the fucking line." The man – fresh-faced, soft-featured, white – swung round, and aimed his metal tray upwards, at the side of Miles's head, slamming it as hard as he could. The tray caught the outside edge of Miles's right ear. The ear split open. The offensive tray clattered on the floor as the white man legged it. Miles threw his own tray down and ran after him. The man made it to his cell, the door almost shut, but Miles stopped it with his foot, then kicked it in. He grabbed the guy by the neck, his own blood soaking his shoulder, then kicked in the door of the toilet and threw him inside. Miles had the white boy by the hair and smashed his head against the toilet bowl and smashed it again, and again. The screws came crashing in and, with great violence, dismantled Miles from around the man's neck.

The young man was fussed over, and never answered to his own behaviour. Word went round that he was from the bourgeois city of Bath, and that he was the son of a politician. Miles was banished back to the old block, with an untended inflamed wound. It was one more scar that he would wear for life. He was put into a cell that looked like something from a Victorian zoo. He lay on the bed. A screw banged the door open. He just stood there, staring down at Miles. Then he said, "Johnson? I heard about you and I'm having none of your fucking antics on this wing, do you hear me?" Miles stared up at him, mute. "I said, do you hear me? Do you understand?"

"You finished?"

"I want an answer."

"You finished? 'Cause if you are, you can fuck off."

"All right. Righty-o." The screw shut the door. A week later, Miles was shipped out to Swansea Prison, another country.

CHAPTER NINETEEN

TIME OUT OF MIND

HM Prison, Swansea, 1981

The whole trip to Swansea, Miles was thinking of what he knew about the Welsh. Memory One: at Gunac, his foreman, Taffy, had been one of the most overtly racist men he had ever encountered. Memory Two: In Bristol, when the football crowd got tanked up, they would sometimes steam into town "looking for Welsh" and the Welsh boys, up for a night of partying in Bristol, would always oblige, with a good, man-on-man, pub brawl. So, in all probability, what Bristolian fighting men felt surge through their system at the thought of Welsh men, Welsh prisoners would feel at the sight of a Bristolian convict, Bristolian and Black as a finally flung insult.

On arriving at Swansea Central, with the simplicity of a toddler, organising red bricks with red bricks and blue with blue, Swansea Prison put Miles in a cell with the only other Black man there, Vernon Washington. Vernon was older than Miles, in his mid thirties. He was a mixed-race Welsh man who worked the doors of Swansea clubs and was a karate black belt. He greeted Miles with the Swansea vernacular, "All right, Jack?" And that one syllable, Jack, had a good ring to it that Miles would keep and make his own. So, the open racism, the name-calling grief, was spared to him, because he was under Vernon's wing and no inmate wanted to answer to Vernon. After a time, a third Black man arrived, Fergie Miller, one of a small Bristol posse who were running round the city, mugging maybe, and hustling on the streets. "Yo, man, what you doing here?" Miles asked with the amazement that you have on bumping into someone familiar in an obscure and foreign land. Fergie was soon in the cell with Vernon and Miles. That was three Black men to four-hundred-forty white.

Miles would go down for lunch. Trays were shifted along the counter, receiving the separate elements of the dinner by a row of be-ladled, disenchanted cons. One of the dinner duty prisoners was a short and shifty boy-man, who looked at Miles from day one with slitted contempt. Miles moved his plate in front of this young man's serving dish, and the man lifted a spoon of mashed potato and slammed it on to Miles's plate, all the while looking at him with a faintly curled back lip and his chin sunk into his neck. Miles moved on. The young man performed the same act of racial vandalism the next day, and the day after that. Miles sat, eating his food, watching the boy, trying to figure out where he was in the pecking order. It was clear the other prisoners moved around him with some kind of deference, joking with him, being oddly matey. One lunchtime came, a few weeks into Miles's time in Swansea. The boy-man, once again, threw Miles's portion of potatoes down as if he were cracking a whip, but this time, the very second the greying mound of potato left the spoon, Miles pulled his tray back, and the mash slumped on the boy's counter.

"What you fucking doing? You fuckin' prick," the boy said, his voice screechy with indignation.

"I tell you what," answered Miles, "You fucking slam my food down one more time and I'm going to fucking *do* you." The boy stood with his shoulders back, his face a nasty red knot of anger.

Miles went for lunch the following day with curiosity. He wondered at the boy's psychology and at how he would play the next round. There was a surprise in store: a screw standing with his arms folded, at the serving counter. Next to him was a prisoner who was older, in his fifties, short and thick-set with a square face and a shaved head. Miles caught the officer give this prisoner a nod. It was a cue for the man to walk over to Miles.

"You got a fucking problem with my son?"

So that was it. Adrenalin coursed through Miles's body, priming him to strike. The surge of energy inside him was so fierce that his right leg began to visibly shake.

"Yeah, I got a fucking problem with him. If he does what he's been doing with my food again…" he looked the father in the eye, "I'm going to kick his fucking head in." Miles was acutely aware of his right leg, now in the grip of clownish spasms, not quite the kicking machine he needed.

"Is that right? Well, you touch him, and you got a problem with me, you cunt."

Miles had kept his breathing slow and level. He didn't feel fear, despite his quivering leg. He kept his eyes locked into the father's, then stepped back, taking his tray to the counter and queued for his food. The son, in a moment of pure schizophrenia, managed to serve Miles with both disgust and meekness visible. Vernon casually told Miles over lunch that the father, Crow, was Swansea's all-time biggest gangster. Miles never saw Crow again, and the son was taken off detail, the name of his job, and kept out of Miles's sight.

****

Every Sunday night, Miles had a date in the dark. It was a moment to which he looked forward. After their tea and an hour's allotted recreation (table tennis, table football, cards) a screw would shout, "Back to your cells!" It would be around 8.30pm. The screws locked the men in. Vernon, Fergie, Miles and a fourth prisoner, a white kid, were in a space 15-foot square, with a bunkbed to the left and to the right. In this tight concrete home they did what they could to pass time. Miles and the white kid did press-ups every night, the white kid teaching Miles to do press-ups on the tips of his fingers. They read, books from the library that were donations to the prison, or books left behind by prisoners who had been freed. Miles was working his way through hardcore Black politics. He had turned the pages of Malcolm X, of H Rap Brown. He also read true crime, liking the journey into a deranged mind. Then a screw would bang the door, shout, "Lights out!"

On a Sunday, at this moment, Miles would get into his cot, the lower bunk on the left. He'd feel for the radio under his bed. Radios were treasures to the prisoners, you got them sent from outside. There was a particular radio, a chunky set called a Bush that gave out a heavy bass, whereas most radios sounded tinny. Inmates would congregate in the cell of a prisoner with a Bush radio set, just to listen to music that had some weight. Miles got a radio left to him by another prisoner and paid for the batteries from the tiny wage he earned sewing bags for HM Prison Service. It was forbidden to do anything after lights out. So, the date Miles had, with *Tony Prince's Disco Top Twenty*, was a secret affair. He had a blanket over his head and a note pad and pen. He put the radio inside his pillow like a burrito filling – that way, with his head pressed against it, the bass was augmented. He listened in the dark. He noted down each thing he liked, blind. Sometimes, he forgot to write because a tune would come on that was so full of life, of desire, of night-time freedom that he would feel grief, sharp and unexpected. Grief at all he was missing, this crucial part of life when you are young and strong. It felt like he was suffocating, under the covers, in a concrete box. The music pulsating in this empty other life, the one with all the friends he wouldn't make, the songs he wouldn't dance to, the girls whose breath he would never hear in his ear, the way you hear the ocean in a shell. On those nights, when a tune pierced his heart, he would release the hold on his pen, just let it drop. He would close his eyes and let the music play on.

Miles was getting closer to his release date. He'd been knocked back for probation a first time, when he was transferred to Wales, but the second time parole was accorded. He had six more months to do. He was moved to the wing that was the antechamber of real life. It was far more comfortable and in an attempt to remind the prisoners that existence was also sometimes fun, there were activities, group games that the prisoners were made to do.

One afternoon, twenty convicted adult felons sat cross-legged in a circle playing a game of tag. One man was "It" and ran round the outside of the ring, touching another man's head, therefore designating him as the one to do the chasing (the kind of game usually reserved for a four-year-old's birthday party). The It man, whom Miles had laid eyes on over a game of table football and hated on sight (it was a mutual contempt) was pelting round. As he took the swerve, where Miles was sat, he used Miles's neck for leverage, crushing Miles's head down. Miles was off like a gunshot, up and running, chasing him, yelling, "You fucking little bastard!"

The officer in charge bellowed, with sing-song Welsh inflexion, "Sit down Johnson, we're playing a fucking game yer!"

At Christmas, the inmates were invited to come into the small common room, where there was a big screen, to watch a Christmas special – an animated version of *Snow White And The Seven Dwarfs*. Twenty of them actually showed up, which is a measure of their desperation. Miles was sat at the front, his legs stretched out. The prisoners seemed to concentrate on the film, it was calm in the room, just the asides of certain inmates breaking the spell. Snow White was trilling to a blue bird, also trilling. Miles was all right in there by now, he had negotiated a year and a half in a category B prison in Swansea, at the tender age of twenty. Category B prisons are for criminals convicted for sentences which are undetermined – or of ten years or more – for prisoners whose crimes have threatened life, for terrorists and those who have been found guilty of offences involving robbery, sex, or drugs. He was thrown in with men guilty of murder and crimes of great violence. Miles, on the day of his arrest, had been standing on a pavement, watching a fight for five minutes, before going to a football match for a further ten minutes, unarmed. Miles was not even on the scene of the crime that had punched a hole out of his life.

The prisoners had gone quiet, they were by now engrossed in the film or dozing. On the screen, Sleepy yawned. The mammoth of a man next to Miles yawned back. Miles smiled to himself and turned, catching an unforgettable image of a roomful of men inured to violence yawning along with Sleepy the Dwarf.

Around about this time, Miles had a visitor. Donovan. In fact, it was the second time Donovan had been to see him, he had received an unsolicited visit when he first arrived in Swansea. Donovan had been concerned about Miles's safety, he knew that Swansea wasn't Horfield. It was a really tough prison, full of very dangerous men and not many Black people. This time he came up because Miles had given Donovan's home as his release address. If you didn't have an address, you couldn't be released.

"All right Buffer?" Donovan asked. He looked at this man, Milo, his son, not his son.

"Yeah, Donovan. I'm good. Counting down the days. It's fucking dragging by now, I'll tell you that much."

"Listen, man, you got your old bedroom. It's ready for you when you free, you don't have to worry 'bout that."

So a small light shone. His father, not his father, had come to get him, to almost take him home.

Chapter Twenty

HOW MANY BROKEN WINGS

The day before he was released, he gathered his possessions. There were the few books that he would give away, keeping back only *Meetings With Remarkable Men*. There was soap and biscuits for his fellow cellmate, Vernon, who had followed him to the release wing. There were notebooks, tens of them, Miles's most precious possessions. From the very beginning of his incarceration, almost three years before, he had tuned in to every John Peel session as well as every *Tony Prince's Disco Top Twenty* on Radio Luxembourg. Radio Luxembourg was murder to catch, right on the end of the waveband. If the weather was stormy, then the reception was compromised, but on a clear day Radio Luxembourg sang. He had a notebook and he wrote rough in the dark. He had meticulously made a note of every record that was of interest to him – the song title, the artist, the label. Page upon page. His notebooks, that had followed him through his life: birds then cars then songs.

"Johnson. Get your stuff."

He said goodbye to Vernon, promising to check each other outside, which they never did. It would be like reuniting with someone you were in a car crash with. He followed the screw to a room where he was handed a bag with his clothes. He opened the bag. It seemed a long time ago that he had carelessly pulled on these jeans and jumper, with Nicky trying to hold him back. The donkey jacket came out rolled up, heavy, smelling of wet dog. The jumble of clothing was like a rip in space-time, taking him precisely to his past life. A bed, bright bed clothes, voices, Punky, laughter. A woman's rounded shoulder, pearl-like skin, the shoulder, shifting, turning away.

He began to change out of his uniform, into these unceremonious clothes. There was a mirror in the small room, its silver dulled and spotted. He stood before it. He hadn't seen his reflection clearly for three years. The man looking back at him was not the nineteen-year-old he remembered. For a start, there was his hair. When he had been arrested, his hair had been in the care of one man only, all his life: Beedo. Beedo was the barber in St Paul's and he cut the hair of every Black man in Bristol in the sixties.

Miles was first taken there by Don, at the end of the summer holidays to freshen up for school. At the bomb site kids said to him, "Man, Beedo is *rough*." And they laughed. The first time Miles went inside the shop, stepping from the bright pavement to the shadowy interior, he saw Beedo. The combination of Miles's low-angle view and the dread the children at the bomb site had communicated, made Beedo seem like an ogre, the biggest and fiercest-looking man Miles had ever seen. Beedo interrupted his work for a beat, looked at Don and Miles wordlessly, then went back to trimming the hair of a small boy whose eyes were like watery stars and whose mouth was a little bridge shape of misery. Men were sat around waiting, or reading the paper At last, Miles climbed onto the chair. He hadn't combed his hair for days. It was pure knots.

Unfazed by this, Beedo pushed Miles's head down and put the large-fanged comb at the nape of Miles's neck, then raked it through to the front in one deft move. Tears straightaway trickled down Miles's face. In three hellish comb scrapes, it was done. Beedo then cut his hair beautifully, giving him the desired, Pelé '62. Miles got off the chair and Beedo said, "See what happens. Next time you come, you comb your damn hair." Miles's neat head burned raw all day. But he carried on going there, maybe minus when he was in care, that he can't remember, but certainly afterwards. Miles's hair was always cut short. Prison had pulled this up to a halt. There was no barber available for afro hair, are you kidding? So, Miles let his hair grow, from day one.

The man looking back at him, in the mirror in this small room, in a prison, ready to leave, was harder looking, stronger and had locks that fell around his face, to his shoulders.

"Johnson! Are you changed?"

Silence.

Louder.

"Are you changed?"
"Yeah."

****

Where did he go from here? Through those prison gates, out, thirty prison quid in his pocket. It was a momentous occasion.

The air smelt clean, cleaner than in jail, fresh air and birds, the loudness of their song surprising him. His desire was to be alone. He had told no one the exact date, he wanted no one there. The shop in the railway station. Buying jam doughnuts and a Tizer. Arriving at Temple Meads Station, the feeling of familiarity. Elation. His racing heart. Walking through the city, walking on air. Free.

He made a bee-line for Paradise Garage. Before being banged up he had spent so many afternoons in that cramped shop that it felt more like home than anywhere else. He pushed the shop door and there was Rich, on his usual perch in the middle of the clothes, rocking backwards and forwards to a song. Richard looked up, "Yeah, I heard you were getting out." Flat as a tyre.

Miles was unnerved. He had been gone for nearly three years, not three weeks. But gradually Richard's enthusiasm mounted, until he couldn't hide it anymore, "Look at this," – pulling out clothes. "Have you read this? Seen this? Heard about this?" Miles got a crash course in underground culture of the past few years, Richard by then as excited as when a new shipment of George Cox creepers used to arrive, so some kind of emotional apex. Miles thinks he left the shop to stop at Don's, but knows for certain that his first night of freedom was spent at Richard's, who threw a little party. Certainly not your "Welcome Home, Miles!" strung up between bunting and balloons, with Auntie Moira passing round a bowl of cheese footballs. This was a gathering of friends from Paradise Garage, an assortment of elegant punks, and maybe Nellee or Claude, and Derrick. His good friend Dennis. Everybody's girlfriends, too. There were takeaway pizzas and a bootleg of *The Thing* by John Carpenter. To Miles, it was a homecoming fit for a king.

****

He threw himself back into life. And life had been waiting for his return. He remembers the period after coming out of jail as one of immense joy. Those couple of years in Bristol, before tracing a line to other places, was kaleidoscopic. For the first six months, he was on probation. Being on probation cauterised a part of his social circle. He could no longer be with the football crowd. It was something that he had thought about in prison, it was a decision that he had made. His circle of friends became suddenly tighter, and its focus shifted.

He was in Paradise Garage, that was a constant. Right after his release, people would come to the shop to see him again, after all this time. They would tell others that Miles was out, so for the first months Miles was like some kind of reluctant monarch, unlikely courtiers coming for an audience, in this singular shop with a record ever-turning. As soon as he was out of prison, Nellee had Miles back on the social circuit, like a mother and her debutante hitting the right soirées. The first house party Miles can remember, which may well have been during his first weekend of freedom, was in the parental home of a girl in Redland. This was his first time around women since his release. He was shy. Going through the care system had stripped him of self-esteem. He wouldn't, couldn't, make the first move. The girls at the party were watching him and what they were seeing was a wildness that he unknowingly embodied. He was more alive than anyone else in the room, that's how it looked. He was a nineteen-year-old, in a twenty-two-year-old's body and was famished for excitement. One girl in particular, Sophie, was on his case. She sat next to him, chatting brightly, looking at his mouth too much as they spoke. Miles was half-listening, half-watching a couple of public school boys getting hopelessly drunk. Derrick was trying to reason with one of them, steadying him by holding his shoulders, "Listen man, you need to get outside and get some fresh air."

The kid looked stupidly at Derrick, taking in Derrick's face and fathoming Derrick's words. Then the kid said, in his nasal voice, "I think I'm going to puke."

"Get outside, go on, before you..." and the kid put his hand over his mouth. He retched. A thin fountain of vomit squirted from between his fingers, arching on to Derrick's face, a bit like those joke flowers that clowns wear, the ones that spurt water. Derrick went mental, "You fucking idiot! Get outside, you fucking plank!"

Miles was on the sofa, head thrown back, shaking with laughter. He said to Sophie, "It's good to be out, just for shit like that."

Later, Nellee came over.

"The girl whose party this is? She's really into you. She's over there." Miles looked just beyond to some girls, all holding cans of Red Stripe. "Here's the thing though – she's got herpes."

"What are you talking about? Hey, listen, Jack… I ain't messing with that for fuck's sake."

"Nah, it's okay. She just went out with this one St Paul's guy and she caught it off him, it was fucking ages ago."

"What you sayin'? She ain't a flippin' negrophile is she?" Nellee told him that it was just one Black bloke and that she hadn't been with anyone since. Then he lectured him, quite earnestly, on the pathogenesis of Herpes Simplex and how this girl hadn't had a flare-up since she caught it. The level of bizarreness of this entire exchange is worth noting. Miles was listening with concern.

"So what? She can't give it to me because it's not active?" Miles looked over at the girls. It was evident that they all knew what was being said, which was incredible to him. Miles was uncomfortable, yet he felt that this was what was required of him. There was expectancy on the girls' faces, this seemed to be a group ambition. "I dunno, Jack. Just tell her I'll meet her next week, something like that." Miles may have seemed arrogant to a lot of people back then, because of the way he looked and the way he dressed. He was closed and kept people at a distance because he was unsure of himself, for no other reason than that. He was also very trusting, as if a residue of his dysfunctional childhood was that he let other people decide for him. He trusted their choices, like he had when he was a small with boy with no control over his life. Why else would he have listened to an argumentation, then agreed to go out with a girl he had no interest in and who carried what was at that time a stigmatised STD?

He left the party with Sophie. He hadn't had sex in two-and-a-half years. He heard that they put bromide in prisoners' tea. He had got through prison without giving women much thought. Now here he was, on a bed, with a girl who was offering herself. He imagined that he would come almost immediately and that the physical release would be urgent and explosive. But he was limp. He looked at the girl, nothing happened. They got down to business. Still nothing moving. Something in him had altered, it seemed to be running faster than him. He tried, he failed. He got up and left.

He felt faintly concerned as he walked home to Don's. Then he thought about how this Sophie had led a twenty-two-year-old dude, who was hot out of prison to her bed. She had probably expected to get her brains fucked out, when all she'd got for her trouble was inept noodling around. That made him laugh. He met Sophie again a couple of times and although he got his performance together, it wasn't really happening for him. He met with the host from the party. That was difficult, too. He met her at her cousin's house and they had sex, sex without a condom.

Miles was trapped in a weird form of kindness: he could never bring himself to say no. He knew what rejection felt like. These encounters after his release from prison set the tone for all the relationships with women that were to come over the next few years. A girl would make a move on him, or sometimes would pursue him with what can only be described as ardour, whether subtle or more frontal. He only wriggled out of it if the girl in question had a dodgy reputation, or had had a relationship with a close friend or acquaintance. After sleeping with a woman with herpes – something he didn't catch, but that wasn't really the point – he had understood this about himself: he was doing things that, deeply, he didn't want to. He flipped through women. He inadvertently hurt some by never falling in love. In fact, he had been trying to be kind by not saying no. It wasn't that he wasn't into sex, he most definitely was, he just wasn't interested in everything else that was required beyond the bedroom door. All that consumed him was music, he was getting up every day for that one thing and, in any case, there was no room left in his heart for disappointment.

CHAPTER TWENTY-ONE

THERE'S A WORLD

Paradise Garage was Miles's headquarters. It was the temple of cool. You got to hang around there if you had sufficient idiosyncrasy, sufficient style. People dithered at the shop door, unsure whether it was possible to go inside if you looked ordinary. Miles felt that way the first time he went to Vivienne Westwood's shop, Sex, in London. Looking through the window at the poker-faced bird of paradise, Jordan, and saying to Dunc, "I can't go in there. How can I go in there? Look at my clothes." And Dunc having to psych Miles into it. Paradise Garage had a similar effect. Miles was down there every day, playing records that he'd just bought in Virgin, and connecting with people who came by. He hung out there with Nellee and sometimes Claude and his brother, Derrick.

A kid came in, wearing a leather motor cycle jacket. He had a look on his angular face, one eyebrow raised, as if to sharpen his focus. He was seemingly going through clothes, when really Miles felt he had his eye on the turntable and the men around it. Miles pulled a record, a black polished disc from the white paper inner sleeve, and put it on the deck. It was, *No Sell Out* credited to Malcolm X, on Tommy Boy Records. Raw hip-hop, a heavy Keith LeBlanc beat and the hypnotic voice of Malcolm X talking over it. Miles had read *The Autobiography Of Malcolm X* in prison, and those writings helped to fragment his received perception of himself and, over time, to free his mind from the rank – the lowest – that he held as a Black man in a white world. A wall in St Paul's was one day dressed with cautionary graffiti, "Niggers Are Scared Of A Revolution," put there by Miles's own hand. So, Malcolm X over hip-hop was the ultimate fusion, the ultimate sound.

The kid in the shop parted weighty leather jackets on the rack, then stopped still, his head cocked towards the music. A week or so later, he came back into the shop. He was very noticeably carrying a pristine Virgin bag. When Miles eventually asked what he'd bought, he pulled the record out of the bag, trying to curb his eagerness a little. It was another Tommy Boy record, *Salsa Smurf*. Miles asked, "Let's have a listen?" The tune kicked in. He looked at the kid and smiled, the song was even better than, *No Sell Out*.

"I tell you what, mate, this is wicked." The kid came into the shop all the time, after that. His name was Robert Del Naja, his mates called him Delge.

*****

Miles was in Paradise Garage with Cockney Pete. He was white, blond and one of the rare men back then who was working out and muscle-bound. He was a slick dresser, something of a poseur, and he was a laugh, a proper laugh. He used to go on blinders and act outrageously. One day Derrick said to Miles, "Fucking hell, Pete had this party last night and he got tanked up like you wouldn't believe. He was only running round bollock-naked. Listen man, he was running round like he had something going on down there, when what he's really got is fucking kindergarten stuff. My new name for him is Cockless Pete." This kind of Derrick anecdote had Miles in stitches.

There they were, Miles and Cockney Pete, the afternoon indistinguishable from any other, when a young Black man in a coat from a second-hand store sauntered into Paradise Garage. He hung around, looking at clothes, but seemed, like Delge, more interested in what was being played. He wandered over to Miles and Cockney Pete, "All right?" he asked. He looked at the turntable, said something – what, exactly, is lost to time – but it was enough to kindle a conversation. His name was Grantley. He lived in Redland. This man resonated with Miles. He was an interesting clash of Black and punkish whiteness in the way he looked, he had an elegance and carried himself with pride. There were the same qualities about him that people have attributed to Miles. Arrogance, for example, that isn't arrogance, but the sum of feeling misaligned with your surroundings and having had to steel yourself, to shut part of yourself away. A goodness also, at least a desire to be so. In some ways, Grantley was the closest Miles would ever come to looking in the mirror.

"D'you know where I can score?" asked Cockney Pete. Which – the love of a spliff rather than a sale – led to the three of them walking back to Grantley's flat. Miles didn't smoke, but he felt like prolonging this new encounter. Grantley and Pete were on the sofa smoking and Miles, who had hit the equivalent of a triple cherry on a one-armed bandit, was stood in front of Grantley's incredible reggae collection. He riffled through, pulling records out carefully, and he played tune after tune. He came across *I Don't Want To Lose You* by Paul Blackman and Augustus Pablo. He turned to Grantley and said, "Man, this is a fucking heavy tune."

Which is what sealed it, music. Grantley, who later took the name of Daddy Gee, had just nonchalantly entered Miles's life.

****

It was Nellee's idea, to go to Glastonbury. It was a first for Miles. You climbed your way in to the festival through a bush back then. No one he knew had paid their entrance. The excitement of going there was immense. Nellee had talked about it a lot since Miles's release, because some of the musicians playing were in their various record collections: King Sunny Ade, A Certain Ratio, UB40. It seemed like all of the Bristol club, the Dug Out – which was the headquarters of Bristol underground nights – was down there, along with the entire student union of Somerset, and residual punks and hippies, pulled up in the surrounding fields in clapped-out caravans, running music from generators. He wove his way around the site with Nellee, until they found their base with the crew from Bristol. The last thing on his mind was meeting girls. Miles and Nellee must have been there for only half an hour before A Certain Ratio walked on to the stage. Seeing them live fleetingly made him think of the first time he had heard them, on his little transistor, in jail.

He can recall that fantastic feeling of being outside, standing on grass. Of staring up at the stage, the Pyramid, which was built from redundant telegraph poles and still used as a cowshed over winter. It was magical, there was only the present time, caught in fields of invisible lines that joined the dots between worshippers here and worshippers gone, who danced beneath the sun and beneath the moon. It was a big crowd, it was brilliant, perfect, all these people milling round under a cornflower sky. Then there were those few moments before a concert kicks off when sound is deconstructed, and a band shows you its mechanics: The guitarist strikes a chord thickly, once, twice, tuning; the drum goes tish tish tish; the singer asks, into the emptiness, an echoey, "Are we good?"

Miles had such a great time, revelling in the music. Towards the end of the set, in his peripheral vision, he was aware of someone in front of him, turning his way. He took no notice. The person turned again. How could you be so distracted? He felt he was being watched. It was annoying. His gaze flicked away from the stage, to the silhouette. Looking up, straight at him, was a smiling girl in a leather jacket. It threw him. Each of us has our own idea of what constitutes beauty, and to Miles, this girl – although outside conventional standards – had it all. He locked eyes with her, and thought, "What's she doing?" He was really puzzled, and turned to Nellee now, who got him by the arm and pulled him away, to another stage. The incident was forgotten. Miles was caught up in the joys of freedom and music, heady with it, awoken from the lost years.

The girl tracked him down to where he and his friends were camping out. Chaka Khan was belting out of their speakers. She stood there, waiting, on the edge of the darkness. This time, there was no question that she was there for him, and he jumped up. His memory has a gritty, saturated quality, like a Super 8 film: her eyes hold candour, she is unaware of how she will last through time. He is walking around Glastonbury holding hands with her; they are in her cousin's tent where they are listening to Spoonie Gee.

Here, the memory ends. He found out where she was from, a village outside Bristol. He felt she was untarnished, he felt she was removed. In the weeks that followed, he visited her in her village. The drawn blue Liberty curtains in her bedroom cast her in a perpetual morning light. She had the worst record collection he had ever come across.

Then, after a while, curiosity must have got her, because she took a night bus into Bristol, on her own, and entered the subterranean world of the Dug Out. Miles was down there, with a girlfriend, he can't remember who she was. The girl from Glastonbury took one look at Miles, at the betrayal, and did what she was primed to do: slowly self-destruct. The girl from Glastonbury comes out of the written story here, although she didn't vanish completely from his life. She has her place in this narrative because he thought she was a girl he could take as a serious partner, it was the first time he had felt that way and it took him by surprise. He was young though, and only recently free and she was younger still, and disturbingly naive. He knew she needed protecting. He didn't have the time to give. The time you must give over to shield a girl like her. He had already had twenty percent of his life stolen from him so on that front, he was down. Also, they were both profoundly fucked up. It took him a while to work that out.

****

It was early 1983. It was just the three of them: Miles, Nellee and Gee, dossing around in their basic flats, spinning record after record. Gee and Nellee had become friends whilst Miles was inside. There was already a project between the two of them to make music, but Nellee told Gee they should wait until his mate, Miles, got out of prison.

Gee moved to St Paul's, to City Road, which was the area's main artery. St Paul's had always been the headquarters of sound system culture in the south west of England. Sound system culture was born in Kingston, Jamaica, in the 1940s. It was a phonographically based movement, with selectors playing vinyl records. A group of DJs would pull up in trucks in various neighbourhoods of Kingston and rig up a sound system run off generators, playing for the people in the street. The basic principal of playing vinyl for party people never changed, but over time the music evolved from being American-influenced, to being island music – reggae and ska – and sound system culture eventually became the most powerful ambassador for Jamaica in the world.

In the 1950s, blues, or shebeens as they were also known, were where the Black people of England would commune to experience music. It was here, in these clandestine clubs which were often in basement flats, that sound systems would set up for the night. Blues were always dark, you could sometimes barely see, so your other senses were heightened. The MCs and DJs were on the same level as the people come to dance, there was no stage, no division. The bassline was deep and physical. Music was a spiritual experience, a part of African identity that had been kept intact from the enemy. It was fundamental to the Black community, and taken for granted. Twenty years on, white people got curious and came down to blues thinking they would just be listening to reggae music, not expecting what they got: an old guy in a corner, smoking a spliff, playing a record and the white people not understanding how they're still managing to stand up, under the weight of this bassline. A bassline so resonant that it made shirts and trousers shake on men and, legend has it, the pressure of the bass great enough that unsuspecting first-time white women lost control of their bladders. They literally wet themselves.

Miles never imagined himself in a band, or as a performer. His Jamaican heritage and community had brought him music, and the only way he envisaged being involved with music was in the way he had been shown, as an offering and a shared experience. He was lucky, during his childhood in the sixties, Bristol had some of the greatest sound systems in the UK. Of the men running them, the MCs, the selectors, some were his familiars. Keith, who was in Tarzan the High Priest's sound system, for example, was married to his Auntie Joy. Tarzan's Sound System was the first one in Bristol. They would receive shipments of singles, direct from Kingston, often on a Thursday and start a party on a Friday night, not stopping until Monday. Count Ajax, who ran a blues for decades, was a family friend. Miles had first gone into Ajax blues really young, maybe aged eight or nine. It was Christmas time and the whole community was out partying. There was a bit a freedom for kids to wander round during the Christmas season. He can remember going down to Ajax, with his friends. Saying hello to Don or to someone's dad, or someone's brother. Having this as an excuse to peek into the darkness. He can remember being a small boy that felt swallowed by the mighty sound. It is a subliminal image in the film of his childhood, a few seconds of a forbidden, adult world.

****

In 1983, England was descending into the bleak heart of Thatcher's Britain. There was the strategic neutralisation of trade unions leading to the miners' strikes brewing. There was the Sus Law ('Sus' being an abbreviation for suspected person), an archaic law that was part of the 1824 Vagrancy Act. It authorised a police officer to stop and search any person deemed intent on committing an offence. It was sufficiently vague to be impossible to frame in objective terms. An officer could claim that it seemed that the Black youths standing on the street corner looked like they were intent on mugging the next passer-by, or robbing a post office, or smoking illegal drugs. It was his view. It was enough to see a man or woman arrested, often strip-searched and held in a cell for the day. It was a law used perniciously, mostly targeting ethnic minorities. It caused much concern in the ghettos of the UK. It was eventually repealed in 1981, after the 1980 UK race riots, where in the ghettos of England Black people went head-to-head with the police, fighting for fundamental human rights.

In Bristol, the St Paul's riots happened in 1980, which was when Miles was still on probation, making it impossible for him to be there without being immediately rearrested. He has sometimes thought of this. He was put away for four years for a crime he was innocent of, but had he been a free man, there is no question that he would have been down on the streets of St Paul's, fighting. The four years might well have stretched to far longer. The St Paul's' riots had an unexpected knock-on effect: the police kept more or less away from the ghetto. In a country where it wasn't so much Big Brother watching you as a crazed nanny taking your temperature, St Paul's was paradoxically a shelter from the infantilising, anti-working class think-tank that was policing creativity, as well as basic human rights. You could run into St Paul's if the police were tailing you, and they wouldn't follow you in. You could have a party in the streets of St Paul's and make a lot of noise and the police would let it be.

St Paul's was Bristol's red light area. Come night time, the sub-bass of reggae vibrated through the doors of the basement shebeens. There were street hustlers, dreads in high beaver skin hats selling ganja from cars, cars which also heaved with bass lines from the speakers laid flat in the boot. There were prostitutes, white women mostly, out on the beat with their *Dynasty* hairstyles and hook lines, "You lookin' darlin'?" spoken in broad Bristolian. St Paul's had a soundtrack to it in the eighties. Gee's place, in the heart of it, was where they set up camp. It was an organic process. They would bring their records, look them over, play them. A few friends would come round, so sometimes there would be ten people at Gee's, smoking weed, listening to music, dancing. It became a thing, and the friends would come back with another friend, who would bring another friend, until one day, these concentric circles had Gee's place overflowing. It was Gee who had the idea to turn what was a splice between a pastime of playing to mates and a passion for music into something more precise, which was to play in a larger space. It was the start of the collective that was to become Wild Bunch.

Their sound was taking shape. Over the first year, the punk, new wave, dub and disco undertone was losing ground to hip-hop, until this is what it became: each of them taking it in turns putting records on with no real format or plan. One minute it could be *Fodderstompf*, by Public Image Limited, then maybe next it would be a Lonnie Liston Smith, *Space Princess* disco track, or Joe Gibbs, or Augustus Pablo. It transformed into set playing times as their record collection grew. They nurtured individual styles, Gee played reggae and RnB, Nellee played hip-hop, some afro beat and what would later be labelled rare groove. Miles played a mixture of disco, new wave, funk and hip-hop. He had also begun experimenting with what was to become his signature sound: the superposition of two seemingly unmatchable genres – a dirty hip-hop beat, underscoring for example, a mellow UB40 track, or even *The Magic Roundabout* theme tune over Adonis, *No Way Back*. Or again, the LL CoolJ, I Need A Beat, instrumental, with Dennis Edwards, *Don't Look Any Further*.

This was close to punk, in its essence. It was a transgressive sound, a subversive, poor man's take on music. Wild Bunch, christened so by Patrick Irie who used to MC for them down the Dug Out – not a direct reference to the Sam Peckinpah film but a statement about the eccentric way they dressed – were signing on and pooling Friday giros to buy records. It was DIY taken to an art form. How to cut up two records in order to prolong the break for as long as possible, how to drop the stylus smack in the right place, the break, on a vinyl. There are the elements of Wild Bunch that can be explained through a careful piecing together of facts. Then there is the inexplicable, which is to say the magic. The sound that was borne, Wild Bunch sound – a crazy, rough, block party sound that held silences, and whistles, then dropped a bass line like a bomb. It was an all-in thing. When they played, party-goers watched them. Wild Bunch were dressed with English eccentricity and street cool – for example, Nellee and Milo would saunter through Clifton, stopping off at WH Smith's, where they shamelessly consulted all the fashion magazines, particularly Face and *Vogue Homme*.

This is how they spotted a pair of Nike Air Ace 83 (in *Face* magazine) and went to London by coach on their giros the following Friday to buy a pair each. Or how, in *Vogue*, they first saw jumpers by Gianfranco Ferré and, again, both bought one. Of course, burning your entire dole money on one item of clothing made eating difficult. Later, in Kosta's café, their daytime haunt, they ran up a tab so ceaseless that Kosta, the owner, was on them all the time. Miles and Nellee both wore jeans ripped up to such an extreme that they had to wear leggings underneath for modesty. Gee, like Miles and Nellee, dressed with a punkish lean but his was a more studenty take, thrift-store long coats or vintage Americana, especially a coach jacket and a baseball cap. They were all interested in fashion, but in fact none of them really cared who was looking. Miles's passion for finding and introducing new music to dance to was what it was about for him. Nothing else. It was enough.

CHAPTER TWENTY-TWO

GOLD IN MY EAR

There is a place in Bristol, up high. The houses in Clifton, in their pale elegance, seem to stand back, letting the Downs, a soft expanse of green, roll outwards towards the Avon Gorge. The River Avon snakes between cliff fronts that face each other – on one side is the neighbourhood of Clifton and, on the other, Leigh Woods. Placed between the two banks, hung in the sky like a wrought iron metaphor, is the Clifton Suspension Bridge. It was designed by Isambard Kingdom Brunel. At the birth of the bridge, in 1831, construction workers with special skills in explosives convened to blast out Saint Vincent's Rock. Then the site was closed, just four months in, as Bristol's militant underclass invaded the lofty quiet and went on a civil rights rampage. This was a group of men fighting to give the industrial towns of England, and the working class in general, greater representation in the House of Commons. They fought, also, to get the destitute boroughs of Bristol safer infrastructures. Private homes in Clifton were burnt down and looted. They demolished the gaol. The rioters, young men five-hundred or six-hundred strong, paid in blood. Many of them perished in the fires and four of them were subsequently hanged. The story of the mighty is always, irrevocably, enmeshed with the plight of the humble. Grandeur is established, but the poor never forget who carried the bricks and the foolish thing the rich can do, is to imagine they have.

The Downs in Clifton, right in front of the Suspension Bridge, was the setting for the first Wild Bunch get together. It seems a fitting backdrop, a bridge, for their beginnings. The boys and their friends, thirty kids perhaps, set up a little system one warm afternoon. They brought music, and picnics and beer and stretched-out in the long afternoon beneath the equally stretched out sky. It was good. They decided to come back, this time at night: Miles, Nellee and Gee. They had beer, a lot of it, which they'd bought wholesale. They were besieged. Word had spread and party people appeared, as magic as shadows in the night, making their way across the grass. Maybe three hundred of them. The crew was bumping out tunes, selling cans of Tennant's and people were dancing away in the dark. Milo remembers someone standing over them shining a bedside lamp on to the records, so that they could see what they were doing. Then the police pulled up and ran them off the Downs. The problem was dead-stock beer, to the tune of a few hundred quid. So, they relocated the party to Nellee's, in Clifton. His flat was in a house with the 2 Bad Crew upstairs. Within an hour, it was heaving with partygoers, the uptown Clifton heads and little posses from St Paul's, come there to sell draw. It was a good party. Gee was already DJing at the Dug Out on Tuesday nights. After the Downs party, Gee negotiated for this small and, as yet, nameless crew to play at the Dug Out on Thursday nights.

So much has been written about the Dug Out. Were you to walk around Bristol with a t-shirt that read, "The carpet stuck to your feet," it has become such a trope that there are people who would recognise the reference, even today. And it's true, the carpet had viscosity. Clubbers chatted each other up with their soles suctioned to decades of candied beer and dust. Some nights in the early to mid-eighties, especially Wild Bunch nights, the Dug Out was rocking, but it was also a kind of anti-establishment club house, so on other nights, it was half empty. People would trundle down the stairs at the end of their working day to share a drink and chat, or to watch a video in the eponymously named Upstairs. On the nights when the Dug Out was rammed, no other club in Bristol, and quite possibly in the UK had resident DJs that drew in such a broad congregation. Men and boys of island descent, the B-boys down to dance and the dreads stood quiet in the corner, building spliffs, heads rocking to the beat. Arty kids with pierced noses and DMs, getting drunk, collapsing in laughter. Black girls from St Paul's, white girls from Clifton. Nurses, who seemed to bring a buoyancy. Punks, still around, dancing sometimes, to this mad hip-hop. All kinds. It was a place that drew in people who didn't fit elsewhere, or who didn't want to. If you dig beyond the social grouping of genre: punks, dreads, nurses and so forth, and wonder at the common denominator, it may have been that most of the people down in those rooms was an outsider of a kind.

You descended into the Dug Out one evening, out of curiosity, or by chance. It was dingy, but that would seem to you, interesting, or at least not a problem. The punters down there felt like people you could deal with. And the music. That was it. The soundtrack to your unfurling youth would be eclectic, wild and groove-ridden – a fine soundtrack for rogue years. The club existed under constant threat of closure (being a rough joint on the edge of affluent Clifton) and was eventually shut down in 1986. But in the early eighties, in the Dug Out's dark recesses, young women and men talked and laughed and watched each other. People got down and danced all night long. Those nights in Bristol were special. The members of the Dug Out – in and out of each other's bedsits, in and out of the same pubs, the same clubs, in and out of each other's lives – thought, most probably, and why not, that this is the way life would always be. Black people and white people together, no harsh lines drawn. Working-class and middle-class people dating, creating, growing up. Or even just ignoring each other, which was also true, but existing in the same spaces, together and apart. It was a decision made by that collective of Bristol youth. They were under the impression that it had always been that way. It hadn't. It felt like being on the right path. Some things only happen once. The shift within the kaleidoscope that backlit punk, hip-hop and reggae lovers, that put them together and gave the world a new musical genre: it was just a blink in time.

A dug out is, literally, a trench that is dug out with a roof built over, for the protection of troops. That seems right. It was a mismatched army of people down there, in the Dug Out. It was worth putting a roof over. In the booth, in the cupboard under the stairs, Wild Bunch cooked up something magic in their cauldron, and the people under that collective spell can remember. It is their small piece of something bigger.

Perhaps at the Downs night-time party, perhaps at the Dug Out, Wild Bunch and the bardic Mark Stewart, met. A looming, Hemingway-like figure, Stewart was, at once, all-embracing and formidable. He fronted The Pop Group, who made the classic, *We Are All Prostitutes* whose artwork featured a demented-looking Margaret Thatcher, her fingers signing V for Fuck Off. Mark took a shine to this punky collective of hip-hop DJs, and must have seen something in them that could translate out of Bristol into the heart of London cool. Mark knew a lot of people, a lot of edgy creatives, who would certainly not have put Bristol down as a hot-house of trendsetters – he would prove them wrong. Mark took Wild Bunch to London. There was a dynamic to this relationship: Mark, like an exalted scientist, bringing his findings for inspection before a certain (picky) establishment. His enthusiasm was infectious. He introduced them to his friend, Newtrament, from Ladbroke Grove. Newtrament had a little crew and he was also in possession of the best hip-hop record collection Wild Bunch had ever seen. The rumour was that Newtrament's father was an American, and from those mystical shores sent his son hip-hop releases fresh off the press. Mark organised a battle at the Titanic club, Wild Bunch and Newtrament against a hip-hop collective, Language Lab, who had an MC with the wonderful name of Dizzy Heights. Milo remembers strutting into that battle with his crew, Mark's confidence in them buoying them up. It was fairly cool runnings until Mark grabbed the mic and, totally indifferent to what was going on (MCs rapping over hip-hop), began hollering insanely, a punk stream-of-consciousness rant, over the beat. Milo, Nellee and Gee stood back, stunned, until an opposing MC yelled over his own system, "Stop defecating on the mic, man!" This memory still makes Milo laugh.

*****

Nellee, Miles and Gee had been hustling money to buy a couple of Technics turntables. It was their single, burning desire. And it happened. It was a game changer. The turntables in question, Technics 1200s, were direct drive, rather than belt driven. Instead of the low "woaah" sound made after scratching, right before the record picks up speed again on landing on a belt drive, these turntables allowed a DJ to scratch, then release the tune, hitting straight into the right speed. They would no longer drop a stitch of time. Here they were, a group of mates – now including Claude 'Willie Wee' Williams, along for the ride – with no great experience, just two spanking new turntables and an explosive level of energy. They took on London and green as they were, they did all right. Maybe they would have made it there anyway, to the Big City, on their own. But each of our stories is a sum of encounters and Mark Stewart is a cornerstone encounter in theirs. It was the hand of punk that took the hand of this young crew, who were a living fusion of so many sub-cultures that had come before.. It is also probable that it was via Mark and Newtrament that Tim Westwood got wind of them, and he, in turn, invited them to a battle at The Wag Club, in London against the local Cookie Crew, a two-girl set. In the end, it was Westwood with his power to arbitrate, who raised the arm of the victorious Cookie Crew. Wild Bunch left London slightly disgruntled at their silver placement, feeling short-changed because the crowd had been very noisily behind them. They weren't, as yet, in a place where the "From Bristol" tag was a badge of cool. From Bristol still smelled a little of cider and hay.

****

Since his release from jail, Miles had been staying at Don's, back in his old room, on East Grove. His bedroom was unchanged. The wardrobe was still packed with his stuff – magazines, records, t-shirts that he hadn't worn since he was twelve. By this point, he had started working for Paradise Garage, but in Kensington Market, London, making the commute from Bristol Temple Meads train station to London, Paddington five days a week. Richard, who was now his boss, was always good to him, holding back one-off merchandise and giving him discounts, so Miles already had some incredible clothes, and he did love his clothes. This is an important point, because at Don's there was no lock on his bedroom door. Miles came home one day to find his coat, a full-length leather La Rocka! that was a prototype and one of only one, gone. Things had vanished before, but this was the limit for him. Even today, he can't talk about it without mounting outrage. It has to be handed to Don, at this point, that welcoming a twenty-two-year-old ex-convict into your home, with his nightlife and his girlfriends, was a show of something beyond paternal. But whatever his kindness, Miles felt that the little he owned wasn't safe and he needed to leave.

Since his release, Nicky had been pressing him, showing up at clubs where he was, waiting outside pubs. When she heard that he had been released, she finished with her boyfriend and had maybe imagined that to be enough for Miles to pick up with her where they had left off. She had been working on him for weeks, asking him to talk with her, to go out with her. She finally went all in, "Why don't you just come and live with me?" All those weeks, he had held her at bay, but that evening, the evening that he found a space where an expensive leather coat should have been, he made the decision to leave. Nicky was the only person he could think of with a place of her own and set of keys for him, so he packed up his bags and called her.

He began living at Nicky's randomly. Their relationship as it had been before he got put away – light-hearted – was gone. She had had a life whilst he'd been in jail, of course, and she was altered. He felt the change in her. Jail had damaged Miles, too, seeming to have finalised his emotional closing down. Even without incarceration, theirs would only have been a passing story, but that time out – almost three years – was unbridgeable. He moved in to Nicky's with a nihilistic approach to his future there. He was in dire straits, which is the sad story of many young people whose adult lives are a sequence that begins: care, jail, freedom. Because freedom is a free fall, when there is nothing solid enough, no real family, no one to help you financially, once you step outside. He was still so young, he had little to give. Some evenings, he would leave a party with a girl and not go back to Nicky's. Sometimes, he would meet a girl on a Friday night and not show up at Nicky's again until Sunday. "I was at Grant's," were his only words. If she had pressed it, he would probably have told the truth, but she didn't press it. They were unfinished, just kids. She was a hard worker, she had the ambitions of a regular girl: to save money and buy her own place, to have a man. Miles wasn't that man, and he had known it from the start. He went through the motions, in a scrappy way, of living with her. Maybe she saw hope, because she wanted him. Maybe she believed. They were on different paths, that was the fact. His life was a vortex of encounters. He was on a critical learning curve. Life was telling him something about himself: that music would rule him.

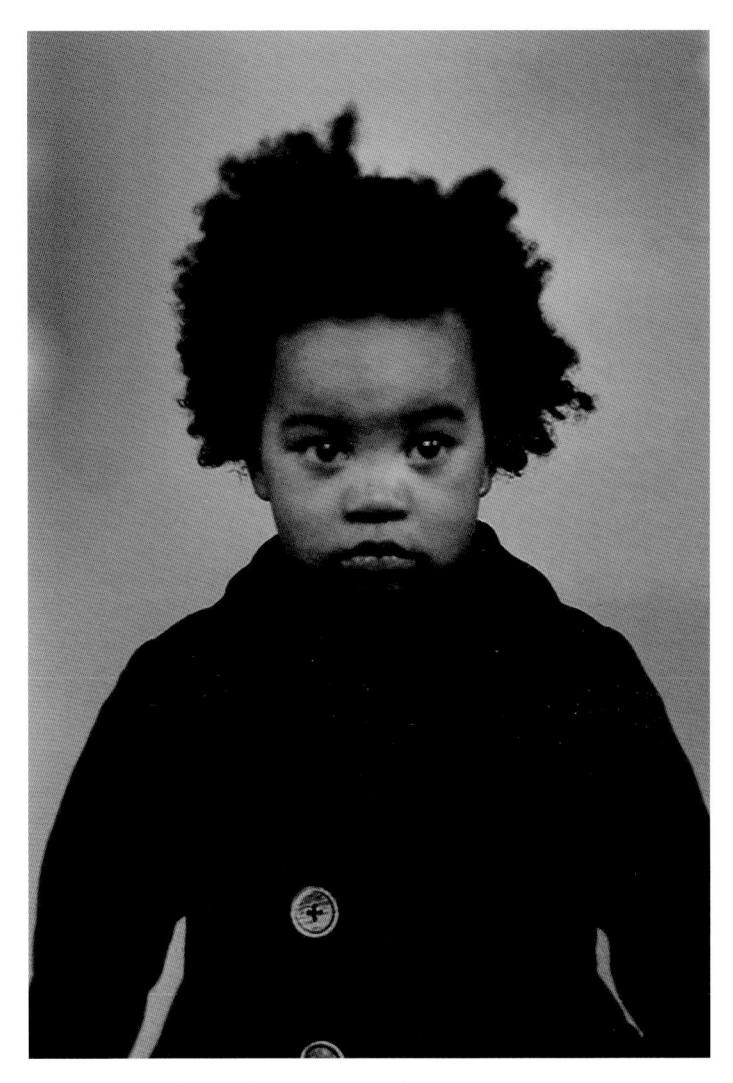

Mum's Barnardo's orphanage processing picture.

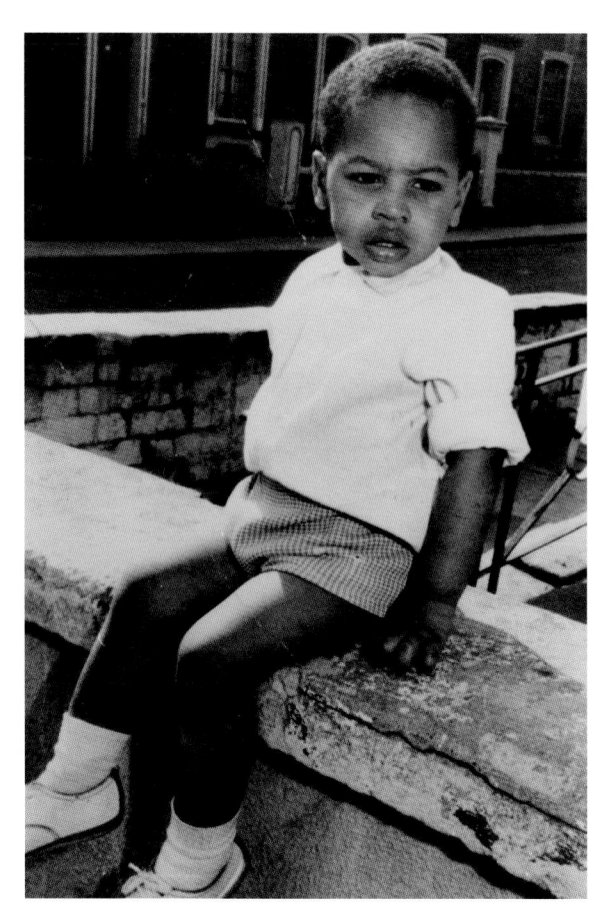

Top: Me in St Paul's.
Above: With my cousin at Bristol Zoo in 1963.

Me and my kid sister.

Before the darkness: Me, baby sister and friend Paul in Fishponds, Bristol.

Mum and Auntie Joy.

Mum and Auntie Joyce in Bath.

Mum and the gang. Mum is standing, second left. That's me bottom left.

Foster mum Marlow and partner Ken.   Bristol City boys. Picture courtesy Steve Bush (centre).

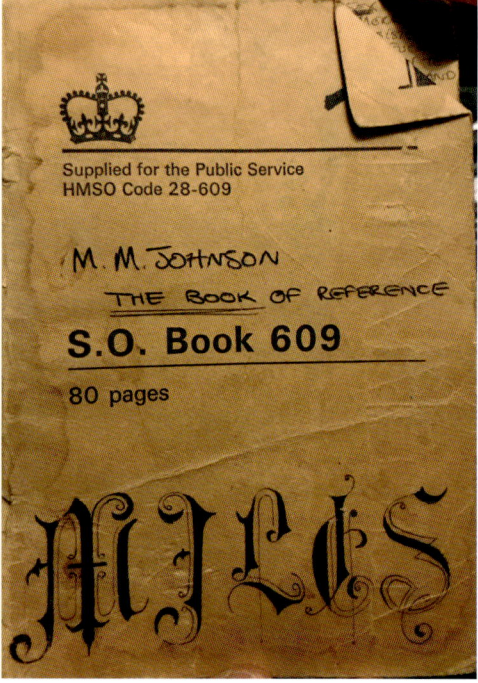

Flyer for a gig by the short-lived Rumba Lament. The cover of my prison notebook.

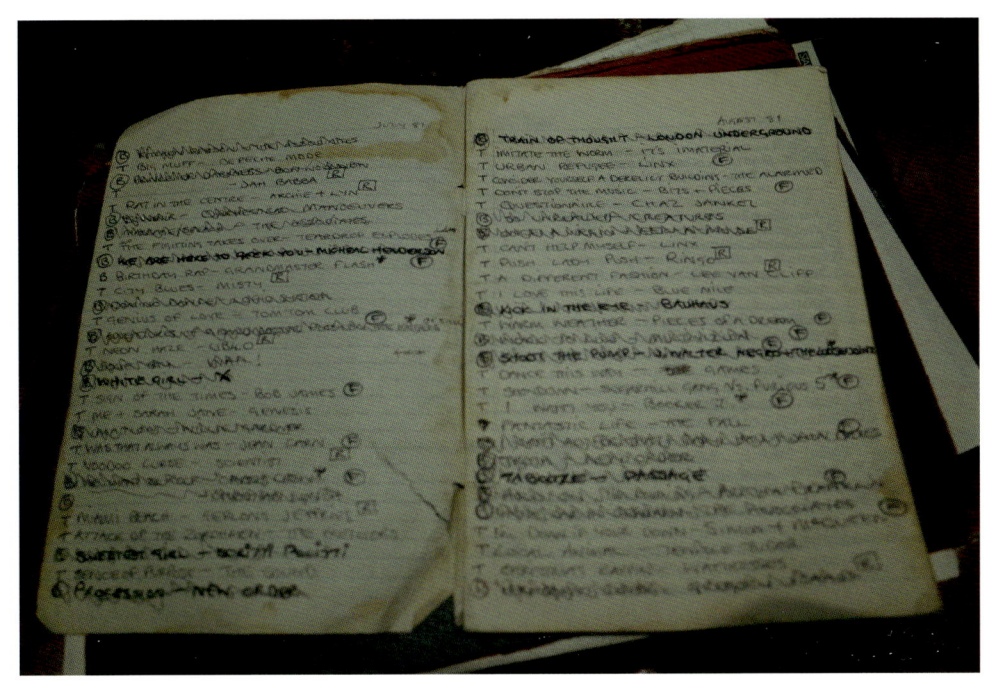

Always on my mind. Lists of all the tunes I wanted to buy.

Free at last. Mum visiting Bristol after my release.

Wild Bunch Downs party. Picture: Julian Monaghan.

A collection of Wild Bunch flyers.

Wild Bunch and Moichi Kuwahara in Japan (Photo Bridget Macklin). Down Time Mood Tape, 1985.

A great reason to be skint. The highlight of our year, St Paul's Carnival, 1986. Picture: Sarah Dunn.

City to city: Moving to Camden in 1986.

The start of something good. Wild Bunch: *The Look Of Love*.

Movements: Wild Bunch press shot by Julian Monaghan. Me, 3D, Grant, Nellee, Willie Wee.

A name of our own. The first Massive Attack graffiti appeared in Bristol in 1987.

Me and G at the Moon Club, Bristol.

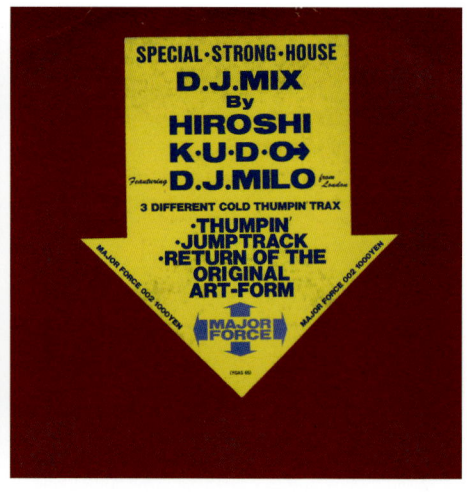

Return Of The Original Art Form, Major Force.

Major Force, 1987: Takagi Kan, Masayuki Kudo and Toshi Nakanishi.

Above: Something had to change Top: With Kudo in Japan. Above right: The best of times with Chica and Hiroshi, Tokyo, 1987

Nagasaki crew.

RUFF DISCO RECORDS

NATURE BOY

RF 001
SIDE 2
33 1/3 RPM
STEREO
© ℗ 1992

Produced By
Nature Boy
Glitch Music (BMI)

1. "The Living Groove" (5:41)
2. "You Want....." (5:02)

Special Thanks To D. J's Choice (Tokyo)

RUFF DISCO RECORDS
(212) 979-8779

A NIGHT ON THE TURNTABLES, BLOW BY BLOW, HIT BY HIT.

TONY HUMPHRIES			JOHN ROBINSON		
Spun on September 5, 1992 12pm - 2am			Spun on September 2, 3, 4 & 8, 1992 12am-1pm		
WRKS -NY			WBLS-NY		
Artist / Title		Label	Artist / Title		Label	Plays
BANANARAMA Last Thing On My Mind		(ffrr/London)	CE CE PENISTON Crazy Love	(A&M/UK)	5
DEGREES OF MOTION Soul Freedom		(Esquire)			
ARTIST UNKNOWN Struggle		(Emotive)	ANGELIQUE KIDJO We We	(Great Jones/Island)	3
REEL TO REEL The Anthem		(Strictly Rhythm)	ARTIST UNKOWN True Love (Import)		
KIM BEACHAM The Reason		(111 East)			
DES'REE So High		(Tape)	MARTHA WASH Carry On (RCA)		2
SUGARCUBES Leash Called Love		(Elektra)	MORRISON Rain Man (Import)		2
VICTOR SIMONELLI Need A Little More		(Tape)			
JOEY ROBERTS Love is Energy		(ffrr/London)	TEN CITY Only Time Will Tell (Atco/EastWest/Atl. Grp.)		2
BRAXTON HOLMES 12"s Of Pleasure		(Clubhouse)			
NATURE BOY The Livin' Groove		(Tomato/Import)	AL JARREAU Blue Angel (Reprise)		1
ANGELIQUE KIDJO We We		(Great Jones/Island)			
THE SAX MACHINE Sax It Up		(S&G)	ALOOF On A Mission (Cowboy/UK)		1
WALLS OF SOUND I Need Your Luv (Right Now)		(eight ball)	BILL ROBINSON I Aye Bye You (Nott-Us/Apollo)		1
NIGHTMARES ON WAX Set Me Free		(Warp)	CANDI STATON When You Wake Up Tomorrow (WB)		1
BIZARRE INC. I'm Gonna Get You		(V3)			
MARK DAVIS You're Special		(Strictly Rhythm)	FIRST CHOICE It's Not Over (SalSoul)		1
MALIKA So Much Love		(A&M)	HAPPY MONDAYS Stinkin' Thinkin' (Elektra)		1
LINDY LAYTON We Got The Love		(Black Diamond/Import)			
HAPPYHEAD Digital Love Thing		(Atco/EastWest/Atl. Grp.)	KAREN POLLACK You Can't Touch Me (Emotive)		1
BAS NOIR Addicted To Love		(Atlantic/Atl. Grp.)	KATHY SLEDGE Heart (Epic)		1
DATURA Brujo		(Trance/Irma)			
HAPPY MONDAYS Stinkin' Thinkin'		(Elektra)	KIM BEACHAM True Love (111 East)		1
SOUNDS OF BLACKNESS Joy		(Perspective/A&M)	LIL' LOUIS & THE WORLD Saved My Life (Epic)		1
ARTIST UNKNOWN Instrumental Track		(Antima/Irma)			
INTENSE Eternal Love		(Ace Beat)	MARTHA WASH Give It To You (RCA)		1
MICHAEL WATFORD Love For 2		(Tape)	PRINCE MARKIE DEE Trippin' Out (Columbia)		1
WHEN WORLDS COLLIDE Track Unknown		(Gold Tone)			
DEEE-LITE Thank You Everyday		(Elektra)	SHEER BRONZE Walkin' On (ffrr/London)		1
THE TORONTO CREW Knew Family		(Tomato)			
KEY CHOICE Rejoice		(Tape)	The above songs are ordered according to the number of plays they received during the five shows produced on the dates above.		
CATHY DENNIS You Lied To Me		(Polydor)			

This is A Listing Of The Actual Show In The Order The Songs Were Played On The Date Above.

FROM MILO

Top: New beginnings in New York.
Middle: Waiting for Mandela, 125th Street, Harlem, 1990.
Above: Independent venture. My first solo release. Right: Nature Boy on New York House DJ Tony Humphries' playlist. All the affirmation needed.

Where to begin: East Village, New York City, 1989.

New frontiers: New York's best dancers on the Tokyo catwalk at the Men's Bigi Show in 1990.

Mum and my son, East Village, NY.

Chapter Twenty-Three

NOTHING WILL BE AS IT WAS

Kensington Market, London

Kensington Market, London, was a three-storey indoor market on Kensington High Street. In the early eighties, it was colonised by the sub cultures of the time. It was there for punks, new romantics, rockabillies and any kid with a leaning for dissident dress. The Paradise Garage outlet was on the top floor and specialised in elaborate cowboy boots, handmade, with extreme-angled Cuban heals and their accessories: silver toe tips, boot chains, spurs. Miles was now employed by Richard to work for Paradise in Kensington. Miles's job was to sell these boots, and to showcase them. His were snakeskin.

He was getting up at six, Monday to Friday, to take a train from Temple Meads to Paddington. He became part of the Kensington Market community. People, amazing, extravagant people, stopped by. Sometimes as customers, sometimes just to hang out. London night life had its royalty in artists like Leigh Bowery, Boy George, Ray Petri and Vivienne Westwood. Kids who blew their wages in Kensington Market wanted to be as wild as them. It was a time of uninhibited self expression, of crossing every boundary, of juxtaposing different cultures and sounds. Miles, mixed-race, dressed as himself and standing proud, fit right in. Did more than fit in. He embodied an ideal of the moment. Freedom and fearlessness. It was a firework display set off from an island, whilst on the mainland, in the darkness, HIV had begun its labyrinthine voyage into the white blood cells of those gifted and beloved. Of those abandoned and consoled in poppy. Of those unfettered in love. Of those stumbling, fresh, unlucky. HIV trawled the waters of the arts, especially. When its net was hauled in, to a shivering shore, its catch was of stories stolen from the future. But we're not there yet. This was Kensington Market, 1984, and life was out loud.

Miles was all over the place. Wild Bunch had residencies by now. Tuesday nights were on Dean Street, in Soho, when Gossips became Krush Groove. Thursdays were in the Dug Out club, and Fridays, still in Bristol, Tropics. He was living with Nicky, in Lockleaze, on a road of semis where everyone's dad was called Dave and everyone's mum was called Pam. He was with a girl who collected snowstorm paperweights, had a building society account and whose parents were married to each other. He was spending his waking hours with what England was delivering in the way of the most incisive, groundbreaking artists. The two distinct lives he led were like icebergs travelling towards each other.

He became friends with the other stallholders at the market. There was a guy across the floor selling second hand clothing but on the quiet he was also dealing vintage seventies porn and ultra-violent horror films, imported from America. Porn, and those b-movie horror films were hard to access back then, so Miles became, in the posh end of Bristol, the underground go-to guy for that. He got his hands on copies of the 1976 film, *Snuff* and that litter of videos found homes embarrassingly fast. It caused a rumour to spread around St Paul's that Miles and Gee watched snuff movies. Most of the time though, not a lot happened in the Paradise shop in Kensington. Afternoons would fade in and fade out. Lunch breaks might be broken up with a welcome visit from a mate, passing through. Daniel Day-Lewis, who used to drop by Paradise Garage in Bristol, was now in London. He was in a play, or a TV show, cast as a doctor. He would stop by on his break sometimes and hang out. Miles liked him because he was a humble guy, who could have been an asshole he was that handsome, but he wasn't an asshole, he was a good bloke. One time, he came by with stack of books, borrowed from the library. Books about anatomy, books about surgery, books about human biology.

"What are those?" asked Miles.

"These are what I'm reading for the part I'm playing."

"Right," Miles was eating, "so you find the procedure for the part you're acting, like if you're going to take out an appendix, you read that bit, is that it, to learn how it's done?"

"I'm going to read them all for this role, mate." Miles hardly read, and when he did, it was a rotation around three things: the *NME*, Black revolutionaries and serial killers.

"Flipping hell, Dan. That's nuts." Miles was stunned. He reflected on Daniel and those books a lot over the following days. Miles was someone capable of going into great detail. Capable of digging. He didn't know what method acting was, but Daniel and his books set something ticking. Miles was still, always, searching for what you needed to do to be a man, what you needed to give, to carve out a life for yourself. The depth with which Daniel was prepared to dive for understanding impressed Miles incredibly. It was the way he felt about music, which seemed to be an endless voyage out, or an endless voyage in. Or maybe both. In the shop that lunchtime, he stole a look at Daniel, and then got up and switched tapes.

One afternoon, a Black man came into the shop. Clearly, he was foreign. It wasn't that he was wearing crazy shit, which he was (cowboy boots, punk studs everywhere, bracelets) it was how he put it all together that gave him away. His trousers were tucked into his boots, his bracelets went right up his arms. The man said, "Yo man, that's my tape." He nodded to the ghetto blaster. Miles looked at him, trying to understand. Miles had this friend, this girl, who had given him a tape called *Zulu Beats*, a recording from Newark, from an off-the-road radio station. On that show, a guy called Afrika Islam played obscure hip-hop and cut-up breaks. A crew with a tape like that in the UK was a crew with an edge. This was the game: some crews had more money than others, a London crew like Mastermind that Wild Bunch respected, would go to New York and bring back treasures that they would play on their radio station. Wild Bunch didn't have that kind of money, but they were resourceful. Miles and Nellee got hold of rare tapes and badgered people to find out what the breaks were. They would investigate until they got an answer. When Miles first got hold of an Afrika Islam tape and took it to the camp on City Road, it was a stun-gun moment for Nellee and it was hard as hell to impress him.

"That's my tape," repeated the big man dressed in US ghetto finery. Then the man said, "I'm Afrika Islam."

Miles, who was DJing under his real name, Milo, had no idea what Islam looked like. There was no MTV, nothing. For hip-hop, just tapes. Now here was this guy saying, "That's my tape, I'm Afrika Islam." Milo and Nellee had been listening to two of his tapes for days on end, stopping, rewinding, trying to catch any little clue as to what record was being played. Now here he was, a hip-hop lord in Milo's shop, buying boots and casually suggesting, "Listen, man, we're in a hotel down the road. Stop by later, I'll give you some more of them." Milo's mind was spinning. That's right, Afrika Islam was on tour with the Rock Steady Crew. Of course. Nellee was even trying to find someone who might get them into a show. This was unbelievable good luck.

Islam and some of the Rock Steady crew that Milo had seen in the film, *Wild Style*, were chilling in the hotel room. It was every Christmas come together. Milo's eyes were all over the place, looking at what the performers were wearing, catching bits of their conversation.

As soon as he had those tapes in his hands, he realised that his only desire was to get on the train back to Bristol, and to share the jackpot with his boys. He walked up to Gee's camp on City Road later that night, barely able to hold it down. Gee opened the door, "All right, Jack?"

"Jack, you ain't gonna my believe my day today. You will not fucking believe it." He was heading for the front room. "I was only with Afrika Islam. I was at his hotel!"

"Fuck off, Jack."

"Check this out," said Milo. He put the tapes on the table. Gee, Nellee and Milo looked down at the collection of plastic cassettes. It was their holy grail. Each was labelled with the dates that the shows were recorded. So, they played them, and they played them again. Rewinding, listening to catch whatever in the way of information they could. The radio shows teleported them immediately out of England, straight to the heart of the matter: these were the beats that DJs were using in the Bronx, the birth place of hip-hop. Afrika Islam performed mixes with maybe a narrative from a movie (for example Mel Brooks in *History Of The World, Part I*), or someone talking in a documentary, incantatory, underscoring this with the two records he was cutting up. The beats could have been sourced from an obscure rock record, just as they could have been lifted from a forgotten funk LP. The way the music was then put together, with the chosen break prolonged, altered the intention of the original tune, tightening it and giving a relentlessness. It got into your head and into your body. It was a rough sound, a savage sound, with an emptiness around it. It was sometimes political and had rage. There was rapping over the breaks, boys and men delivering their realities like a eulogy to their lost innocence. And it got you dancing, too. Most of all.

Once they had identified as much as they could on the tapes, Milo, Nellee and Gee went out to find the records that had been used to make the breaks in the shows. They were also actively sourcing to build their own, reminted body of sound. They weren't scared to turn over every record, the unlikely and the naff, sifting for a few bars of magic. To say this involved the patience and temerity of a butterfly catcher is not so far fetched. The records they looked for were mostly out of print. They spent entire afternoons in second-hand record stores, in Bristol and London, at the 50p bin, flipping through LPs. They would come away with scuffed cuticles, dirty fingers and a slab of vinyl in a bag. They would then spend further entire evenings listening to everything, enduring many supremely shitty records waiting for the one special catch – a break that had it. Those Afrika Islam tapes, along with the jewel in the crown – a half-inch master tape of the *Wild Style* movie's breaks that Nellee had brought back from New York – were to be their secret weapon. If Wild Bunch were going head-to-head with another crew and it was a contentious battle, if it got too hot for them, they would drop one of these tunes, from *Wild Style* or *Zulu Beats* and bury the opposing crew on the spot. This was what they were aspiring to, not to be Islam, but to be as heavy. These three men had in common a desire to be independent and to excel at this thing, at being this crew.

Delge, 3D to the world today, was now on board with Wild Bunch. Gee, Nellee and Milo had felt that it was time to get an MC. Milo had gradually begun spending more time with D, sharing a love of hip-hop, horror movies, and Robert De Niro in anything. Once they became friends, it was with D that Milo would hang out in London every other Saturday. They would buy movie stills from a shop in Soho, then go to Groove Records, run by the seemingly incongruous Jean Palmer, coined the disco granny, who in fact knew her shit and loved her music. The last stop would be in a huge store full of dead stock music, where the top angle of every vinyl sleeve was snipped off, not for resale. It was basically the knackers yard of records. If you were patient, and if you were lucky, you sometimes struck gold.

D was a fledgling street artist, covering walls in Bristol. Milo was sometimes D's lookout, the pair of them stealing out in the dead of night, so that in the morning colours covered a blank wall, graffiti for the early morning commuters, appearing as mysteriously and slyly as buds that bloom in the dark. The two of them would revisit the scene of the crime the next day, because of course, at night, you couldn't get any real idea of how the colours looked, or how the scale worked. Milo remembers one wall D did on the roundabout at the bottom of City Road, where it leads on to Sussex Place. The walk towards the wall was drab, urban, grey, beige, grey, then suddenly, bam, a fist of colour in your eye. It was Milo's favourite piece. Milo was D's lookout because he believed in D's talent. Milo would never have helped him that way out of love alone, it was just too risky for an ex-con.

****

The rush in Milo's life over the next couple of years was such that it is impossible to pull the threads of a precise timeline, to give each event absolute chronology. It's like watching a tumble dryer, trying to pick out one garment with your eye. People's recollections don't necessarily concord. The Wild Bunch years are a patchwork of flyers that have come down through time like pressed flowers or of websites whose investigative skills are sketchy. Sometimes there is proof-positive of a date in the form of a dub-plate, or in the careful lettering on the hundreds of tapes that Milo has kept. Sometimes it is people pin-pointing a party on a map of their lives, "Yes, definitely, July not June because it was my birthday, my eighteenth, and I got my nose pierced the same day," and so forth. As Milo remembers it – and what is overwhelming to him – is how much was happening, concertinaed, in such a short span of time.

He was still doing the commute Bristol-London five days a week. He was playing the Dug Out every Thursday, Tropics every Friday. London on Tuesday. In between all this, he was running through women with alarming casualness. He looks back on that time with a sense of having let himself be used. Women rushed him, giving him their home phone numbers, hanging around at the end of the night, on the pavement, or sending a friend over to ask if would go out with them. Which meant follow them home and have sex. He did, often. Far too often not to write about it. The sex itself is a blur of faceless bodies, bodiless faces. There was no erotic epiphany. It was not necessarily joyless sex. It was sometimes good sex, for him at least. But it was definitely soulless.

One night, he left the Dug Out with a white girl who lived in St Paul's. He doesn't remember much, even precisely whether or not they slept together, but he does remember this: he was on the sofa and she looked at him. She asked, "How many women have you had this week?" It caught him off-guard. He felt uncomfortable. "I've been watching you, this past couple of weeks. Go on, how many?" He had to think. He had to count. He looked at her, ruefully.

"I don't know. Well, I do. But listen, this ain't a good week to ask me." He laughed. She just carried on staring him in the face. "Okay. Seven." She didn't take her eyes from him. Then she spoke, "Don't you have any pride?"

It was a judgement he took away from that night, and turned over and over. All that sleeping around had done something for his status quo, yet he understood that it was, at the same time, demeaning and something else, that he would understand later – it was damaging. What of the sex? What of desire? He remembers that walking back from a club or a party with yet another girl, the thought that would often run through his mind was whether she would have an interesting record collection, not what she would look like naked. (In fact, recollecting this time in his life, he said, half joking, "I've been with so many women. Do you how many records that is? That I've sifted through?")

He remembers never wanting to stay the night, and sometimes having to. He remembers, one time, waking up in a flat in Clifton to the sound of a song playing from another room. The woman he had had sex with was sleeping and he lay, listening to the music. It was the haunting, graceful, *Win* by Bowie. He left the bed and knocked the flatmate's door. He was faced with a girl from his school, from Pro-Cathedral, a kookyish girl. They were both surprised.

"Oh hello, Ginny," he said, "you live here, do you? Hey, what album's that on?"

She handed him the sleeve of *Young Americans*.

"Second track."

They played it again.

The morning light filling her messy student-girl room.

Just sitting there. Listening together.
He remembers that.

Chapter Twenty-Four

RIVERS OF MY FATHERS

Wild Bunch played their first St Paul's carnival. They put every last penny together to hire the biggest sound system that they could. They set up in the morning, at the top of Campbell Street, a towering rack of equipment, two mighty bass bins. A dread walked by. On seeing the extravagance of the equipment, he smiled, "Ras!" It was the spirit of carnival. Milo had been coming back to St Paul's, to see Don, but the connection to his community was broken. Did anybody recognise him? Remember him? He wouldn't have told Donovan he was playing. And Charlie. Milo has thought of that scene, since. Of them playing all day and right through the night. Their noise absolutely crushing every speaker in the neighbourhood, the sound travelling as far as Knowle West. They each played what they wanted. One of the things Milo enjoyed the most, in those Wild Bunch years, was when they played carnival. He would move to the side, Gee taking over. He can remember just sitting, looking out, listening to Gee's music, loving it. Watching the community dancing. Every carnival they played, they stacked up an outrageously heavy system. The sets they played in their residencies felt lifted out of the confines of a club and the songs were sent into a space without walls, their sound to the power of ten. There was something in the alchemy of an industrial sound system and dancing right out beneath the sky that gave you a feeling, an ongoing jolt, of being alive. That first carnival, Campbell Street was covered, revellers out all night long. At three in the morning, it hit its spike. The road was packed, rocking away under the stars. Was Charlie there? Somewhere? What would he have made of this, of his son sending out music to make you dance, he,

Charlie, who could dance like no one else? Donovan told Milo that when Charlie took to the floor, the crowd would move back, making a circle around him. Does rhythm have a genetic memory? The Italians say that the groove above your upper lip, beneath your nose, is placed there by an angel, who leans over your crib, placing a finger to make the indentation, "Shh," to silence you, so that you will not tell everything that you are born knowing, because you are born knowing all. This mixed-race boy from the ghetto, like his father before him, might have been told to forget, to forget the most primitive and spiritual expression of life: dance. Neither forgot, father nor son. Blood to blood, heartbeat to heartbeat, this is all that I gave you, my son. Rhythm.

****

There was a gig in Seven Sisters, that was one rough North London place back then. D would be MCing, along with Willlie Wee. Willie Wee had an attitude on the mic, an effervescence and real party warm-up banter, but it was D, aged only maybe eighteen, who had the lyrics:

> *3D on the mic, the day the law died*
> *Putting on my fat cap, stepping outside*
> *Had the munchies in the night*
> *Walker's or Murphy's*
> *Like tagging up on a crisp, painted surface*
> *Buff jacket on my back, you know it's vicious*
> *Open up a can of brew cos it's delicious*
> *Je ne sais quoi*
> *I'm looking like a vandal*
> *Girl next door*
> *Got me burning like a candle*

To Milo, there was no MC in Britain at that time, right across the board, who could touch him, lyrically, no one else who could frame the extraordinary in the mundane in quite that way. Milo felt they had a secret missile in D. The gig was in a big hall, it was a beat-up and draughty place. The party-goers, five hundred of them, were Black, one hundred percent, Black. Wild Bunch was clashing a local crew. The space felt tense, as if the night could flip from being a dance to a cautionary headline in tomorrow's paper over nothing – a dirty look, a spilt drink. From the other side of the room, the London crew span a record and the whole room began to move. D was drained of colour, looking like a hip-hop Count Dracula, livid with apprehension. The crowd was heating up and the wave of sound crashed from one shore to the other, to where Wild Bunch were: This side now. Their bass was bumping, Willie Wee was chatting. They were minus D. Milo, on the decks, turned and saw D, in a state of suspension. D and Nellee were the only two white boys down there, that's how it seemed from where they were. He could sense the hostility.

"Get on the mic, man." D looked at Milo and seemed to suddenly spring into action, with the words, "Where's the fucking Tennent's?" He slugged from a can and took the microphone. There was a lull, all these London hip-hop heads forming just one, circumspect ear. There was a boo, and another. The beat kept on. D held on to his mic for dear life and then he took off. The room started shifting, dancing. D was in full flight. Milo says he was laughing inside, it was like they were machine-gunning the enemy with this white dude and his brilliance. That evening was also the first time that Wild Bunch met Soul II Soul, who were down for the party. Nellee couldn't have known that in the crowd of working-class Black Britons, here in Seven Sisters, he had just changed his destiny. He was to jump, a few years on, from one posse to another, from Wild Bunch to Soul II Soul and take the whole world hostage with Jazzie B.

****

It was an all-dayer, at Tropics in Bristol. Milo had been looking forward to it. Wild Bunch had a space in the basement, out of the way, which meant they could play right through, whereas DJs were rotating in the rest of the club. Nellee was playing, and Milo was due to take his turn. In his mind he was revving up, but he felt a little weak, floaty.

He got behind the decks and played two records, before turning to Nellee, "Listen, Nells, you got to take over."

"Eh? What d'you mean?"

He knew how much Milo loved to play, but maybe he saw in that second something that had been staring them all in the face for weeks: just how sick Milo was. "All right, man," Nellee got back behind the turntables, in a slight panic, scrabbling to pull out a record, his eyes, surprised, followed Milo as he made his way out through the club. Milo had felt weird for weeks, bad enough to go to the doctor, who ran some tests. Now he felt his legs might not carry him, he was dizzy, barely able to move forward. He felt immeasurably tired. The music was thumping, people were dancing, it was dim in there. He pulled open the door to the street and the sunshine almost knocked him out. He steadied himself against a wall, feeling like he was slipping from consciousness.

A voice cut through to him, surreal in its timing, welcome in its familiarity, "Miles! Miles! Miles!" She was shouting. Running. It was Juliette. She was before him, looking into his face, "Miles you got to go to the hospital, Don got a letter. Miles, listen. You've got TB. It's really serious. You've got to go now."

"What are you talking about?" Now he was dizzy, walking beside Juliette, his eyes on his feet. He didn't know anything about TB, for him it was out there with malaria or the dengue.

Within minutes of arriving at the Bristol Royal Infirmary, he was isolated. He was put in an ambulance and driven away. There are elements here that seem to echo back to Kray House: the outbound drive, the thinning cityscape, the powerlessness that he felt. There was being taken inside a place that was secluded from view.

****

His life, since his release from prison, had been that kind of spinning round and round that children do until they stagger, their vision smashed for an instant – that kind of unabated devouring of life, piling on parties, work, women and music, always music. It was noisy, unreasonable, exciting and the only blanks, the only rest, had been sleep that would fell him, for a few hours in a bed, or a few minutes on a train. All those missed nights' sleep had come crashing down at once.

The hospital, Ham Green, in Abbots Leigh, had only recently dropped the sobering appellation of sanatorium. Much like inside a church, it was dark and cool. People spoke in whispers. The single sound was a trolley being pushed along a corridor, with its rattling bottles and pots. He was taken to a room. The curtains were drawn. There were two beds. His fellow patient was an old man whose arm, like a branch of driftwood, rested on the blue sheet, spectral and still. Milo lay down, too. He left his mind, he left the present, he disappeared into the secret world of sleep and from the outside, had you pushed the door of this hospital room, you would have seen two men, their faces ashen, sunken, and the only movement was their struggling chests, rising, falling, and the only sound was the breath fighting in and out of their bodies.

They gave him medication that shook the phlegm from his lungs and turned his piss luminous orange. He lay for most of the day. Getting up, walking a few shaky steps, was enough to exhaust him. A week, maybe two, went by and people began to visit. Carla showed up. She was a girlfriend from his teenage years. Now she was back, at his bedside. She took one look at him and teared up. Sitting beside him, holding his hand, she began to chatter. She went on and on. His eyelids ached, his ears couldn't focus. She stood to leave and said she would come back the next day, with food.

"No," he said, "There's no need. Nicky's coming tomorrow."

With this she sat back down, saying, "You shouldn't be with her. She ain't good enough for you. When you were inside, she was shagging that bloke you don't like. Lance. She told him she wanted to have his baby."

Milo was half-dead, three quarters of his lungs were drowning. This fresh news could have finished him. There were a lot of promiscuous men and women on that Bristol scene in the early eighties. Milo was one of them. But there was a code even within this quite depressing free-for-all. Number one: you didn't sleep with a mate's girlfriend. Number two: you were careful not to catch a dose but, if you did, you took yourself out of circulation. Lance followed neither of these guidelines. Milo had felt stalked by Lance. Although they were from different worlds – Lance ran a small construction company – they were vaguely similar, physically, and Lance seemed to hover around Milo's exes, without a particularly good strike rate.

Milo closed his eyes.

"All right, Carla. I need to rest. I'll see you when I get out."

So that was it then. Done. He lay in the torture rack that was his body and tried to think. How did he feel? Angry. Angry but so tired. He had no energy to talk this through with Nicky, nor any desire. If he could have found a way to do it, he would never have seen Nicky again. But he felt as trapped with her as he felt trapped inside his own failing body. Later, he would confront Nicky and, although she probably had no idea just what Lance was like, she had the good grace to flush red and babble on about how she had been looking for Milo, that was all. That Lance had reminded her of him. This was the worst thing she could have said. Milo had reached a place of no return in his feelings, or his lack of them, for Nicky.

Word got back to Bristol that Milo was in really bad shape. He left a space, there is no question. Wild Bunch nights at the Dug Out fell a little flat without him. Like all interesting art, Wild Bunch worked as a composition, this one's gravitas a counterpoint to that one's edge. With one member down, no matter which of them, Wild Bunch was slightly off its axis.

Removed from his life once more, Milo had time to think. It was unlike the years in prison, when what lay ahead was uncharted. Now he wanted to recover, to get strong because he wanted to get back to music. It was his calling, and that is the one thing this enforced bed rest brought home to him. The old man was gone from his room. Healing was taking a long time. Milo had lost a lot of body mass, he looked bony which he never had before. He lay in the dark, trying to sleep, feeling his lungs half drowning, feeling the need to piss. Feeling dog-tired. He needed the bathroom. He got up, carefully, sitting on the edge of the bed before standing. He shuffled down the darkened corridor to the bathroom and made his way slowly back. It took all his energy. He pushed his room door and the shadowy space illuminated. Gee, Nellee, D, Willie Wee and Julian Monaghan, who had driven them there leapt out of nowhere. "Yes, Jack!" they boomed, but in the same second their faces froze. It was as if their breath alone had almost knocked him over.

They stared in shock at this gaunt, grey Milo, and Gee, with his priceless honesty, said, "Fucking hell, man, you look really bad." Milo was deeply happy to see them, but he was in a hinterland of sickness, unable to sit, unable to talk. He remembers how dismayed, how concerned, they looked and although he appreciated them coming he just wanted them to leave immediately, so that he could lie back down in the dark and wait for sleep to take him away from his aching, frightening self.

Chapter Twenty-Five

FEET FIRST

Lockleaze

He was sat in the kitchen, at Nicky's. Looking through an *NME*, drinking tea. He heard the front door open, and Nicky come in, back from work. Before, before everything – TB, prison – they had been all right. It wasn't a love thing, but she had his attention, she made him laugh. She was like a quintessential British barmaid. It had been a normal relationship, or a normalising one, maybe. It was ordinary and that was good. He had felt safe, but his soul was punctured. He was meant to give back, to love back, but he could only gesture to these expectations. Now, any connection to Nicky was burnt through, it was ashes, in the shape of its own past, suspended and ready to collapse into nothingness. He didn't want to be in her home, he didn't want to be around her. But he was poor, almost penniless, and his only family was Donovan. She gave him shelter. He still had sex with her, infrequently, and although before there had been a young lustfulness between them, now the sex was a way for him to buy time, to keep his possessions in one place. He was on his way out. How could she not have felt it?

From the moment she walked in through the door, she was talking, non-stop. About what they were having for tea. About a colleague. About a council grant. Whatever. Anything. A soliloquy of terrifying cosiness that was masking a more sinister narrative, one that Milo would not hear, until it was too late.

Down at the camp, life was getting frantic. Wild Bunch were now visible on the London club scene. They had a new kid with them. Milo had got him into the Dug Out, even though he was underage, because he was Adrian, Marlow's nephew, the little boy who used to listen to records with Punky and him years before. Milo called him Tricky Kid. One thing Milo has always had an innate feeling for is the creative potential of others, and his is never the obvious choice. One afternoon, down at Gee's, Milo was cutting up two records and Tricky took the mic. Words tripped out. Words from his interior world, peculiar and compelling. From then on, whenever Tricky felt like it, he had permission to grab the mic.

Dave Dorrell, one of the team behind the planetary hit, *Pump Up The Volume*, was a lynchpin of the London club scene. One night, down to visit his girlfriend in Bristol, and wandering through the streets together, they caught the sound of Wild Bunch playing, quite by chance. The music soaked the streets around the venue. He pushed the door, wondering what was behind it. He says he was blown away. Dave, back in London, got them a gig at the Wag Club, but this time not an afternoon affair, this time, at night. It was the real deal. The Wag Club was riding high. The punters in there at that time were from *Face* magazine, from *i-D*. They were Bowie and De Niro. They were those Magnificent Seven supermodels and this was highly intimidating stuff. Right up until their set, Milo felt ill at ease. It was the impostor syndrome that comes from a childhood of disinterest and neglect. Then they played and his doubts evaporated. Nellee was networking like a man possessed. He was a star at that. Maybe Nellee stayed on, maybe not, but Milo took the train from Paddington, to Temple Meads at daybreak. He walked to Lockleaze. The sunlight was the colour of straw. Seagulls were bleating in the sky. He was alone.

****

One afternoon he was sent, by Gee, to a girl's flat in Old Market. She was a student – of what, Milo has no recollection. She was interviewing people around St Paul's, or maybe she was interviewing musicians, for her studies at Bristol University. She had asked Gee if he would fix a meeting with Milo for her. Milo went there once and then was asked to go again to finish off the interview. A word befitting this girl, if it weren't reductive somehow, would be "nice". She was a nice girl, she was nicely spoken. But not only.

There was a loveliness to her, a freshness. Her name was Izzy. She was from another city, Manchester or maybe London, creating instant curiosity around her, since Bristol's underground scene was quite village-like. Miles didn't think anything of the renewed request to see him, until a few days later, Gee dropped, "I think Izzy's into you, Jack."

"I think you might be mistaken, mate," Milo replied, laughing. He forgot about it instantly, this girl was not in a league that he was dealing in. Gee had insider information and also obstinacy. So, he returned to the subject and this time told Milo, straight up, "I'm not making this shit up, Jack. She told her best friend that she really fancies you." Gee, the unlikely matchmaker, knew this best friend very well. Milo had to think about it, hard. He had had brief encounters with a few university girls. Girls who wanted nothing more than that one night with him. Who would drag themselves from an unslept-in bed, barely washing, hair mussed up and head straight for a lecture. He would never contact them again. What Milo got right away, was Izzy's difference to all these Dug Out girls. She didn't really fit in with that crowd, because most of the young women down there and probably most of the men, had a fault-line. There was an edginess and volatility to some, a recklessness and an abandon in others. There was a song by Black Uhuru around that time, *Shine Eye Gal* – a shine-eye girl being one whose eyes burned bright, looking at men other than her own man. Milo didn't have the confidence to deal with that kind of woman, it was something he watched for very closely. Izzy, plainly, was more focussed.

Milo understood that he couldn't do with a girl like Izzy what he had done with all the other girls he'd interacted with since moving in to Nicky's. There were too many people watching this one. He was being auditioned for the role of the decent guy with a decent girl. It was time for him to cool the sleeping around, it was a good time for a girl like Izzy to enter his life.

This was all one-sided: what he could gain, what he could learn. He wasn't ready to let a woman in, he wasn't about to let Izzy see the real-life him. This was to be a balancing act and a dilemma. Because he was keeping Nicky in his life and keeping his life in the cupboards in the spare room in Lockleaze. There was nothing, ever, to stop him making a choice between those two girls. His choice was not to choose. He reasoned his way into this new relationship with Izzy by thinking of himself as a kind of lodger in Lockleaze and Nicky as a landlady from whom he was renting a room. Nicky was closer to his past and Izzy was an embodiment of what his peers aspired to. There was a virtuous and cleansing side to being with her. He was still so wobbly, just finding his feet as a man around women. His trust level in womankind was smashed the day after day after day that Betty didn't come back for him at Kray House. He didn't want revenge, he did need comfort. The rightness and wrongness of all of this, he found hard to think about. So, he didn't think about it. He started going out with Izzy, it was a public relationship, he didn't tell Nicky. He kept his room at Nicky's and he didn't tell Izzy.

****

Back to City Road and Gee's place, an afternoon similar to so many others. Gee was a welcoming man, and his flat was a good place to be. He was in his kitchen, he would stop everything to make a meal. Milo, in the front room, sorting through records, heard the phone ring. Then Gee appeared in the doorway.

"Hey, Jack. Neneh's on the phone. She wants to speak with you."

Wild Bunch had met Neneh Cherry through Mark Stewart. This was the Rip Rig + Panic, Cotham connection. Milo knew Bruce, Neneh's first husband, from school. Neneh and her crew, all from London, had come to the Dug Out a couple of times, there was an instant affinity. She was young, with a powerful physical presence – the strange, snubbed profile that gave her remarkable beauty. She was a happy bundle of energy, burning brighter than anyone in the room.

"Hey, Neneh?"

"Hello, Milo. How are you and do you fancy coming to Japan? To DJ?"

"What?"

"Next Tuesday." It was Thursday.

The only time Milo had been abroad was on a giro with Nellee, to Portugal. They were so broke that Nellee almost got battered because he had discovered the delights of sangria, and had been syphoning off someone else's glass in a bar, unable to buy his own. They had gone on temporary passports from the post office. He told Neneh that he didn't have a proper passport. Neneh explained, with precision, the emergency passport drill. He would have to go to Newport. The last time he had been in Wales, he was in a cell.

The following Tuesday, he and a model-cum-DJ named JP, took off for Tokyo Airport. Milo thought about Japan and what it signified to him. Not a lot. His only recurrent image was of Don's Japanese Datsun. Hours and hours later, he and JP were being driven through Tokyo by a personal chauffeur. The city, captured in his car window, was a hundred frames a second, flashing like a disco. At a traffic light, he lowered the car window.

A lull.

An elsewhere.

The air was warm, how strange it was to discover that it had a different quality to England's air, a sultriness. He asked their chaperone, "Is there a record store that sells hip-hop and rap? Stuff like that?"

The chaperone had a think, "Yeah, go to Winners. It should be open."

It was midnight. He had been in Tokyo half an hour, and he was already negotiating the flickering night. Billboards were covered with words that looked like vertical ropes of intricate beads. Being taller than the crowd, Milo had a view down a sidewalk, busy even at this hour, it was a river of black hair. He found the record store and, space being at a premium, it was packed rigid, floor to ceiling, with vinyl. It blew him away. There was every hip-hop release from America, records impossible to find in the UK. Newtrament's entire record collection was in there. He called Nellee as soon as he was done, "Jack, we've got to get out here with the crew. This is where it's at."

The next day, Milo was pushed blinking into the furious lights of fashion. The shows were styled by Ray Petri and the iconic Buffalo gang was present, their off-beat beauty a reference even today. Milo was there as a DJ and as a model. He modelled for a few years, for Buffalo, in Japan and in London, catwalk modelling and photographic work. He did it for the money, it was really that clear. He is as camera shy as a kid at the awkward braces-and-spots stage of life. He could not understand why anyone would want to use a picture of him. He borders on having body dysmorphia. He will look at a picture of himself, young, where he cracks the lens with his beauty, and say, with feeling, "That face is absolutely gross to me."

Milo did a show for Takeo Kikuchi and Men's Bigi, and there was an after party, in Akasaka. The music grabbed him, it was hip-hop, it was music that was hard to source. He made his way excitedly through the crowd.

DJs were swarming the booth. They all seemed to have long hair, straight down their backs. There were rocking quite a style, black leather Adidas tracksuits, Vivienne Westwood buffalo hats. Milo was fascinated. They were a mash-up of punk and hip-hop. This was like looking at a Japanese Wild Bunch. Milo moved in closer, right up to the turntables, almost knocking the needle from the groove. He put his hands up, "Sorry, mate." And the DJ said, "Move away." Milo had a brilliant time, dancing down in that club. A few nights later, there was a Mega Dance City party, in a cathedral of a place, and Milo was DJing. He was on the second floor, cutting up *Shack Up* by Banbarra. He was running two seven-inch copies and was towards the end, letting the song play out. He saw a figure bounding up the stairs. It was the DJ who had shooed him away for his clumsiness.

"Hey man, how are you?" asked Milo.

"Good. What is this record? I've been asking people." Milo looked at this guy. Then he put the two copies in their sleeves and handed them to him.

"Have them," he said.

The Japanese DJ, furiously focused, youthful and luminous, was Hiroshi Fujiwara. Milo and Hiroshi became friends, there and then. By the next day, Milo was at Hiroshi's house. He had no clue what Hiroshi did for a living, DJing maybe. His home was full of strange, mesmerising things: pictures, records, magazines dedicated to bizarre enthusiasms, quirky objects that caught the eye – a bold colour, an unexpected shape. It was one big curiosity cabinet. There was a pet reptile crawling around the place, an iguana perhaps. Milo kept his eye on that. The connection between Hiroshi and Milo was profound. Milo could never express his feelings, they were banged up in some inner chamber of pain and shame, he was a man of few words. The Japanese culture, with its innate modesty, suited him. Hiroshi and he have never spoken to each other about their friendship. It is like the air, it is just there, all the time.

What Milo didn't know was that Hiroshi was already clued into the sharpest subcultures of the Western world. He was friends with Malcolm McClaren and Vivienne Westwood, and with Chica and Toshi – the godfather and mother of the Tokyo street scene – who had wandered, as you would in the 1980s, on this planet, if you were touched by the hand of dissonant creative grace, to New York City. Chica and Toshi hung out there, with Warhol and Basquiat and the recusant alumni of The Factory. Hiroshi has a quality that Milo identifies as purely Japanese, of being able to sift through other cultures, like running river sand through a pan until he finds gold. The Japanese have the ability to pick out a musical trend in Chicago, a family shoemaker down a cobbled street in Italy, a wine from a single hill in France, and understand their calibre, as far removed from their own culture as these may be. Hiroshi is the master of that.

Hiroshi and Milo had their routine, during those early days. Milo would go exploring Tokyo and come back with bags full of wizardry. He would meet up with Hiroshi, in a thimble-sized café in Daikanyama, and Hiroshi would ask, "What did you find?" They would sit, drinking tea, examining the morning's haul. Hiroshi was twenty years old, Milo twenty-four. In a sense, Hiroshi was a natural follow-on from his friendship with Nick, then Dunc, then D. Milo had always found a mate to go treasure-hunting with, or at least someone able to appreciate that an interesting aesthetic can appear in the most unlikely places. Hiroshi, however, has a power of vision that can transfigure something that you don't know you like into something you burningly desire.

Milo was on a high for weeks after his return from Tokyo. The crew could feel he had been hit by a cultural bomb. Japan was all he could talk about, and the plan was to get Wild Bunch back there, but how that would ever be possible, they hadn't yet figured out. In the meantime, Milo brought mementos from Japan for his boys, all these bits and pieces of outlandish, crisp Tokyo street gear, to keep his crew looking fresh, the freshest.

He was spending his days between Gee's and Special K's cafe on Park Row. Right then, at that very instant in time, Milo caught the light. If you saw him in a club, it would often be with his head thrown back, laughing. He would have seemed strong to you, and joyful. He was wriggling out of a past life, shedding a skin, right at the start of the journey out.

Chapter Twenty-Six

SOMETHING'S WRONG

Bristol, 1984

Milo dipped into the house in Lockleaze, to pick up some clothes, at an hour when Nicky would be at work. From the hallway, he heard her. Shit.

"Miles? That you?"

"Yeah, all right, Nicks? What you doing home then?"

"I need to talk, Miles."

"I'm on my way out, got to be at Gee's in an hour."

"I'm pregnant."

He was halfway up the stairs.

"I'm pregnant, Miles."

"What the fuck are you talking about? How can you be pregnant?" He was coming back down the staircase, one heavy footfall after the next, "You are joking?" She walked to her front room and sat, her arms folded across her belly. The sofa was dark, she looked like she was floating on an autumn leaf, this vanilla-coloured girl with her knees tucked under her. "You're going to have to explain this to me."

"There's nothing to explain. I missed my period, I've done a test and everything. It's definite."

He stood there, absolutely motionless, sizing up the situation. Then he walked out, to her bedroom, to the drawer where she kept her pills. Each rectangle of silver contained twenty-one blisters, unpopped. He walked back into the room and threw the packet at her feet. The walls were closing in on him. Please, don't make this real.

"Look Miles, it's not like that. No, I did take some. I don't know, maybe, yeah, I did forget. I got lost, then it was too late, so I came off. I just came off the pill, that's all."

"You fucking stupid cow." Those words were spoken with deliberation, spaced, as if each syllable brought this new truth closer to home. Then, quickening, he said, "You can't have it. Nicky, listen, I am in no position to be a father. I can't be that, do you get me? I don't have a job. Man, I'm all over the place. I don't have any money. I'm just not ready for fatherhood. You know that. There's no way this can happen."

"I can't get rid of it. I can't have another abortion."

Milo was surprised, his mind rushing, trying to remember a past abortion and failing to. He stood there, frozen, as she explained that she had to keep this baby. Her voice trembled. He didn't want to feel it, but he did feel her love, or her desperation. In Bristol, in the ghetto in the eighties, being a man's baby-mother had weight. It was a definitive status. It kept a man around. What was she doing? She must have felt, since coming back from the hospital, that Milo had pulled away. She may have heard about this new girl he was seeing. Up until then, he had never been faithful to Nicky, because she wasn't his to be faithful to, but the women he was sleeping with mostly disappeared with daybreak. Now there was a girl out with him in public. That must have hurt.

"Call your mother, get her round here."

The mother appeared, Mary, appley smiles and warmth. She liked Milo. "Tell her." Nicky sat on the sofa in stubborn silence.

"Nicky is pregnant, Mary. Apparently, it's mine. She just came off the pill. I had no knowledge of that. I cannot have a baby. I don't want a baby. We can't be parents. It's not happening. Tell her, Mary."

Mary stared at her daughter, blinking fast, "Bloody hell, Nicks, what are you doing?"

"I'm keeping it, mum."

Milo felt hollow. Women, they find a thousand ways to fuck you up. It never once crossed his mind that Nicky when they were barely speaking and he was sleeping with another girl more often than with her, would pull a fast one like this. Of course, the basis of their relationship was in itself sick. He was sleeping with her for the shelter, which is quite close to hustling your butt. He had never lied, though. He had never promised her anything more, he had never said he loved her. This was a calamity. He was twenty-four. One year out of jail. He felt like he was walking right back into a cell.

Nicky would keep the baby, she had decided for him that he would be a father. He told Izzy, maybe not straight away, but soon into the pregnancy, that she might hear that another woman was carrying his child, "I wasn't with the mother. I was on my way out. I didn't make any plans to have a child, I didn't have any plans with her at all." He didn't lie. Izzy listened and she was kind. She must have wanted to believe that it didn't matter that another woman was about to bear his child, at least not enough to forgo seeing Milo.

What was in Milo's mind? For a start, the words of the girl from St Paul's, don't you have any pride? They had stayed, disturbing him like a submarine disturbs the ocean's depths when nothing on the surface shows. He was trying to work out what he wanted and what he had to give. Did he think it was right to be sleeping with one girl when another was pregnant? No. He knew. He knew how wrong that was. Did he feel guilt? No, again. The pregnancy was maybe his seed, but not his desire. He felt it was entrapment, and it hurt. He did not feel sorry for the future mother. He felt sorrow, and fear, for the unborn child. Until the baby was born, until the baby was older, he more or less stopped messing around. He tried to stick with Izzy, although he knew that it was going nowhere. She was so different to him. He stayed by Nicky, too, in a fraternal way, because he didn't hate her. Without understanding his own psychology, let alone another human's, he could sense that Nicky wanted him. She was having his baby because of this and the pregnancy made her happy. He was in a state of inner conflict. He didn't want to become his own father.

****

Milo had never mastered swimming. Izzy said she would teach him. They would go to a pool in Clifton, week after week. He couldn't float, the density of his bones weighing him down. It was a struggle. He swam underwater, he was trying to get to the surface. Across the city, in a poorer neighbourhood, Milo's baby grew. There they were, father and child, evolving in aqueous worlds, unfinished.

****

Wild Bunch were still going strong. Gee was walking in front of Milo, towards Portland Square. He was excited. He had found this place, an abandoned warehouse. Milo stood back on the pavement, arms folded, as Gee – who had put his own padlock on the warehouse door – got it open. Wild Bunch, by then, had gained quite a following, they had gone from being promising to what should have been bankable. Money was the one thing that they never made. Sometimes, like carnival or parties, they were actually out of pocket. The Dug Out fee was nominal. Milo didn't drink alcohol, so the Dug Out's free-drink-for-a-set meant he played all night long, more or less, for a pint of orange juice. Eventually the fee increased and ended up being £200, making Wild Bunch the best-paid DJs at the Dug Out. They spent all the money on buying more records.

Gee showed Milo around the warehouse, with that look on your face you have when someone is unwrapping a present you know they are going to love. The warehouse was on a few floors, with junk furniture and office debris scattered throughout, but the top floor was one mighty space. Milo smiled, "Jack, this is wicked, man."

The crew cleared the space, they put out flyers, Strictly freaks, ravers and butt-shifters. Newtrament with his Krew from Ladbroke Grove would come as their guests. They were in business. It was perfectly illegal and in a building that was a health and safety hell zone.

The Red House jam was the first warehouse party, and it rocked. They had a makeshift bar upstairs, and they had Derrick on the door. Party goers started to arrive, quite early on. Suddenly, Derrick appeared at the decks, frantic. "What do I do with this?" he asked, money bulging his pockets out. They hadn't thought of that. "Flippin' hell, I got nowhere to put all this cash."

They sent Derrick back to the door with a collection of bin bags as his till.

They had hired the heaviest sound system imaginable, it was raucous. The place was rammed, it was just a sea of heads. Around about midnight, Derrick was back at the decks, this time the panic was unbridled. "Cops are coming up!" Milo pushed his way through the party, in time to see a group of police officers, at least the crowns of their helmets, bobbing up the stairs. The first copper was an older man, clearly a chief constable. Milo stepped back. The chief put his head round the door, and took one long look inside. He was dumbfounded. He stared at the party, there were at least six hundred people in there. Black kids and white kids, hanging off the speakers, break dancing, people packed together, bumping away, or clamouring the improvised bar. The sound was enough to flatten the hair cells of every cochlea in the neighbourhood. The chief shook his head, and signalled his men, "Let's get out of here."

The party went on until day break. Wild Bunch washed up at Gee's. They had paid Newtrament and Derrick. Nellee looked at Milo. Looked at Gee. There were bin bags stuffed with money slouching all over the floor. They tipped out hillocks of banks notes, kings in their counting house. They were counting until lunch. They had made a killing. It felt good.

Chapter Twenty-Seven

LITTLE GREEN

Late May, the baby came. Milo stuck by Nicky in the delivery room. It was a drawn-out labour. In the final throes, as the midwife became busier and Nicky wilder, as the words, "Baby will be here very soon," were pronounced, Milo walked straight out of the room. Nicky was screaming for him. He told the nurse that came for him that he couldn't deal with blood. He didn't fool her. This was where he had unexpectedly drawn his own line – he couldn't fake this part. He knew that to be beside your woman as your baby is born has deep meaning. It is the baby that you created and desired as one, an embodiment of your love. He couldn't pretend.

When he finally went back into the room, the baby born and Nicky elated, it was an out-of-body experience for him. He could see himself going through the motions, hear himself saying the right words. He was observing all this from afar, a satellite of his own self. The baby that was born was perfect in every way. The baby needed unconditional love, the baby needed an adult for a father. The baby deserved so much better than this.

****

The Wild Bunch chapter was coming to a close. Nellee and Milo hustled enough money to get themselves to Japan. It is interesting that Milo's only experience of Nellee, who went on to a life of crazy fame and fortune, is of being stone-cold broke. Milo may well be the only person on earth to have seen Nellee hungry. In Tokyo, once again as Giro Brothers, they came to the shocking realisation, early on, that the Wild Bunch tour they were pinning on their friend, Moichi, putting together within a couple weeks, would take much longer than that. Their money would have to stretch. Moichi found them a house in the suburbs, dirt cheap. They were able to eat only once a day. They were walking through Shinjuku one evening, famished. A street vendor was dishing out traditional soup to a couple of working men and a woman. Nellee and Milo could have cried they were that hungry and the steam that came to their nostrils was ambrosial. They stopped, deciphering the menu, drooling invisibly.

The lady diner considered them, then said, "Take a seat."

"Oh no, we don't have any money," one of the two replied.

"It's okay. Take a seat."

You would like to read that never to a man, has a meal tasted so divine. I would like to write that, too. But the soup was teaming with slimy eye-like tapioca and choppy bits of the body of an animal they couldn't identify. It terms of disappointment, it was as bad as the first time Milo had sex after prison. Milo and Nellee exchanged the briefest and most eloquent of looks, then got the soup down.

****

After a month of Tokyo life, abstract and nocturnal, but also blindingly different from anything they had experienced before, they were ready to bring the crew over. The Wild Bunch Japan Tour was in place. Up until then, Milo and Nellee had hung out in the most interesting bars and clubs, because knowing Hiroshi, Toshi and Chica had got them a pass to the heart of the matter. They had managed to make a little money, DJing here and there, and modelling. Once, they DJed in a hip-hop nightclub run by a Yakuza gang baron, a brazenly handsome man, tanned the colour of tandoori chicken, who seemed to have sauntered straight off the set of Miami Vice. This man took a liking to them. Milo has an image in his mind, of Nellee ensconced in a booth in this gangster's club, surrounded by Yakuza. Nellee was completely at ease, spooning noodle soup down his throat, just chilling. Milo said how he loved that side of Nellee, how much it amused him, this ability he had not to care about being a total oddity and just keep on doing his thing.

It had been risky, the whole Tokyo adventure. It's one thing gatecrashing parties in Camden, or even going to Portugal near enough skint. This was Japan – a place where people are born private, where, at least at the time, it was impossible to wander from one acquaintance's home to another's and crash, sofa to sofa. It may have been foolhardy, but Milo and Nellee believed in Wild Bunch, that was all. Wild Bunch was in fact the first thing Milo had had faith in, as a man. Those boys were like brothers. Milo was the only member of Wild Bunch with no family. Gee, D, Nellee and Claude all had stable families, in fact all of them had parents still alive and together. Sundays, during the Wild Bunch years, were the worst for Milo. His crew would vanish back to Sunday dinner and he would be out on a limb.

****

Back to Japan, 1986. Daddy Gee, Willee Wee and 3D at last graced Tokyo with their presence. Pretty quickly, they discovered vending machines that popped out warm saki. Gee, spread-eagled, all six foot four of him, totally soused, on a Tokyo pavement, is a mental polaroid that Milo will keep forever. All five of them doing a fashion show with dodgy choreography, styled as African-dictator-meetst-the-cast-of-*ER* is also pretty priceless. Gee and D were staying in the French man's house in the suburbs, that had been Milo and Nellee's first address. Milo and Nellee had both hooked up with women by then and were elsewhere. A bit of a myth has grown around that Japanese tour – that Nellee and Milo were living it up in some kind of Trump Tower, whilst Gee, D and Willie Wee kept a low profile in squalor, in a semi-squat with Yakuza swarming the neighbourhood. Milo feels that this needs a little moderation. He and Nellee were in the kind of hotels that offer sheets full of static electricity. The Frenchman's house that Gee and D were in was otherwise let out to TEFL teachers, so the only danger there was splitting your infinitives.

They were a week from the tour's kick-off. They were in good spirits. All, except D. He had confided in Milo that he wasn't doing so well. He was missing his girlfriend. She had stopped writing to him. He was worried. Now, at this point as a reader, you have some insight into Milo, so you already know just how unrelatable this was to him. All he could think of in the way of comfort, was, "Well you'll be back in a couple of weeks. Don't sweat it, Jack."

One morning, just before the tour was due to start, Milo showed up at the French man's house. Gee, Nellee and Willie Wee were sat at the kitchen table, grim-faced. "What's happening?" asked Milo. One of them pushed a piece of paper his way. It was a note from D.

"Sorry, I had to leave."

Milo was stunned. They explained to him that D had gone AWOL, slipping out in the night because he was scared Milo would try to stop him leaving otherwise. D, their prized MC, their front man, absconding like that – abandoning them – right before kick-off. No.

Milo was livid. They all were. The anger persisted well after they returned to Bristol. D was sent to Coventry. Milo remembers D coming into Special K's and sitting quiet as a librarian, in a corner, stirring his tea for five hours and – this was how it was said in Bristol back then – the whole crew blanking him. D did his penance; he tells of a time when he found himself having to repay his father the money he had borrowed to get to Japan. He took a job at the BBC canteen. He was running around in overalls with frozen lamb chops for Sue Lawley. Sort of. You get the picture. What is certain is that the gifted lyricist who just months before had been centre stage of Wild Bunch was having to rethink his ambitions. He picked up his cans of paint, and turned his back on the world.

Eventually, D was needed because D was special, and he was forgiven. He returned the fold. Milo understands those months of their lives differently today. Everything that was happening was so crazy, as if they were in a globe snow shaker together, under falling snow that gave their days an air of constant Christmas. Milo had no stability, had no comfort in his life, so the down side of Wild Bunch bounced off him like a bullet on reinforced glass. The Wild Bunch adventure was putting hope into his heart, and making him feel he had a place in the world. There was no woman who could touch that, as a sentiment. He was incapable of understanding love, even young love, the kind D had for his girlfriend. It was like explaining red to someone colourblind. Milo is older now. He gets it.

City Road, Bristol, 1986

He was walking through St Paul's. He was wearing a hat cocked on top of his dreadlocks, a silver puffa jacket, crazy sneakers from Japan. Milo walked with a bounce, it always looked like he was listening to music when he walked. On the opposite side of the road, a very tall man appeared to glide down the pavement his way. The man crossed the street and walked towards him. As they got closer to each other, the man looked right into Milo's face, and he smiled. A quiet smile. Milo held the man's gaze, his own face closed, and walked on.

Then he realised: it was Charlie.
Milo didn't slow down, nor did he quicken his pace.
He kept on walking, just as before.
In his mind was this: don't smile at me.
It's too late now, I'm fucked up already.
Fuck you, Charlie.
Fuck everybody who has failed me.

****

In his fifties, Milo understood that not turning back, not acknowledging Charlie, was one of the biggest mistakes of his life. You think you have time. You always think you have time. But you don't.

One day, decades from then, someone would tell Milo, "I heard Charlie died." Milo asked around. That was how it came back to him, as reported speech, as second-hand knowledge. His father's death. He has nothing of Charlie. Just a first and last name and one verified fact: Charlie danced.

****

There was Gee's camp, that was the base, and then there was Special K's, a favourite hangout. Special K's was a café whose exterior was tiled in Victorian moss-green and white. It wasn't far from the Dug Out, further along Park Row on the angle of a slow hill. Kosta ran it, he was Gee's closest friend. Inside was scrubbed and simple. It was the golden age of the jacket potato, a time when in English cafés an entire menu could consist of spud and an ever-eccentric choice of filling. Kosta did jacket potatoes, he did lasagne and he did the job of creating a quieter, brighter place for young hip-hop heads, graffiti artists and Wild Bunch followers. Plus, there was a pool table. TB had put paid to Milo's job at Kensington Market, there was no way he could put his body under the duress of the daily commute. He didn't want to be in Lockleaze, so he spent entire afternoons of his life in Special K's. This is where something fundamental to Bristol cultural history happened.

In prison, over three years if you include his time on remand, Milo had religiously tuned into the John Peel and Tony Prince radio shows. It was Milo's date with music. In his cell, by only a smudge of moonlight, or sometimes completely in the dark, he listened and he filled notebooks with songs. He wrote blind, sometimes writing over himself so that he would have to decipher his own words the next day. In separate notebooks, in careful print, he covered the pages with columns. These were the songs, from John Peel and from *Tony Prince's Disco Top Twenty*, that were of interest to him. Three years of these columns and it became a map of his musical mind. These notebooks have survived. In them he lists records, TP or TR (To Purchase or To Record). His handwriting looks printed, the lettering maybe echoing a graffiti aesthetic. Some of his 'E's were exactly like Basquiat's – three horizontal bars with no backbone – although he was unaware of Basquiat when he was in jail. There is a star system of classification, concerning the song and the interpreter.

Over a two-year period, after his release, with a trainspotter's intensity, Milo tracked down most of the songs in those notebooks. On his downtime from Wild Bunch, he put together mood tapes labelled simply, *Mood Tape #1*, *Mood Tape #2* and so on. Six in all. The notebooks are poignant; the tapes are something else – a precise sonic library that later served to define what is known as Bristol Sound. On these tapes, there is also music from his past, his childhood, that he sourced, wanting to redeem it and use it again. There is everything that he wanted to hear, one day, as a free man. This was his body of sound. The tapes are introspective and mellow. His mother's tunes, Donovan's songs. Movie scores from movies that no one he knew had watched, except him. It was an aspect of himself he had never revealed in public. His public image was that of a Black man with a punk aesthetic and a taste for dirty, heavy basslines. Although, live, he mixed ethereal melodies over, for instance, a *Sucker MCs* instrumental, it was the beat that people danced to. So when Milo passed one of these tapes to Kosta, one lunchtime when the café was empty, asking him to put it on, he didn't think anyone would really notice.

They noticed.

Milo told Kosta not to give the tapes to anyone, and Kosta didn't. But copies were made, some with Milo's okay, and copies were made, without his okay, for different people. For quite a few people.

People talk about the Bristol Sound, write about the Bristol Sound, and do so in earnest. Often, it's the bass line. The "Bristol bassline", the "Wild Bunch bassline", "reggae bass", "drum and bass". It isn't. Or, at least, not only. It's the super positioning of singular, specific voices, like the ones on Milo's tapes, over a loaded bass that is at the inception of what has been given such a strange name, trip-hop. It is a sound that mirrors what Milo was mixing live: the surprise of a tremulous melody or a plain, northern girl's voice when lifted and placed over a slow hip-hop bassline – that seems rather than to wash it out, to give it weight. The magic was in the marriage of the two. It was Milo who earmarked voices like those of Tracey Thorn or Liz Fraser – five stars in his prison notebook. No one else in the crew was listening to The Cocteau Twins or Everything But The Girl – Milo is certain of that, he raked through everyone's personal record collection. Milo's *Mood Tapes* had many Wally Badarou tracks, including *Mambo*, so identifiable as a trip-hop signature sound. The atmospheric beat of Les McCann, on Massive Attack's masterpiece *Teardrop* is also a running theme on another. Listening to these tapes today, because they have survived against all odds, the most surprising thing is that Milo isn't even mentioned on the Wikipedia page dedicated to trip-hop. These *Mood Tape* songs, the melodies and voices, were an expression of his soul, his captive and already damaged soul. Like Bristol itself, the tapes told the story of displacement and yearning, of loss and of hope, renewed. They were the only way that Milo showed his fragility.

Chapter Twenty-Eight

SEARCHING FOR THE RIGHT DOOR

Although Juliette had kept a connection with Betty, Milo hadn't. He saw Betty once, at a family meal. It's a bad memory. He was still living at Nicky's for the baby, but he was on the point of leaving for good. Only their child sewed a thread of conversation between them. It was a birthday meal, for Juliette. Nicky was invited. Betty had come. Here she was, at a table with all of her children. She was the queen, and yet she was the child. Milo, Juliette, Troy, Joanie. The way humans can deal with so much grief, the way a family gathering can happen, each drawing a chair to the table, and suspending, in the space of that communion, all of the pain. Breaking bread. Being blood. Trying for meaning.

Then Nicky kicked off. Round the table, Milo's family and Juliette's friends, aware of the tension, got on with the moment, laughing and talking over it. Although Milo was not Nicky's man, she was gunning for him. About his absence, about her expectations. Quite publicly. She was a little bit drunk. She was slightly flirtatious with Troy. Maybe she was trying to make Milo jealous. Certainly, she was testing the boundaries.

Milo didn't know his mother anymore, but more than that, Betty didn't know this son, nor the man he had become. Here in a pub, around plates of chicken and bowls of pasta, was Betty's first view of Milo, the man. With what looked like a girlfriend, running her mouth off. Although no one came out and said so, this occasion (the Johnsons together) was special to each of them. It was perilously close to being ruined by Nicky's rage. It is the only time in his life that Milo felt himself tighten inside and the only time that he ever felt like punching a woman out. With Betty there (oh, how life enjoys a repeat). Except Milo would have rather shot himself, truly, than hit a woman. As a small boy full of promise, he had seen his mother, the woman sat here, stately and serene, and for so much less than the issue with Nicky, get beaten half to death. Milo got up from the table. "Have a good one, Ju." Nicky was up, following him out on to the car park, shouting after him. He walked away.

*****

Becoming a father had changed Milo, he was calmer, though a deep sadness settled within him that was never to go away completely. He continued to see Izzy and he was still living in Lockleaze. Occasionally, other women broke into his world again. The girl from Glastonbury, he still sometimes saw her. She remained on the cusp of his life, a girl who was the right one and the wrong one all at once. His darkest strokes were with her. They made each other angry, and his anger came through as a harshness, yet what he felt towards her was unlike anything he had felt for anyone else. He watched as she got herself into all kinds of trouble, it might have been funny, she was certainly that, funny, but it made him sad. She let the wrong people in. She seemed intrepid in the most foolhardy way. Yet he saw her once, in the phone box on Ashley Road. As he drew nearer he saw that she was holding the receiver with both hands, cradled between her hunched up shoulder and her face, so that these – her hands and the phone and her shoulders – were all packed in the same small window frame. She was crying, her eyes were closed and just her chest jumped with the tears. And another time, she was hit in the face in the Dug Out. Without knowing her side of the story, without needing to know, Milo had grabbed her and taken her away from there. His instinct was to protect her. Milo and this girl were made up of the same negative charge and they pushed each other into the far corners of their respective minds and held each other there. She was the one that he had wanted for his own – and maybe still did – but she hadn't understood. She had wanted to be his, but kept her mouth shut, unable to say words of love. They were young and broken kids, who were moved along on the floating debris of their childhoods. One day, she was gone. From the clubs, from the streets of St Paul's, from the grass where he sometimes saw her, lying reading a book. She left without saying goodbye.

Nicky and Izzy were two entirely separate and watertight lives. Just once, at the St Paul's carnival the year that the baby was born, the two worlds that he held apart walked into each other. Wild Bunch were in full party mode, on Campbell Street, in the middle of the afternoon. Out in the sunshine, there was a big gathering of the neighbourhood, but also Wild Bunch followers, and Campbell Street looked as culturally diverse and vibrant as any carnival in Brazil. Izzy was hanging round near Milo, with her friends. From where he was, behind the decks with a view out to the street, Milo spotted Nicky moving up towards him, the baby in her arms. This was unannounced, an intrusion, breaking an unspoken understanding. The sound system was as heavy as possible, the bass making everyone's body buzz. It was no place for a baby. He left the decks and bounded through the crowd. Izzy saw him, watched. She saw Milo stop before a woman, lean into her, speaking. The woman frowned, then nodded. Milo moved in close to the baby, he was smiling. Then Nicky turned and made her way out. Izzy looked on, her expression betraying her shock at this corporality perhaps. Milo's other life, out in a working-class neighbourhood, with a faceless woman and child was suddenly made real.

He was a father and a boyfriend and a partner when in fact, in his heart, he felt like none of these things. He had a sense of bewilderment and frustration, that his hand had been forced. He looked after the baby all through the first year of its life. He put a barrier up and was unable or unwilling to bond. He behaved more like a good big brother than like a dad. He couldn't see himself in the baby, yet the baby was his. He was scared of the baby loving him too, it would only cause pain – to the baby, and to himself. He felt, somehow, that the younger the baby was, the easier it would be to forget him. He had no understanding of child psychology, no idea that leaving would hurt his child, just as much as staying. He knew he would leave Bristol, it was something he felt compelled to do and it was just a question of time. He had been trying to figure a way out of the relationship with Nicky long before the baby was conceived. He felt no guilt towards Nicky, but he was conflicted and lost. Leaving Bristol for good was still a hard decision to make. There was even a wild and fleeting idea that if he took the two of them with him – Nicky and their child – away from

Bristol, to a place where everything would need to be written from scratch, then love might grow. Maybe they could become a family. He asked Nicky if she wanted to come to London with him. He was scared of humiliating her in her parents' eyes, he didn't want her to seem worthless. He was scared of being a bad man. He was scared, if he's truthful, that Nicky might say yes, although in his heart, he knew very well that she would never follow him on a wild and unmapped journey. There was the house that she was buying, a job to keep and her baby to care for. She said no, of course she did, she couldn't follow him. She may not have realised that she would never be near him again. She had forced him to make her significant, the baby as a small hostage against the ransom of his presence. She had taken a gamble, that a man so damaged would miraculously mend for her. It turned out to be a game with no winners.

Nellee wanted to go to London, to this metropolis, where each encounter was like a hit on a pinball machine, illuminating a labyrinth that led to interesting people, who led to yet more interesting people. Milo? He just needed to be gone. In Bristol, he was drowning in his own local celebrity. He had gone from being a child rejected by the fundamental people in life, his father then his mother, being put into care, then imprisoned to – without transition – being quite the Prince of the Night. He had felt it closing in. He had fucked around for years. He had slept with all kinds of women: plain, pretty, Black, white, mixed-race, from the ghetto, or from Clifton; working girls, university girls, a seamstress, models, a stripper, the future wife of a future world leader. Then he had found himself in a double life where he didn't fit, where there was no sense.

He left both Nicky and Izzy together. Strangely, the relationship with one had enabled the relationship with the other. Without Izzy's presence, he would not have stuck it out at Nicky's for as long as he had. Izzy made Nicky an impossibility. And without the reality of Nicky underscoring his time with Izzy, that relationship, too, with Izzy, would have ended sooner. Without Nicky, he would have had no excuse for not giving Izzy some kind of status in his life. The truth is that Milo couldn't give anything more, to either of them. It was just a mess.

Chapter Twenty-Nine

FOREST OF FEELINGS

Tokyo, 1987

Nellee was clear-cut. What Nellee wanted was to move this show on, he wanted momentum. There is the story of the Gordian Knot, a knot so intricate that it was impossible to undo. Alexander the Great reasoned that it made no difference how the knot were undone. So, he slashed it apart with a sword. Milo's life in Bristol was a little like that knot, woven with sorrow, tightening over time. He couldn't go backwards, unpick life, start over. If he could, where would he travel to? How could he have changed his trajectory? He had not had the distance on himself, the guidance of elders, or even the recognition of his own pain to have been able to change a single thing. Not yet, not now, but it would bloom, later, in the streets of Harlem, in the Black soul of the Earth. Now, at the age of twenty-six, like Alexander the Great, he solved his problem with one swift move. He took what little he had and jumping at the chance to get away, left Bristol.

He and Nellee moved to Mornington Crescent. Milo had a room in a flat with Nellee and Nellee's striking and surprisingly grounded best friend, Zohra. They were hooked up with the Soul II Soul posse, and spent afternoons of their lives hanging out with each other, listening to music. Then Milo got a place of his own, in Camden, with just one bedroom and a tiny garden that led on to Camden Lock. It was the first time in his life that he had a place to himself. Chica and Toshi had moved from Japan to London and they often came by. Some of his friends. Not women, hardly ever. He listened to music, he watched films. He organised music for the parties they would play. He was undisturbed. How did that feel? Being quite alone? Fucking brilliant, that's how.

Milo was involved in fashion, not only as a model but designing hip-hop clothes. He and Nellee were working for Moichi, gathering footage for Moichi's style-setting TV show, *Club King*, in Japan. Nellee and Milo trawled London clubs and shops, interviewing underground creatures and club legends. At the Astoria club, Milo tried to interview John Lydon who looked square at him, then told him to fuck off. Just how you would imagine it should be, a badge of honour. Nellee and Milo were industrious, they were filming and making music. They were still very young and, in London, unleashed. Island Records approached them, probably having heard their dub plate on Tim Westwood's show. The long and the short of it is that, as Wild Bunch, they were signed as the first UK hip-hop artists to a major label. There was a dinner, in an understated, laughably expensive restaurant where the Island team, from A&R to the bosses, gathered round Nellee and Milo. What to make of these two Bristol boys? How to market them?

The boss, who had been carefully watching Milo leaned in, "Can you sing?" he asked Milo. In the beat of time in which Milo tried to collect the right words, Nellee answered,

"Yeah, you can sing, can't you, Jack? He can sing."

Milo looked at Nellee, this was unbelievable. "I ain't singing, mate. I can't sing, what's wrong with you?"

Milo was laughing. Check out this kid, he thought, looking at his friend. Nellee was on a grift, operating on the correct level, in fact, for the situation, because what else was this, but a supper of disciples out to spin money from music, any which way? Nellee knew that Milo couldn't sing, but it was something he would have found a way around, even though Milo's idea of a living hell would have been to appear on *Top Of The Pops*. Milo was an anarchist at heart, he was truly disobedient. In this, his very first rebuttal, he showed what he didn't need at any cost: to compromise his integrity. He wanted to make music. He wanted only that. Though there was something else at play, an understory – fame that he didn't want at all. He didn't mind signing a record deal, but he did mind the idea of being objectified. Fame also scared Milo. Fame is only a litmus paper that shows up the acid hurt of your past, or its alkaline tenderness. The disproportionate cosseting that comes with success and the drugs, the women, are only attendant to the status of celebrity, to be taken or discarded. Milo had seen his pathological inability to deal with attention from women, how he had given his intimacy so easily that it had no worth. He figured out, all alone, that fame might be the same. There was a spirit in him, come from somewhere, who can say, that stopped him from ever drinking or doing drugs. He says he feared what might come out of him, after so much violence and abuse as a child. What enraged soul he might become, whom he might punish. He stayed in control of himself, always. Even in love. He decided that if you swim out towards love, towards anything, you'd better make sure you have the strength to turn and swim back to the shore. This fame thing, it seemed to control some people and reduce them to less than they were before. A man with a lack of love for himself, caught up in the narcotic that is fame, would need luck on his side to survive.

Milo and Nellee cut those four tracks: three straight-up hip-hop and the fourth, *The Look Of Love*, sung by a young and tremulous Shara Nelson. This song was Milo's desire, he had to push Nellee hard to have it included. The beat of the song is slowed-down and the end effect is one that Milo described back then as 'lover's hip-hop' – it was a coming together of lover's rock and hip-hop. This was Milo's own signature sound. It is the song that created a new music genre, trip-hop. Wild Bunch were excited, they had made no money from the deal, but they were truly happy with their record. It felt as though they had come to a clearing, and the future was glinting with promise.

Milo was in Japan more and more. As a DJ, he had a residency in a Tokyo nightclub, Bank. He was getting hip-hop t-shirts and jackets made, too, travelling alone to South Korea where his friend Kwazz had advised him to go if he wanted clothes that were fairly priced. Some of that clothing has survived: B-boy bomber jackets with hip-hop imagery from a New York breakbeat compilation emblazoned across the back; an octopus rapping, holding a microphone; a B-boy skeleton with gold chains and gold teeth.

****

Around this time, he was in a nightclub, sifting through records for his set, when Moichi's girlfriend came to him, "My friend wants to meet you," she said. Milo was busy, he glanced up. Stood there in clothes that looked like she had pulled them on in the dark, with an indecipherable look on her absolutely immobile face was a woman, Hitomi. He had seen her before and each time she seemed to be placed in a different setting: on the door of a reggae club, taking the money (she looked wild, her head was shaved up one side, she had dreadlocks and spray-gunned punk make-up); in a light-flooded high-rise office, being a secretary. Now she was before him waiting and, just behind her, touching her shoulder, was her boyfriend. He was distressed. Milo asked Moichi's girlfriend, "What's going on?" She explained that Hitomi and the guy were over, they were done and that Hitomi wanted to speak with Milo. He answered, "I can't speak now, I'll maybe speak with her another time, then?" The situation seemed odd. He didn't want to be a part of any drama. Milo would always remember Hitomi in that first instance, how strong she seemed. Her total disregard for her pleading ex-boyfriend. The directness of her gaze. He saw a spirit in this woman, she wouldn't be stepped on. Weeks went by, and then they met. They suited each other. She was fierce, she was funny. She was an outsider. They were strangely alike. They grew close, closer, until she became his whole world. Hitomi was a mate, the ultimate mate. Years later, he was with her and Tricky and addressing Hitomi, Milo said, "Hey, Jack, do you remember that?"

Tricky looked stunned. "Do you call her Jack?" he asked.

"Yeah, I do."

"You can't call her that," Tricky laughed. It was to him as if Milo had called his wife bro', it was so incredibly unromantic. It hadn't occurred to Milo that Jack was for his crew, that Jack was man-on-man. It hadn't occurred to him because Hitomi was such a natural follow-on from his friendships with his male friends. That's the kind of closeness they had. A partnership. A laugh. There are far worse things to take a chance on in the name of love. Hitomi and Milo rented a little flat in Tokyo, in the Daikanyama area. He still had his place in Camden. He went there less and less. The people at Island Records were depressing to him. They had signed a hip-hop collective and they didn't know what to do with them. Maybe Milo could have stayed, fought his corner. A year or so later, hip-hop exploded. Milo would have made sense to the A&R by then.

Inside himself, he was gone from England. He had found this place on the planet that wasn't immured in latent racism. Japan was a monoculture. Yes, he was a Black man but it didn't carry the myriad of knock-on associative ideas. The Japanese didn't seem to care about whether or not he was handsome, either. Girls would come to his gigs, or the gigs with Nellee, and there was no loitering around at the end of the night, no eye-fucking hunger. He didn't miss the attention. The words of the girl in St Paul's had been grinding away in the back of his mind all that time: don't you have any pride? It seems that this is where his pride in himself as a man would begin, in Japan, with Hitomi. One day, not so very far away, she would become his wife and the line would be drawn, black ink, beneath which clean white pages of faithfulness would be turned and turned, twenty-five years of them.

The year in Tokyo, with Hitomi, was the most liberated he had ever felt. He was building a relationship with her, yet they shared no common language. They pieced together an understanding of each other through music and DJing and all that they were excited about. There were aspects to Hitomi that Milo found hard to deal with: she was a heavy smoker and she would drink until she couldn't stand up straight. She changed. She pulled herself together. She learned English. He was making a different, unseeable effort. He was letting a woman in, trusting a woman, for the first time in his life. There is a Japanese art, Kintsugi, meaning golden seam. It is the tradition of repairing broken pottery with lacquer mixed with powdered gold. The mended pot is veined with these gold lines. It is strangely more beautiful and stronger than before. They were this to other.

He spent a lot of his time in Tokyo with Hiroshi. Hiroshi, with his crew, Major Force, had a record deal going. Hiroshi, K.U.D.O, Takagi Kan, and Toshi. These new friends whose names were now on his tongue, names to turn over, percussive and soft as the sound of a glockenspiel. Milo was their new recruit. They recorded *Return Of The Original Art Form*. It was Milo who found the title on one of his old Afrika Islam tapes. He was turning out to have quite a knack for that. The record was a cut-and-paste style, loosely based on the Lesson series by Double Dee and Steinski, but less hip-hop, more disco. Milo did a bit of scratching. Imagine it, five years before he had been scrubbing the cold cracked floors of Swansea Prison, now here he was, making music in Japan. The posse of Tokyo DJs and MCs taught Milo how to start to make music. They broke it down to him, especially K.U.D.O. It was through them that Milo bought his first sequencer – a Q40 – and a four-track mixer. He began to make original music and continued to DJ under the name DJ Milo. He toured with Major Force, a collective made up, among others, of Hiroshi and Tagaki Kan, Toshi and Chica (Melon), ECD and The Orchids. They toured Japan with Public Enemy. Somewhere out there is an interview in a magazine, Milo interviewing Chuck D. It was during that year that Milo met some of his heroes: Jungle Brothers, Flavor Unit, Kool DJ Red Alert, DJ Cash Money. The idea of moving to America was germinating. The dialogue with these Black American men was easy to Milo, and liberating. He was freeing himself from the way the outside world had tried to define him. The shackles were coming off.

****

The last of the Wild Bunch days were in Japan. Many years before, 3D and Milo had done a movie with Dick Fontaine, *Bombin'*. Fontaine had brought down graffiti artists such as Goldie from the UK and the Tats Cru with Brim from New York, to Bristol. Brim did a piece on the wall of the Malcolm X Centre in St Paul's. Beneath it he wrote, "Massive Attack." It had a ring to it. 3D and Milo decided to use it, in fact they wanted to call themselves, "The Underground Massive Attack." Milo, who was about to begin the tour DJing with the Jungle Brothers and Major Force, asked 3D to join him. Because Milo didn't want there to be any confusion, or false promotion, they didn't advertise as Wild Bunch. The two of them toured under a different name, one whose promise was unimaginable: Massive Attack.

****

It all became a little overwhelming for him, maybe for all of them. Milo was now, for work, spending most of his time in Japan, coming back to England only once in an entire year. At the very end of the eighties, he came home. Down in St Paul's, at Gee's, everything was the same, but busier. Gee's front room now had a couple of boxes of production equipment, paid for with their record deal. It was the deal that would give the world *Blue Lines*.

On this last visit, Milo played for a gig called Artists Against Apartheid, at Temple Meads. Tricky was crashing at Juliette's house, a house she shared with her boyfriend. Juliette had grown up. Of a life of chaos and abandonment, it seemed she had responded with love and yet more love. She and Tricky had a good time back in those days, they were mates. He slept on her sofa, for a long time, and her front room was his home.

She reappears. Here. Betty.

She is old now, in Milo's eyes. Though she isn't old, not really.

Betty still lived in Southampton. She had turned into this lady the children of her neighbourhood adored. She would go down to the forecourt and marshal a straggle of inner-city children into skipping games and football matches. She brought down a ghetto blaster on sunny afternoons, and she danced until they all remembered how to dance, too. Betty loved music, it had always been part of her life. She played the cello. Betty's mother, Amelia, played the cello, too. All that is known about Amelia is this: she played the cello, she was Jewish, she married a Black man and she died when Betty was a baby. Of all the instruments, the cello is the one that draws you in to the deepest, saddest parts of your soul. Of all the instruments, the cello is the one that is cradled, its hourglass weight resting against the cellist, who feels the vibration as a melancholic hum within. It isn't a wild thought that the first cello Betty drew towards her was probably Amelia's. The cello's bow, made of horse-tail hair, greased, pulled across the four strings, makes a sound like honey and end-of-day shadow. As the bow travels above the bridge, there is a slip sound, a slight buzz. The mechanics of cello playing create these imperfections and they are a part of its beauty. This was the only language Betty shared with her mother, the language of the cello, which has the same range as the human voice. The music Milo can hear in his head is that dreamlike blue, too.

When visiting Bristol, Betty would stop at Juliette's. One afternoon, calling by, Tricky was in the front room, surrounded with what might have been the paraphernalia of semi-depression: ashtrays brimful, scrunched biscuits packets, mugs ringed with tea stains.

Betty told him he needed to get up and do something with his life. Milo had left behind reels of his music, recordings from Japan. Betty said, "Adrian, just take my son's music and make some songs. Do something. Get yourself a record deal." Which is exactly what Tricky did, signing his first recording contract using Milo's beats. Tricky's mother died when he was small. Betty had vanished from Milo's world when he was twelve. She could never reach him after that. All these bruised lives are entwined. One woman's voice whispered through another's. One boy heard for another. Mothers and their special sons.**City Road, Bristol, 1988**

"Well, I should make a move," Milo said to the posse, Gee, 3D and Mushroom, in Gee's camp.

"Yes, Jack, listen, we'll see you soon." Milo pulled on his coat. Mushroom was at Gee's, trying to figure out how a piece of equipment worked. Mushroom was the last man to join Wild Bunch. Milo had sometimes played with him, but mostly Mushroom stood in for him and would get behind the decks and mix at parties when Milo was away. They became friends, Milo and Mushroom. Later, they made a trip to New York together, running wild around the city.

The crew had grown up and were – necessarily – growing apart. The bond that Milo felt with them, Gee, Nellee, D, Willy Wee, Tricky and Mushroom, was unchanged and irreversible. They were his idren. A sound system has a particular basis, different from a band. Its basis is in sharing: sharing records, sharing the microphone and the small space in which you play. The only wealth really is the records, which a sound system holds on to like a rib cage holds the heart. Wild Bunch is a collective founded by three men, becoming seven men. It is based in this fraternity and like all the best friendships, you are free to walk in and out of it as you choose. If you represented the connections between the seven members of Wild Bunch by an electric light board, then you would see different patterns illuminating the circuit over forty years. There has never been a time when all of them were lost to each other, the circuit has always stayed lit. It was decades before Milo and, without a doubt, each one of them, would look back and realise what an incredible thing they had made.

Milo lifted his hand, "See ya."

"Later."

He wandered out, on to City Road. Hitomi was at Juliette's. He would go and get her. He had his Sony Walkman on, bought in Japan. He was the only man he had ever seen in England with one of those. It changed his life. He took the long route to Horfield, Bristol gliding past to the music of a mood tape, a segue to the next dance.

Chapter Thirty

THEM CHANGES

Hitomi thought that they should marry. He considered it. Hitomi was a woman who got things done. She was older than Milo, by four years. She was different from Milo, there were tiny coloured bulldozers in her mind that could flatten any obstacle. She was stronger than him in ways that he needed. She was braver. He felt himself steadying. He was becoming a clearer version of himself, in that way that you do in your late twenties. Marrying Hitomi was right, he could feel the weight of tradition and of honour, he connected to it. It would give them both a sense of moving on, of growing up.

One afternoon in late summer, they walked through the streets of Daikanyama. It was raining. The rain left mist on Hitomi's arms. From the top of a flight of steps, he saw an avenue of open umbrellas, advancing like a long, peaceful New Year's dragon. They walked for an hour, into an office. There was no more ceremony than if they had opened a bank account. They wrote their names on the bottom of a piece of paper. They were man and wife.

New York City, 1988

His first time in New York City, in 1987, had been with Mushroom. Milo had gone there on a quest to walk onto the set of the films that he admired, films like *Midnight Cowboy*, like *Taxi Driver*. He wanted to be inside an atmosphere like that. On their very first morning, turning a corner, they saw a man being filmed. Mushroom seemed to have been electrocuted, "That is Herbie Hancock!" he exclaimed. There was nothing Milo could do to stop him, so he stood back and watched Mushroom accost Herbie Hancock with childlike joy, with the candour that let him say, "You are my hero." Herbie Hancock was gracious, and smiling, and Milo took a picture: an ultimate jazz master and a young man who was just at the start of his musical odyssey.

Milo and Mushroom hit Times Square come night. As soon as that sun dropped, the city became vivid with danger. They kept their money in their socks. Times Square, in the craziness that it was – porn theatres, strip clubs, hookers, dopeheads, billboards and lights everywhere your eye could travel studding the black sky, luminous, the colours of boiled sweets – in all of this, they found a record shop stuffed with hip-hop, they spent hours in there. Milo left the city with treasure: graffitied t-shirts, records, the poster he had seen in *Wild Style* (black-and-red velvet, with zodiac symbols, each one of a different sex position). He left with the gold caps he and Mushroom had had made for their teeth on Times Square. In photographs from that time, Milo and Mushroom, who both had fur hats and teeth bucked with gold, look like rakish pimps.

They had run all over downtown New York. Just two invisible young men in a city of continuous movement and clamour. Milo loved that place, right away.

The second time he went to New York was with Hitomi. They had to negotiate the teeming streets with all their worldly possessions in suitcases and bags teetering on trolleys. Their first address was the YMCA, on 34th Street. Those opening months in America were the hustle that is the lot of every poor recent immigrant to the USA. They had disembarked with a plan. Hitomi's sister was to open a store in Tokyo, selling hip-hop and house records, street clothing, video tapes of American music shows – cornering a tight, select market. Milo and Hitomi would have to set up an export business. Their days were spent scouring the city, exploring the recesses of Delancey and Orchard, of Brooklyn and Queens, taking random turns and getting lost. Looking for the supplies that would secure them a future. In those days, vinyl records came in sleeves that bore the name of the record label and, incredibly, the phone number. This was Milo's new life, his American dream: sat on a bed in a rundown YMCA dormitory, sorting through records. Copying down the phone numbers of the record labels. Going to a pay phone on the corner of 34th and 9th. Talking to a record company with authority, the word "Tokyo" causing lights to flash at the other end of the phone line. This was New York, 1989, and the Yen was pulsating. Being, always, practically broke. Being happy.

At night, they went out, suckered to the energy of downtown NYC. They had come with an idea of where to go, friends had tuned them in to the right clubs. Hitomi, like many Japanese people of her generation, could DJ. It was a thing, in Tokyo back then. Almost every kid on the scene, whatever they were by day, had a couple of Technics turntables and their own little vinyl collection. They would mix in their front rooms, just for kicks, just for themselves. Hitomi loved these New York nights. She loved music, she loved to dance. She had a little rap crew of her own, all-girls, and they toured with Major Force. She was a singular woman.

****

There was no time to rest. Their first year of married life was dominated by the urgency of getting their business up and secure. The shop in Shibuya, DJ's Choice, had opened. They had found a niche market that Tokyo clubbers and hip-hop fans were curious about. It became a pressing need for Milo and Hitomi to find a place with enough room to house their mounting stock. They were just about breaking even. They rented an apartment, but on the kind of street that had marauding rats. Young Latino men across the way dealt drugs to skinny women in denim mini skirts and to men with swollen veins and no socks. It was a Hispanic block in Alphabet City, on 4th Street. It was The Village. Mention of The Village throws up a Polaroid in our collective mind, of a place made famous by Warhol and The Factory. Although The Factory had disbanded by then, it had irrevocably shaped the neighbourhood, and many of the artists who had moved there to claim or be claimed by that scene, remained. Downtown Manhattan was a pinpoint in space-time. It was colonised by anti-establishment artists. The allure for Milo was the demographic, not unlike all that he had loved in Bristol, down the Dug Out for example. This was the neighbourhood that had invited hip-hop and graffiti out of the ghettos of the South Bronx, and a place where there was something punkish in the coming together of Blacks and whites.

It was in this neighbourhood that Milo learned to read New York City, and its rhythms. In a city of perpetual human exchange, the trick was to know who was the guy on the street corner having a rough day, who was the man you did not answer, or even look at, when in his need to let off steam he threw his hook out at you. Carrying a gun, having death coolly at your disposal, evens out the Alphas and the Betas, it becomes nothing more than the luck of the draw.

****

This was the golden era of hip-hop and house and the epicentre was New York. Milo's life was predominately nocturnal. He went to block parties and clubs: this jacket, that colour, this record, that graffiti artist (it was his new notebook, there had always been a notebook in his life) that he would later go on to source. The clothes they were sending to Tokyo were the clothes worn that same month in the clubs in downtown NYC. Most of the clubs he went to were in Manhattan, below 34th Street. There were small clubs in East Village, like Save The Robots, near their home. Down the road there was club called Choice where Larry Levan played after the legendary New York club, Paradise Garage, closed. Milo was a punter like any other. Nobody knew his face, remembered his face, nor cared who he was.

He went to block parties, these without Hitomi. He went to rough clubs and saw up-and-coming artists. He saw Wu-Tang when they were beginning to blow up in New York. It was just before Christmas. He was waiting in a crowd on the sidewalk for the door of the small club to open. It was below zero. The Black gathering was wrapped in big jackets, low hats. Their eyes and the fleeting clouds of mist from their mouths as they spoke were all you could see. Milo was wearing a North Face down jacket, it had cost him half a month's wages. There were other men wearing the same one, probably drug dealers. Winters in New York, the air paralyses your fingers and hurts your face. To hustle, to be outdoors and shift your gear, you needed to be wrapped up warm. This particular Sagarmatha Series jacket, the biggest they made, was of armchair proportions and designed for North Pole expeditions. There were only a few New York outlets for North Face, Tent 'n' Trails was one of them, so the model was hard to find. These jackets were utilitarian status symbols. Outside the club, the people were excited and expectant. There was a sudden movement. A gang from Brooklyn rushed the door, trying to force their way in, without paying. Within seconds, a fight broke out. Milo knew that it was a thing for a razor to be pulled, and a North Face jacket to be slashed, out of spite. So, he stepped back. There was a lot of shouting, a surge in the crowd, a bouncer cursing, "Yo back the fuck up, man!" Then a quick, furtive blade, pulled in the scrum of bodies at the door. On a puff of frosty wind, a small storm of white feathers billowed into the black, Christmas night.

****

Once a year, there was the *New Music Seminar*, which took over the hip-hop and house clubs in NYC, hosting events. Everywhere you looked, like popcorn bursting in a pan, there was a DJ battle or an MC battle that would go down, years later, as legendary. At the battles, there would be twenty or so guys DJing, fighting it out, rhythmically. They were exhibitionist DJs, scratching and juggling or quick mixing. These men were performance artists. They were there to show off their skills with two records, which decades later would be termed "turntablism" and this required musicality, imagination and dexterity. Sometimes, back in the early eighties, breakdancers would perform with that kind of DJ, in clubs downtown. There was another type of DJ who would be the headliner at that same party, one whose job it was to make people dance rather than be watched. These neighbourhood DJs also made mix tapes, it was almost the only way to promote themselves. They would hand their tapes out, often to their friends and in this way, their sound stamp would be out on the streets. Typically, on these tapes, the DJ would introduce himself before the beat, often through an echo chamber: Now you know it's goin' on…What's up New York City?… City… City… City… echoing out. The cars parked up the length of 125th Street on a summer's night would blast out songs, or drive around the grid of the neighbourhood, windows down, mixtapes playing.

They made the tapes in their rooms. These guys were like sonars, scanning their world for a record that no one had, to make their playlist unique. Their musical ideas snaked their way (often without permission) from uptown to downtown, out, gone. They sometimes gathered momentum, so that in the strangest of transmutations, a beat that had been isolated and taped in a tired one-room crib in Harlem, wound up underscoring a sixty-second, hundred-thousand dollar film made to sell sneakers the planet over, or relit the career of an obscure, or has-been funk or rock band. Music inside one person's head wound up being part of many people's lives.

When you have nothing, and your spirit is creative, you will find ingenious ways to express yourself. Blues and jazz, just like hip-hop and soul, are the flowers that have bloomed on the landfills of oppression.

****

Milo was in a car, at a Harlem traffic light in the opaque August heat. WFMU on loud, playing Soul II Soul, *Keep On Moving*. He had already heard the demo, D had played it to him Japan. New York went crazy for it. In every car – Black, Italian, Jewish, Latino, it didn't matter – cars were pumping the song. it sweetened the summer. For Milo, the fact that he heard his friend's music, and had Nellee travelling, this way, with him through New York City, made all his world feel closer and it gave him happiness.

CHAPTER THIRTY-ONE

DON'T STOP TO WATCH THE WHEELS

Hitomi and Milo worked with a Japanese clothing company called Men's Bigi. Milo modelled for them, and the designer was Hitomi's friend, Yuji Imanishi. The company asked them to find hip-hop dancers in New York City, to bring over for a fashion show. Milo was in clubs most nights of the week. He had seen kids on the dancefloor here and there who were remarkable dancers. Most of them worked with rappers live, or danced on music videos, so he had recognised faces, but he didn't know who they were. To find them again took him a few weeks. He went to every hip-hop event on in the city, composing a team of dancers with the passion of a football scout. One of the first guys he connected with was Prancer, a dancer for the rapper Special Ed. Through him, a little collective came together: James, Rome, Tonga, Prancer, Sound and Kazo. Then a few others were drafted in: Roger, Michael, Peter, Miguel, Lenny, Brian, Emilio, Stretch, Stephen and Adé. They were young, these dancers. Born in New York. They were defined by their neighbourhood, by their block, by America's static view of ethnicity. They were also gifted, open and up for an adventure.

Milo visited each of their homes, in Brooklyn, in Queens, in Harlem. Mostly, but not only, these were fatherless boys, just like himself. He entered kitchens, met with a mother, still young, watchful, careful. The mother often had another family member shadowing – an uncle, a cousin – for back up, or a second ear. He tried to explain the journey, the show, his own role as chaperone. He tried to reassure. The women listened, moved from the doorway to the kitchen table and, finally, pulled up a chair. Chin on hand, or sat up straight, they listened. My baby in Japan. Milo could feel the boys willing him on, to find the right words, until at last the small triumph, or not so small: trust.

Tokyo, Electric City, 1990

Milo had been in Tokyo with his dancers for one day. They were wild with excitement. They made their way down the streets, decked out in full hip-hop tradition. The shoppers stared at them with open curiosity. Electric City was lined with buildings twelve storeys high, heaving with electronics. The equipment – stereos, ghetto blasters, speakers, Walkmans – turned each store into Santa's grotto. Astoundingly, for boys from the poorest districts of New York, these wares were stacked on the pavements, just sitting there, nothing strapped down.

Milo saw himself reflected in these young men as in the clearest of waters. He recognised the rush of freedom without the monkey on your back that you had back home, that reading of suspicion, or fear, in a stranger's eyes who wasn't Black like you. Then there was the beauty of Tokyo, the eccentricity of its overpowering consumerism, the bewildering gadgets, the city painted with lights. Milo's first helium days in Tokyo had been the same. Now he watched his dancers exploring the central street in Electric City, he watched as they stopped at shop windows, "Look at this!"

And another of them calling from a different store front, "Yo! Come over here, look at this shit man!"

Their smiles, their buoyancy. Outside one shop, sitting big as a farm cat, was a ghetto blaster. "Anyone got a tape?" one of them asked. Milo did, in his pocket. It was a mixtape and on it was the hottest tune in Black America at the time, *Hold On* by En Vogue. It's a tune that starts out a capella, an all-girl polyphony, with the surgeyness of gospel. As the voices gathered intensity, the dancers began circling the pavement. Shoppers slowed down. People watched from the other side of the street. The voices of the singers climbed a note higher than the note before and then, on the boom of the thudding bass, the dancers, with breathtaking synchronicity, dropped to a crouch on The One. That was the theme, dropping down on the first beat of the bar, and here also was the miracle, because this was spontaneous, and done with the intuition and intelligence of jazz musicians improvising. One dancer, Miguel, was Puerto Rican. His hip-hop had a Latino ripple, an almost flamenco bravado. Each of them came with his own signature, and each was able to dovetail into the corps. Milo, now surrounded by a small enthralled crowd of Tokyo shoppers, watched. These boys whose bodies carved shapes, all made the same step, with subtle, clever variations. The way they moved together as one was tribal, and looked so other-worldly, here in a retail hub in central Tokyo. The contrast was unbelievable and mesmerising. These boys could move like cats, like kings. Milo says that in all his life, it is a moment he regrets not having being able to film, because it was beautiful. Back in New York, after Tokyo, Miguel and Milo stayed in touch. Miguel was making bootleg Louis Vuitton for some Japanese customers, and Milo helped him collect contacts. Miguel came from the streets, and he returned to the streets. One day Kazo called Milo, said, "Hey 'Lo man, how's it going? D'you hear Miguel's been shot?" That body – young fluid burning with life – was gone. He was here. Then gone.

****

Back home, in East Village, life with Hitomi was happy. He loved her. They had started to think about having a child. At first, he said, "Maybe." Later, he said Yes. Hitomi told him,

"You can't have only one child. You've got to have two, close together."

He believed in her more than in anyone. It didn't cross his mind that she couldn't magic up two children, one after the other.

He was working, a lot. There was never much money, it was constantly ploughed back into their business, or else spent to make music. It didn't matter. He felt safe. After returning from Tokyo, the dancers were galvanised into making a group. They called themselves Zhigge. After them, "Zhigge" became the latest slang on the streets for looking fresh. They knew a young guy who was just starting out, beginning to make music. His name was Salaam Remi. Salaam seemed to come from a wealthier family than the Black guys Miles had met in America up until then. He had a studio in a block that was predominantly white. He had a warmth and was genteel. He was, already, about music and the making of it. Zhigge wanted to work with Salaam and with Milo, whose beats they had heard back at Milo's crib, so they came together and made a record. It was Salaam's debut, in the sense that it was his first full production. Milo was surfing on nothing, here.

He was going from the ground up. In a dark studio, surrounded by Black American hip-hop heads, making music. They recorded an album. One tune Milo made on it was Harlem.

It was as if he were sending a letter to the future: Gonna take you uptown, baby. To Harlem.

****

He rode through the city, it was autumn. There was a downpour, briefly, the rain sounding like waves hitting shingle. He rode a long way, into Central Park. There in the arc of his vision, were trees in blocks of brown, then sudden strokes of incandescent red and yellow. The smell of autumn, of gentle decomposition, earth and smoke coming from some invisible place, reminded him of Bristol. He sat on a bench. He thought of his child. Sometimes, he would call Nicky's home. Nicky would be in his ear. First, with a lot to say, the checkpoint between him and their child. She could be friendly or passively aggressive, chatty or guilt-inducing. She had no notion that he had so little money, that he called to speak with his child, not her – that his coins were literally running out. So he would listen, unsure of how to curb her. Her speech felt like a physical pressure applied to his chest. Then his child's voice would come into the ether, and how can such a disincarnate notion as a voice down a phone line feel so real? Yet here it was, the baby sweetness, the always renewed novelty for the child at hearing this man, this dad. These occasional phone calls were now the sum of his parenting.

He thought, fleetingly, of his mother. He tried to conjure up her face. Then he brought his father to the forefront of his mind. He had never done this before, placed them together. His mother and his father. The people who made him. There was nothing. No feeling, no reminiscence. Right in his line of vision, were cherry trees with leaves heated to crimson. He watched a man and his baseball-capped spindly son make their way between the trees, towards the practice fields. He let Central Park take over, he couldn't think. He had no emotions to link to words, or maybe the other way around. A woman ran by, her sneakers patting the ground. Milo got up then, and began the ride home.

****

Nu Groove was a record label based in New York, the first label that Milo connected with. It was owned by Frank Mendes, and his wife, Karen Kahn. Frank hooked Milo up with the other labels in New York and New Jersey, there was no rivalry from one company to the next. Most of these record label owners had come up through Larry Levan's nights at Paradise Garage, or Dave Mancuso's parties and the like. They were disciples from the New York underground club scene and, just as underground dwellers in the animal kingdom do, they could feel vibrations, movement, so the process of developing parties into labels was an organic one. Clubbers who hung out together turned their nights into musical anthologies. Many people – record store owners, established DJs and DJ newbies trying to come up – knocked on the doors of those record labels, asking for promos. These were white-label vinyls, not for re-sale, but destined for the biggest DJ's across the country to play, in order to send the feedback of their respected audience. Many people walked back down the stairs with bags as light as when they had gone up. Milo's advantage may have stemmed from his accent, still resoundingly English, or again, that he represented a store in economically booming Japan. Whatever it was, Frank let him in.

Milo never stopped making music. At this point in his life, relatively isolated as an artist, experimenting, and green to independent production work, his songs were basic and rough. The sound was raw as it maybe had been in clubs six or seven years before. As a DJ, he had played a couple of records of this kind of quality, tunes like *FASG* by Dem Niggas, or *Can't Stop* by Plez. He was pretty confident he could put the music he was making out there. He pressed up a few promo copies. *Ruff Disco Volume One*, was his first release, under the name of Nature Boy. Frank was friends with Tony Humphries, and Tony Humphries was a house DJ revered by Wild Bunch. A while back, Milo had given a copy of the promo to Frank. Then, weeks later, Frank said, casually, swilling coffee round in a Styrofoam cup, "Hey man, I gave your record to Tony. He really likes it." It was a childlike thrill to hear that, it was enough for Milo.

When Milo's first track was released, he was happy, happy to have reached his goal, which had been to make music, independent of record companies or anyone else, in America. He didn't need more in terms of satisfaction, this alone was good. One afternoon he was in his crib, taping another Tony Humphries show. He would do this routinely: press 'record' then sometimes go out for the night, into the clubs, to see what was new. The next afternoon, he would duplicate a copy of the Tony Humphries show for himself, listening and all the while working, invoicing or boxing up products for Japan. This time, he had stayed in the room and sat, listening to the show live, watching the sky, lazy golden clouds, behind the grid of the security bars. Humphries' show on Kiss FM, Kiss at the time was one of the biggest and most influential Black radio stations in New York, quite possibly in America, for the audience span it reached. Record companies, majors and independents, inundated him with their promos and even their reels. Tony would make a learned selection, then entertain his cult-like following for two hours. Milo had stopped his day, just for this. To the Black community, this part of each weekend was like Christmas, Tony was Santa throwing out gifts for them. A song came on – Michael Watford, a hot new artist who had been getting a lot of attention in recent weeks. He was a vocalist Milo loved.

As the song came close to the end, Tony started to mix the next track underneath as Watford's vocals remained. Milo looked at the radio, as if for an answer. For a few seconds he thought somebody had used the same sample as he had, on his own release. Then Milo recognised the texture of the song, recognised, with amazement, his own signature and all the while Tony Humphries was working the tracks, and all the while Michael Watford was still singing. Milo's heart skipped. *The Living Groove* from his *Ruff Disco* release swelled, then took the lead, Tony Humphries masterfully blending the two. This was so far beyond any expectation he had had, fresh off the boat from England. As much as he had never been looking for adulation or attention, it did feel good to be part of this community. It felt even beyond that: his work had been given the seal of approval by one of his heroes. It was a momentous occasion, it was almost unbelievable to him. This was his own, private, award ceremony, and he received his spiritual prize alone, in a small and dusty East Village room.

CHAPTER THIRTY-TWO

TILL LOVES TOUCHES YOUR LIFE

Their son was born in December. Hitomi hadn't fallen pregnant easily. There had been trips to a doctor, Japanese, who seemed less concerned about Hitomi's age – she was already thirty-six, making her fall into the unfortunately named category of elderly primigravida – and more about Milo's gappy sperm count. He made adjustments to his diet, and one day it happened, a life began to bud. He remembers his excitement. He remembers his fear, all through the pregnancy, a dark corner in an otherwise sunshiny room. He was in a state of suspension, waiting for something to go wrong. Because this, happiness, this, life being okay, being normal, was something that he had yet to experience and it felt like wearing a jacket five sizes too big. Where was the catch?

He sees Hitomi in his mind's eye. It is an ante-natal class. It's a big room, functional, white. There are only Japanese couples there, all sat on the floor, the women forming an inner circle, the men behind. Everything that is spoken is in Japanese. Hitomi turns, tells him the important things, tells him what he needs to know. It is calm in the room, there is a bright, clear feeling. Hidden in the tight scoops of belly are secret lives, new souls. They are here, too. Hitomi is smiling. She turns to him. Her eyes shine. She wears a soft grey roll-neck sweater, that is how he remembers her, pregnant. Sat quietly, studious, dove grey.

One day, Hitomi said those modern day and time-honoured words, "We need to go to the hospital, the baby's coming." There was the labour:

long, hard. He stayed by her, trying to follow every instruction he was given, absolutely subservient to the matter in hand. It was hard for him to watch her pain, to watch it fully, not to look away. To witness womanhood, an aspect of it, that is so brutal, so fierce, so actually virile. The child was born. He was a big baby, with a thatch of night-black hair. Milo was transfixed. They gave him the baby, placed him in his arms. Milo began to cry. To shake with tears, to sob. He hadn't cried since he was thirteen, in the front room at the children's home in Hartcliffe. He was weeping so hard, so unstoppably, that the nurses began to cry. Hitomi was crying, the whole room was caught up in this emotion: unchallengeable and pure. For weeks after his son's birth, he would well up, and every time these tears, though surprising, brought an unfamiliar feeling of peace.

****

Life was ticking over. DJ's Choice was up and running. Milo's days had more structure. The promo distribution companies he worked with were mostly around Times Square in those days, and businesses like Sony and Warner had headquarters there. Visually, Times Square was an assault of neons and billboards, hookers and hustlers, screaming for your eye, and for your patronage. Limos would pull up and pull away, leaving in their wake Guccied rappers, Puffy or Biggie, down to do business with their labels. It was a head-on collision of the needy and the made, neither taking any notice of the other. If he was down there around lunchtime, Milo would stop in a video arcade, and empty his mind. He played a game called *Virtua Fighter*, which was the most realistic martial arts game around. The game could be played alone, or by two players, and men would queue up their quarters on the ledge of the machine, and wait their turn. Just like the surrounding sex shops, the arcade brought in a wildly diverse cross-section of New York men: delivery boys and suited traders, Mexican guys around a *Virtua Striker* soccer game, Black and Hispanic guys on the fight games. Milo was getting a good level on *Virtua Fighter*. Occasionally, a Japanese salaryman came over to play him, a big guy with an expressionless face. Milo would be firing every neurone in his brain, to try and put a beating on this opponent, but he couldn't even touch him. There was never any accolade, never any eye contact. The Japanese man would come next to him, beat the shit out of him in thirty seconds flat, then stand silently waiting for his next victim.

The light in the city that afternoon was dazzling, twinkling. Fingers of sunshine filtered through the massive buildings on Broadway, picking out sleazy details: a neon silhouette above a strip joint; the magazine covers layered over a crackhead, who dozed in a doorway. Milo was in the arcade, wrestling the with fighting game alone. A hood guy came in, Milo had played him before, and their gaming powers were in a kind of arm lock. Milo had been on a winning streak, about to bring in a win and wanted to continue alone, but the dude silently put down his dimes and the fight was on. They went through a few rounds until they reached sudden death. The guy was attacking, and Milo blocking every strike. Both of them fixing the screen, the tension between them real. The guy slipped up, for a second, and Milo struck him. "Yes!" he boomed, fist punching the air.

The guy kissed his teeth, "Man, don't fucking shout in my ear." He had a look on his face, a look Milo had seen so many times, in his football years, in jail – the guy wanted to fight for real. It made Milo laugh out loud.

One day, Milo was in there, in the arcade, it was a regular day, plain weather, ordinary business. He was playing by himself, against the machine. He was losing. That was when you welcomed another player, their dimes prolonging the match. A Black man strolled over, Milo knew him, he was a sharp player. He reminded him a little of Gregory Hines, that kind of face, that kind of grace. Milo had wondered about him, about how he had got so agile on this game, when he was clearly a man who had a lot going on, businesswise. They played together for a while, him beating Milo more often than not. He asked Milo, "Where's that accent from?" Then, "So what is it you do?" And they struck up a conversation, something Milo rarely did with strangers. Their talk ambled and the man told him he was on his way to L.A. They wondered who they might have in common. After a while, the man said, "I could help get you a job on the radio there. If you're interested. You have a great voice for it." Milo was curious, and the exchange deepened. "I'm Stevie Wonder's personal manager," the man explained.

There was absolutely a blank right there, a few missed beats. Milo stopped playing, turned to him, mid game.

"You have got to be kidding me. That's my fucking hero, right there."

"I'll tell him that, man. I'll tell Stevie you said that," he said with a smile.

The offer of a job on the radio had been so untimely in Milo's life. Just as he was getting a small, balanced routine going in New York, he didn't feel capable of upping sticks to LA.

Years later, in an eerily empty airport in Fort Myers, he was returning from a break with Hitomi and the children. They were occupying a row of chairs in a corridor. There was silence, except for the occasional airplane taking off and the prattle of a TV screen hooked up high. Suddenly, his younger son said, "Hey, there's Stevie Wonder." Milo, arms crossed, feet stretched out before him, almost nodding off, opened an eye, looked at the screen.

"Where?" His son prodded him, then pointed. Down the corridor. There was Stevie Wonder, great like a Soviet statue, walking, holding the arcade friend's arm.

"Fucking what? I know that guy, I know the guy with him!"

As they approached, Milo jumped up and the arcade guy smiled, a warm smile, "Stevie, this is one of your greatest fans, right here."

Stevie said, "Hey, man, how you doin'?"

Milo could barely get the words out: thanks, love, joy.

As his plane cruised through the night, the low-pitch babbling of the airflow sending the entire cabin to sleep, Milo, his head resting against the window, was smiling. He had met Stevie Wonder. That is all.

CHAPTER THIRTY-THREE

TOO REAL TO LIVE A LIE

It is 1994. He is at JFK airport. In Arrivals. He's standing back. There is the trick done by the automatic doors. They close behind an incoming drift of travellers, then reopen. Like magicians who speed change, the faces coming through switch from Asian to European, the clothes from neat and muted, to billowing and creased. With each unveiling, you travel, yourself, as a visitor, around the world.

In an arrival of people, mostly white and tall, there is a woman. She is an older lady, she wears her hair in a tidy afro. She looks around, wide-eyed. She sees Milo, and her head bows a little, she is smiling. He walks to her. They don't touch.

"Hello, mum," he says, smiling back, "how was your trip?"

Betty visited Milo in New York when his son was a baby. She stepped into his life, for the first time in twenty years.

It was early morning, a Saturday. Milo was sat on the floor, in the front room, his baby crawling around. They played a game, Milo pinning the toes of his son's onesie down so that he couldn't crawl away. It made the baby laugh. Betty came from the kitchen, in a dressing gown with two cups of tea and sat down. They watched the baby together and chatted about this and that, about nothing in particular. The TV was on, and Betty was fascinated by the brazen American commercials. The baby crawled to his grandmother and looked up at her. She seemed to study him, and they held each other's gaze. Then Betty looked over to Milo, nodded, smiled a faraway smile. Faded, it's a faded memory, there was everything in her smile, their tenuous love caught between the lines bracketing her sad mouth.

Hitomi had arranged a thoughtful sequence of things for Betty to do in New York. Her own parents had died, so she wanted this link, for her son, to the previous generation. The first Saturday afternoon, Milo took Betty to Harlem. Betty, who had been a housewife, a nurse, a factory worker, a single mother. Betty, who had been strong-bodied and joyous and reflective. Betty, who had lost her children, had seen her life cave in and had been to a mental institution had also been this: a Black activist, probably the most vocal female for Black human rights in St Paul's in the sixties. She was well-read, she had worked out on her own parts of the collective history of Black people in Britain. Perhaps retracing the upside-down story, from herself back across the waters to the West Coast of Africa helped her to understand the chaos and the grief that she had been handed as an opening gambit.

Betty loved Harlem. She stopped at every book stand, lifting books, getting out her reading glasses and examining the back covers. She seemed lost in thought, in no hurry. Her eyes were on the life here, imprinting it within herself. All these purposeful, Black New Yorkers, this life that seemed self-sufficient, that existed without the slack-stomached whiteocracy that ruled the land. She stared openly at the men and women she passed in the street. Seeing how they wore their Blackness, the myriad interpretations of their ancestry, forming tribes of a kind: the men in Ghanian robes beneath fat North Face anoraks, the hip-hop kids mixing their western labels with clothes cut from kente cloth, the men and women whose hair was natural, African, in dreadlocks growing in these crazy, beautiful, free ways. This she took in, and must have wondered how it felt to be from here. At once a hundred-thousand miles from your homeland and yet from a place that was defined, that was Black, that had a history, a future and a sense of purpose. She and Milo passed a couple of teenage girls. They had a cockiness, a body language that was unseen in Bristol. The girls laughed as they reached Betty, laughed at her.

"Mum, you can't stare at people here, do you know what I mean? It isn't like in England. You got to cut that out." He said it kindly.

They went to Chelsea, in Manhattan. At the time it was quite an affluent area, with a sizeable gay community. It was predominantly white. The sky was darkening, taking on a dusky New York pink. They were walking along the street, just him and her, and there was no one around, except some kids playing football in the road. They were about seven or eight-years-old. Super Bowl was pending, it was early February. They were little Jewish boys, wearing kippahs and New York Giants vests over their coats. One of the boys caught the ball and ran with it, towards them, yelling Yeah! and laughing. When he reached them, in a celebratory burst, he grabbed Milo by the hand and hit him with a high five, then ran off again, leaving this man and his mother surprised and laughing, too. These are snapshots that Milo has of those days with Betty, when for all the world they were just a mother and son, wandering through New York City. The great gap in their relationship, all the years without each other, quietly shadowed them. To see a small New York boy running, full of joy, full of trust, down a dusky street – the fingers of time must have caught Betty, tugged at her: remember? Do you remember, many years ago, when you were a young woman in the ghetto? When you made saltfish and ackee for Donovan and you had children? Little children. And Milo was a bright light, a sturdy boy, who would run down East Grove to the bomb site, who would run everywhere, just as the creatures of the forest do, free still, green still? Do you remember?

One late afternoon, Milo and Hitomi took Betty down to the Hudson River, to a helicopter launch pad, where tourists queued up for, "A View of Manhattan like a Bird." Neither Milo or Hitomi had ever flown in a helicopter, it simply seemed the golden gift for a visitor, it was the best they could think of. Betty only realised before take-off that she was going up alone. She was a little scared. It was the end of the day and that skyline, probably the most iconic on Earth, lay like a sleeping giant whose nervous system is illustrated in a million lights. Betty's helicopter rose, with the vertical ascension of the Madonna, then veered away. From where they stood, Milo and Hitomi saw the beetle-like craft make a graceful curve and fly, on and out, right between the Twin Towers before disappearing.

There was no before and after to Betty's visit. Milo's view of her, Betty the mother, Betty the woman, was still a partial portrait. As a teenager and young man, he had shut down his love for her completely. He had seen her as an idiot, as absolutely worthless. He had left England for Japan, five or six years before, without glancing over his shoulder. The only connection that he would maintain, throughout the years after his departure, was with Wild Bunch, one or other of them, sometimes all of them, but never none of them. They were the only people he ever gave his trust to, as a young man in Bristol. There was no end to Wild Bunch in Milo's mind, they were his family, but by the late eighties the time had come for all of them to move on, yet without closing their story down. Gee and D had wanted to get a little band together and that's what they did. Nellee had his own plans. They were all trying to figure out what to do next. Milo had cut himself loose. In Daikanyama, in small rented rooms, he had had a lot of time to think. He made a decision not to go back to England, because what he had left behind, aside from Wild Bunch, was nothingness. His mother was the figurehead of that emotion.

Over time, he had started, tentatively, to dare to think a little differently. It was in New York that he began to understand his fate as being within a bigger story, a historical one. He was drawn to Harlem, to its very heart. This was where the rivers of his fathers' met. Men and women had left messages in confluent songs and stories. They had left words in print, between the covers of pamphlets sold on stands in Harlem that flew African flags. When Betty came to visit, Milo saw the guilt on her. Each time she looked at her son, it was there, she couldn't shake it. Milo could hold that gaze. Let's face it, mum, I should be in jail. In jail, in and out of jail. That was what I was set up for. One more Black man caged. It didn't happen. I got away. I have built a little something for myself.

He didn't want her to feel bad, to feel this dreadful shame. Somewhere, in the books that they picked over together one sunny afternoon on 125th Street and on the tapes that Milo played in the background in his crib, as his mother made tea, were the answers. He and his mother, stood side by side, had a wall of constraint between them and a history of neglect, abuse and rejection etched in their palms, sequenced in their souls. At that point in his life, Milo was only just starting to fit together his story with Betty, with Charlie, with Donovan. With the Windrush generation and with Africa. He had only come so far in his understanding of geopolitics and in his understanding of the human condition. It would take more time, more knowledge, for the day to come when he would give Betty his absolution. All around them in the small New York apartment were the writings, like needles and thread, that would sew, stitch after stitch, the rift between them.

When Betty visited New York, Milo took her into its African core. He could have taken her to the Jewish quarter, to Jewish museums and certainly would have, later. This first visit, though, was Black. Milo took Betty to an African restaurant in Chelsea. It was a simple place with an elderly Nigerian woman in the kitchen. Betty and Milo never spoke about anything concerning their family. They had never spoken about Milo's life in care. They had not alluded to family since they lived together on East Grove. In this African restaurant, Betty began, quite unexpectedly, to open up. She talked about her father, she called him Mbakwe. She spoke about the Kru people of his lineage. It was the first time that Milo felt her, felt what she was trying to impart: that she had been raised by her father, only her father. That she was the daughter of an African man before being the child of a white kingdom.

*****

A little more than a year after his first son's birth, a second baby boy came along. There was less worry. Maybe the journey made once before helped, the same doctor, and then the same rush of euphoria upon holding his new son. It was a joyous time in his life, this boy made him feel complete. Their second child was full of spirit and raging for his independence, right from the start. Milo saw himself reflected in this boy, although a sharper, brighter version of himself. Milo had stopped making records, there was no time for that anymore. For the next few years, his life was that of a more regular man: keeping the export business going, raising his sons. He has very few memories of this period. There is a French saying that happy people have no stories, maybe that was it. He had had to stop releasing his own material, as it was time-consuming and involved putting money upfront. His focus was on what paid the rent, and that was the export business. His focus, mostly, was on being a father, and that he was, a New Man, really, before the term was coined. He did as much for his sons as their mother.

He was still working with a collective of rappers, Harlem High. They were members of Zhigge, and other rappers, from the same block. There was Kinny still, Chauncey and Fruquan. There was Spinner, he came in a little later. He was older than the others, short and chunky. Milo says, "Man, that brother was incredible." He knew very little about Spinner. Just that he was from the same Metro North part of Harlem's East Side as the rest of the crew.

This was when, out of the blue, Bristol, Milo's past, something as familiar as Digestive biscuits, or the football results being read on BBC 1 on a Saturday afternoon, or drizzle, came back to him. Tricky. Of all of the Wild Bunch, none could have been closer to his childhood than him. Tricky reappeared in Milo's life when Tricky was on fire. Milo says of Tricky's first album, *Maxinquaye*, that it absolutely blew him away, that it is a musical jewel, one of the heaviest British albums ever. Tricky reappeared in Milo's life, having moved to New York. He and Milo hooked up again. For Milo's sons, this was the only person from their father's past that they would ever really know over a period of time. Milo was happy for Tricky's presence.

Here's an anecdote, it has such Hartcliffe overtones: Tricky wanted to buy a house, and he and Milo visited one in a gated community in Orange County, New Jersey. A place where other music-makers lived. They walked around, Tricky interested. Milo said, "You can't live here. You ain't got a car. How are you going to get to the shops, man?"

Tricky shrugged, "Dunno. Hire a cab." Later, Marlow came to visit, and her opening line on arriving in the house was, "How am I going to get to the shops, Adrian? What are you trying to do, starve me?"

Milo introduced Tricky to the guys from Harlem High, they hit it off right away. Tricky had started a label, Milo was possibly the first artist he signed. Tricky wanted to work with Harlem High and he and his manager asked Milo what kind of budget he needed to record a few tracks with them. Milo presented the quote, which the manager thought excessive, and definitely above the going rate, but Milo felt it was deserved. So, it was paid. The guys from Harlem High were happy with this, it was a lot of money to them. They had done their job, it was good stuff. Spinner was paid. He bought a gun. A week later, Spinner was dead. Milo heard then that Spinner had had a long-standing beef with a man from the area. Spinner had bought a burner, the other guy had a burner. They must have just gone at it.

Milo had never seen the corpse of someone that he cared about. In a church in Harlem, resting on velvet in an open casket, he looked at Spinner. Milo only knew this capsule of men from Harlem, and each one of them had talent. Spinner here, in eternal rest, had more talent than most rappers who were was out there, front-lining, at the time. So, multiply it, multiply the talent, the possibilities, per building, per block, per Black neighbourhood. But this was Harlem, and things could go left in a split second. You are here.

Bam bam. You are gone. Milo stood back, as Spinner's family grieved. It made him think about time, about the fact we none of us can know whether the cursor is near the middle, or just heartbeats from the end.

****

They had moved from the squatty address in East Village during Hitomi's first pregnancy, to a more salubrious place a block away. For a long time now, Harlem had been tugging Milo to it. He went there often, to visit his friends and do business, so when he had taken Betty, he had known what she would see. What he felt for the neighbourhood, Black Mecca, was love, it was that simple. Kazo told Milo of a new building, on 125th Street, just near completion, with a place for them if they wanted. It was a lucky day. They had to wait, to move from one place with their two small boys, to this new address. But the switch from their old apartment to the new one would see them homeless for a few weeks. With two toddlers in New York, it was a problem. On the phone to Hiroshi, Milo talked about their plan and their dilemma. A few days later, without having been asked to, Hiroshi called them. He had found them somewhere to stay. It was friendship stepping from the shadows, so discreetly, lending a precious hand, then stepping back again.

Harlem at that point in time had the most soul in the Western world. Walking down 125th Street which would go on to be Milo's address for twenty-five years, there was no getting away from facts. The book sellers he had shown Betty were fiercely Afrocentric, lining the sidewalks, flying African Unity flags. The stands continued on, from the sidewalk into arcades, processionary, with still more wares: radicals selling videos of Farrakhan, Doctor Ben and John Henrik Clarke. The first time Milo went there, and came face to face with a life-size laminate of Rubin Stacy's lynching in Fort Lauderdale, he stopped dead. The laminate was hung from a beam and the breeze moved the image horribly, heartbreakingly. The white girl to the side looks up at the dead man, at his broken neck, his bowed head, and it is mirth on her face. Mirth. Behind her, grown men, white men; whose sadism is beyond the realms of the human experience, contemplate the scene casually. They are glad. It is horrific, the most horrific of images taken as a souvenir, a postcard from depravity. Along the streets of Harlem, this picture, and countless others showing the bestiality of the white man, served as a backdrop to Harlem life. Milo at first saw these stands and these sellers through an English man's eyes and was disturbed, as much by the pictures as by the way life bustled around them, unshaken. As time went by he understood that these pictures were integrated into the collective psyche of Black Americans, who were not apart from the images, distant observers, they were of them. The forefathers, in these sepia scenes of death remained in the present, a part of life in the heart of Harlem.

What Harlem had, too, was that it was self-supporting, like an independent state. The commerce there catered to the community. There was Dapper Dan, a gentlemen's tailor, by the Apollo. It was the number one place for hip-hop singers and stars to get their clothes made. A Mike Tyson or an LL Cool J might come by the shop with an idea – a leather Gucci suit or one in the pattern of Louis Vuitton – and Dapper Dan, with none of the means of a European fashion house but with skill and a certain amount of wizardry, could make it happen. It was hot-housing haute couture, making every fashion code bigger, flashier. It was bootleg taken to an artform. There were music shops and jazz clubs, food stalls and restaurants and these places were Black-on-Black, and mostly for the people of Harlem. Even the guy on the bookstand selling his Black power bibles was selling primarily to his neighbours.

In summer especially, there was a vibrancy. Harlem appeared red, that is the colour Milo remembers. Red beneath a hammering heat. The neighbourhood came alive, people out on the streets, music flowing from the windows of cribs and cars and shops. There was a sneaker, a high-top Air Force 1, in white, that would blossom, everyone had them, brand-spanking new, at the start of every summer season. People's feet dazzled, the dancing white was what the eye picked out in the afternoons that were corrugated by the deep heat of those Harlem summers.

It was here, in this neighbourhood, that an old guy selling tapes first asked Milo, "You heard of this man? Listen to him." Milo handed over a few bucks and the seller whose eyes were milky and sad, whose cheekbones stood out like pieces of flint, smiled, nodded. Milo, back in the privacy of his home studio, the magnetic tape running, listened as the story of all the fathers before him slowly unfolded. The tapes began at the start, and the start was Africa, its civilisations, its politics, its art and philosophy. The narrator, an African historian, had a rumbling bass voice. He took his time, "So sit down and listen. In the beginning was Africa."

Milo had returned to a life that was normal to him, that was like his childhood in St Paul's where he was a Black boy within a Black community. He was beginning to piece together an understanding of himself, as a man originating from Africa, shipwrecked in a white world. He would have made this move, to Harlem, married or not, a father or not. His younger sons were to grow up Harlem boys and that was a choice. Deep inside it felt like he was placing them within a magic ring of fire, that no predator could break through. Harlem would teach them without even needing words to put the fire out when they were ready, giving them a foundation as to their identity. Wherever they went – and they did travel out of Harlem, to schools on the Lower East Side, for example – the answers to those difficult questions about race were inside them, as a feeling rather than as rhetoric.

He came to realise what four-hundred years of relentless persecution meant. You would not expect a single soul to have intact mental health being born Black, in America, but Harlem was the most conscious of places. Of course, there was crime, there were drugs, there were crazy ladies and strung-out men. How could there not be? Yet here was the place known throughout the Black diaspora as being the most forward-thinking and insubordinate in the struggle against the choke-hold that is white supremacy.

Those were the honeymoon years, for Milo, a honeymoon that lasted a long time until, gradually, Harlem changed. From without. Its dangerously advantageous position on the map of New York City left its beating heart exposed. Over three decades, Milo watched this beloved neighbourhood shrink, as buildings were emptied, then left vacant, then were reconfigured for other people, people who weren't Black. With every scrape of the hungry fingers of a digger that removed a jazz club from where music had flowered, with every hard-hatted architect who moved earnestly through a project tenement, imagining more light here, and greater space for the next wave of occupants – not only whiter, but richer – with every adjustment made by that sharp and clever pencil, something as vital to the world as rain or night, was being dismantled. Milo had seen how money – extreme wealth and the need for it – makes places, people and institutions absolutely soulless. He had seen it in London when all the punk clubs got bought out, and again in Notting Hill. He saw it in downtown New York in The village, when the legendary clubs folded to be replaced by condos. Then he saw it in Harlem, creeping in. Watching Harlem bulldozed by people who had no idea what they were destroying crushed him.

Milo felt Harlem fading and knew that if Harlem were to disappear forever, then the world would be without whatever it is that takes the pain away.

Chapter Thirty-Four

THE SILENCE THAT YOU KEEP

He made a connection one day, maybe the most profound musical connection in his life. He had been working in a studio, Pro Jam, on 145th Street and Amsterdam, on the verge of Black and Spanish Harlem. He was making hip-hop music at that time, and he would switch, from hip-hop to house and back again, but never run the two together, his brain preferring to be immersed in just one genre. He worked with the studio engineer, Greg, who knew many people on the scene and was connected to a lot of session musicians from the seventies. It was cold in the studio. They were waiting for a musician to arrive. Their conversation ambled and the name Gil Scott-Heron came up. When he was young, in his Wild Bunch days, he, or the crew, had owned a Gil Scott-Heron record, which led Milo to the radical artists, The Last Poets. Their poetry, which was perhaps the most embryonic form of rap, had an unrefined honesty, a spell binding intelligence, that blew Milo's mind. Greg was eating, he wiped his mouth with a paper napkin. "You can see Gil Scott-Heron down on the streets some nights," he said nodding towards the window, "It's where he cops his heroin."

Milo frowned, "What do you mean? That's where he buys heroin?"

"Yeah, look out the window, he might be there now."

Milo went to the window. He had a slanted view of a straggle of addicts and one of them was indeed Gil Scott-Heron. Milo, in disbelief, ran out of the studio, down the stairs, with no plan. He looked around, but Gil Scott-

Heron was gone. Milo went into a convenience store, bought something to eat and wandered out again. On the sidewalk, he came face to face with the man himself. Milo was profoundly shocked. A musician that gifted, of that intellect, whose liquid eyes stared his way in dull ecstasy, not really at Milo, but at some fourth and lonely dimension. Milo would learn over time that heroin was endemic to the world of Black music, especially jazz, almost as though the intensity of feeling needed to make that kind of music was too hard to bear without a shot of oblivion.

Back upstairs, the musician they were expecting showed up. He was Fred McFarlane. He had come by to play some keyboards on one of Milo's tracks. Greg had said, "You know, Fred was in D-Train?" Milo was impressed. That had been a big group for Wild Bunch. It turned out Fred had made *Show Me Love* and the bomb that is *Somebody Else's Guy*. He was Madonna's main keyboard player during her Shep Pettibone production years, he was a big name. Unbelievably, to Milo, like many other brilliant musicians of that era, Fred would play on Grammy-winning records, but would sometimes round out the month's earnings putting down keyboards for underground artists, like him. Fred knew hundreds of musicians across the Tri-state area. When Milo needed an instrumental on his songs, he would go to Fred's basement studio in New Jersey and play them to him. Fred would sit in studious silence, listening to the tunes. Then he would sit up, saying with a bloodhound's sense of direction, "I'll get such-and-such guy on track two, to put in a sax. This other guy would be great on track five, on flute. I'll do you some keyboards on one and on five, too." Milo always went to the studio knowing which instrument he needed for each track, but Fred made the home run, bringing a musician able to sublimate the score.

For the men whom Fred brought into the studio, Milo's music was a different canvas to their usual work. All of them were used to working with major recording stars, but all of them continued to work with brothers, with sisters, cash in hand, no middleman. It was humbling for Milo to have men like them, legends, most of them a generation older, collaborating with him. It gave his work another depth. When they had finished recording, they would stay in the studio awhile, shooting the breeze. Milo paid them, they would count out their dollar bills, and each would peel off a few notes for Fred, his back-hander for getting them work. This is where Black solidarity (and Black musicians have got to be one of the most exploited categories of workers ever) and Black art met. Making a little music, sharing your wage.

Spending many, many afternoons and nights with Fred was the beginning of a profound change in Milo. Fred was a churchgoer, hired to do the acoustics, or play keyboards in churches across America. Around Harlem, on a Sunday morning, some of the heaviest bass players, the earthiest soul singers on this planet welcomed the congregations in. The musicians Milo met had church on a Sunday and the other days of the week... Milo smiles... they had life, you know, other stuff. Milo had no regard whatsoever for religion at that point, he found it incomprehensible that a Black person would worship at a white altar. Slowly, his understanding grew. Church was one of things that had helped Black Americans survive slavery and its residual effects. It was the only time they could congregate and exchange information; it was where they spread their news. Black people may well have crumbled into the nothingness that was intended for them after abolition, were it not for Sunday mornings, when they could see and touch each other, when they could give each other the strength to carry on. One day Fred asked Milo, "Do you go to church?"

"Nah. I'm not a religious person."

Fred paused, then said, "I get that. If you ain't lost, you don't need to follow, right?"

But Milo had been lost. An errant soul, a stray. Until he came to live in Harlem, he had felt no attachment to any place, to few people and could not see that anyone would feel attachment to him. Fred talked about all kinds of things, and, in the jumble of wisdom and anecdotes and advice, Milo found the answers to the questions he had been unable to construct. He began to think about his child in England. He began to see that he was a fatherless Black child who had engendered a fatherless Black child, and this was part of Black history: the removal of the Black man from the home.

The seeds of radical thought were planted by his mother when he and his siblings were very young, it was almost subconsciousness. Things that he saw, growing up, things that were unfair. Things that he did not like. He was waiting for the truth to be spoken. In jail, he had read Malcolm X, he learned about the Soledad brothers, he read H Rap Brown, *Die Nigger Die*. He was looking for himself. The first words he rapped on *Friends And Countrymen*, were his own lyrics, he and 3D rhyming: *Afro, albino, Black or Puerto Rico, welcome to the birth of the new rap negro...People call me Black, but my skin is brown, I don't care because my soul is blacker.*

Then Public Enemy came and it was a bombshell. They vocalised in the rawest manner, no compromise: we want this to fucking end. Decades on, and Fred, his stories, the breadth of his experience, the gentleness of his soul, seemed to smooth everything out flat before Milo, he could see the picture now, all of it.

Fred let Milo into his inner circle. Each summer, Fred held a party in his father's back garden, in Inglewood. His father had been a big player on the jazz scene. That first summer of their friendship, Fred invited Milo to the summer garden party. The neighbourhood was full of old jazz cats and soul singers. George Benson lived down the road, as did Dizzy Gillespie. Milo has this memory, perfect as a painting by a great master.

He was in Fred's garden. It was a sultry summer's afternoon. The garden was shaded by tall trees, their branches banks of emerald. There was a little stage, some friends were playing, jazz filled the garden. Black musicians, men and women, were laughing, talking, sitting in the shade. Fried chicken was being served, there was a trestle table laden with soul food. Milo wandered, through the guests, with a plate of food and a smile. The smell of the food was divine. Fred introduced Milo to his father, who was seated, "Hello, Mr McFarlane," Milo said, almost bowing, "It's so nice to meet you, thank you so much for inviting me."

The sound of a couple saxophones billowed lazily and a phrase got Milo's attention, it stopped him, it almost hurt, it was so graceful. The sax player hit another phrase, again, beauteous, this was no accidental magic. Milo looked to see who was playing, he was a white man, one of only a few white men present. Milo said to Fred, "Fred, that player is incredible."

And Fred said, "Yeah, that's Harry Connick's saxophonist. I can get him for you, if you like. He'll do it within your budget, no problem. You have to catch him though, he's always on tour."

Milo sat on his own, eating. He sat, watching, taking it in. He sat listening to the very fine music, all afternoon. The smile never left his face. There are as many Americas as there are people to describe them. This America here, caught in a dreamy afternoon in Fred's back garden, is an America that was good, that was right.

****

At one point, in the late nineties, Milo weighed two-hundred-and-forty pounds of solid muscle. He was working out and carrying the bulk beneath loose clothing, discernible but not on display.

Because his life was in Harlem.

One time, he had a bullet shoot past his ear like a hot bee, within a millimetre of killing him, studding his front door.

One time, he had a gun pulled on him, whilst marooned on black ice, his car and his assailants' butted up against each other, their owners figuring out whether the collision (Milo's car cut up at an intersection by two ghetto brothers), was worth losing a life over.

One time, he went to his window curious at the commotion down there: a dog barking non-stop. It was a pit bull, running round the street with its owner, a Puerto Rican guy high as a kite. The neighbours down on the stoop were looking on. They were just hanging there, it was a nice afternoon. Then a man grabbed the Puerto Rican, said, "You got to put your fucking dog on a leash, man, I got kids down here." As he spoke the dog came for him, and the man, still with the Puerto Rican in his grip, pulled a gun and shot the dog.

The people in the street let up a collective, "Woah". The dog's bark went up an octave and it ran off, in a whimpering daze.

This is how it was. Life could leave you any time, ready or not.

Washington, D.C., 1995

They: Milo, Kinny, Kazo, Wayne and Theo were in a car on Interstate 95, heading to Washington, DC. It was late morning, forty degrees Fahrenheit. The sky was a vigorous blue. Milo drove. They listened to a tape of the Stretch Armstrong show. Every car and every bus driving in their direction was carrying Black men. The closer they got to Washington, the more there were. They reached the city around midday. There were buses, vans, cars parked in every imaginable space. Men climbed down the steps of coaches, holding plastic bags containing their lunch. Men closed their car doors and looked around. The faces held pride and seriousness. Milo wondered if he would ever find his own car again. Washington seemed as though a mighty wave had crashed on its shores, washing up tin shells from many seas, everywhere your eye could travel. There was a calm amongst the men. The overriding majority seemed to be working class, simply dressed, quiet in their demeanour. Milo rounded a corner. The National Mall revealed itself. It took his breath away. He was reflected in this infinite hall of mirrors, by thousands upon thousands of Black men, hundreds of thousands of Black men, a million Black men. Their collective energy had a cosmic quality. They had dignity, their heads upturned, their faces showing deep concentration, listening, listening, listening to the orators who one after another, with gospel cadence, with lyrical genius and with unflinching clarity spoke to their brothers.

Minister Louis Farrakhan took the podium. He stood in the bright sunshine, he wore a bow tie. He looked out upon the greatest gathering of Black men that America had ever seen, and these men looked back at him with a desperate sense of expectancy. They listened to Farrakhan and the venerable speakers present – Rosa Parks, Martin Luther King III, Maya Angelou, Dr. Cornel West, among many others – as though these were captains handing out life rafts on a rapidly capsizing vessel. The orators taking the stand one after the other spoke to their people, straight to their hearts. They addressed this river of men, stolen from Africa. A million men aiming a right fist to the clear American sky, like the arrows of a lost tribe. Milo was among them.

****

Back in New York, there was the repetitious comfort of family life. Saturday drives to the Japanese supermarket in New Jersey. At the book store named Kinakunya, Hitomi and the boys chose books. They would buy the Japanese food that stocked their cupboards. They would eat in the restaurant there. The boys ate noodles and took apart the clever little toys that they had just bought. There were Sundays in Central park with their beloved dog, Chi-Yo. His sons ran all over the grass, the dog bounding round them. There was coming out of his studio in the evening, catching a glimpse of his sons beyond the doorway, lying in dinosaur pyjamas in front of the TV, laughing their heads off at a cartoon. There was the absence of violence. There was faithfulness. What else? Being sat at the table, all four of them, eating Hitomi's noodles, the boys, hair in cane-rows, their small feet swinging from the chair, far from the floor. The boys, at the same table, with a comic book between them, reading it as they ate. A different table, in the same place; the boys, sullen, teenage, eating in silence. Or again, the boys, now nearly men, laughing uncontrollably, the elder son with his head in his hands, the younger son the funny guy. Hitomi and Milo pausing their meal, laughing too, until it subsided.

Chapter Thirty-Five

NATURE BOY

For a few years, to pay the rent, to save for the boys' schooling, Milo took a job as a driver. He drove a shuttle, doing the NYC-JFK/Newark/LaGuardia run for a local car hire company. He didn't have a name, just a number. Five-O-One. That's all he was ever called. He made journeys at night through thick snow, or in crazy New York peak time traffic. Journeys when every second of time counted, his passengers with their hair stood on end as he hit his foot to the board, and sped down the highway. He was just the chauffeur, the Black guy who pulled over on his break, listening to WFMU whilst eating his lunch.

There was a schizophrenic quality to his life. He was skivvying for the international travellers arriving at or leaving JFK, five days a week, but on the plus side, he was his own boss, choosing his own hours. He had never stopped working in music, one way or another. He toured with Tricky for European and US stints, he put out his own music with the Harlem High crew. Later, in 2010 as DJ Nature, he began Djing and releasing dance music again. So, he might be driving a miserable lady with tremor and hardly a thank you passing her lips, or some such person, from the airport in the afternoon. That same evening, he would be lost in a world of music, still umbilically connected to the minds and the hearts of those like him, travelling on sound alone, without a destination.

When he came back to the underground club scene as DJ Nature, it was an enlightenment. He had no following. It was unlike his Wild Bunch days. Down in the Dug Out, for instance, it had been a love affair between his crew and their following, they were friends with so many of them in real life, too. He never spoke of his connection to Bristol as DJ Nature. He was out there on his own.

Today, Milo DJs in select clubs all around the planet. He plays to music heads. He plays to clubbers who come to listen to music as a spiritual experience, just as some people go to church, or the mosque, or the temple. Milo still gets joy, forty years on, from watching party people free their minds from their bodies and dance.

****

In the middle of that swathe of time, was this…

His phone rang. Hitomi asked, "Where are you?"

"In the park, I'm with the dog."

"Have you seen the Twin Towers? I'm looking at them."

He could not see the towers, but in his mind's eye he could see Hitomi. She was working for a Japanese woman, downtown, who had just had a baby. Hitomi was helping with the adjustment, easing the mother into her new life. She was stood by the window, straight backed, the baby resting on her forearm. That's what he saw, in his mind.

"The tower has smoke coming out of it, like it's been hit, I can see a hole." She seemed to move the phone away, he heard fuzz, then the television. From beneath a cedar tree in the breeze, he could hear commotion through the phone line, from the television set, far away in the high-rise home. "Oh my god! Milo. A plane hit the tower."

He called his dog over and they walked back, the walk breaking to a jog, as around him he felt a surge in tension in the neighbourhood. Back home, he switched on the TV. Channel after channel was the same image, the smoking tower. You could feel the cameramen, you could feel the emotion. The frames moved, the lenses scanned, focusing in on the horror far up – horizontal banks of smoke – then backing out, a wide shot, the cubic mountain range, the raging fire. Suddenly a line, a bird, no too big, too quick, straight, silent, a plane, a plane fucking god almighty, surely not? An explosion that went around the world. The South Tower was struck. There is footage that the whole world has seen. Screaming. Holy cow, holy shit, holy crap. The incredulous voices of newscasters gabbling over newscasters. A report, a plane has hit the Pentagon. The sky is alive. The War of the Worlds.

At this point, right across the globe, human beings were riveted before screens. What is going to happen to those people in the tower blocks? Are they calling their loved ones, are they saying their prayers, are they saying goodbye? Will they die, with the world watching? With me watching?

At 09:59, the South Tower collapsed. Milo ran out of his home. Got on his bike. He cycled along 125th Street, through Harlem, getting to West Highway, an elevated road running along the Hudson River. There was a cycle path the length of the river bank that would take him downtown. Ordinarily, West Highway was a continuum of traffic, the cars making the sound of a never-ending ocean rush. On this day, 11 September 2001, West Highway was deserted. He could hear his tyres tracing along the tarmac, he could hear his own breathing. In the distance, he saw something headed north, on the southbound side of the road, towards him. He couldn't understand what it was. It should have been cars, it was only ever cars, breaking speed limits. Then he saw that it was a slow procession of people. Forty people, maybe fifty. He neared them. They occupied the highway, forming a group. They walked in absolute silence. They seemed to be office workers, the men wearing suits. Some carried briefcases. They stared straight ahead. They were monochrome. They were covered in ash, as if obliterated by a volcano, and resuscitated. He cycled on.

****

The junction of 11th Avenue and 34th Street was usually the busiest part of this road. There were still no cars. He stopped. Right the way down, to a disappearing point in the Godzilla of advancing grey clouds, were fire trucks, lined up side-by-side, a red river of loss. There was such chaos that, without realising, he was already beyond the barriers, into Chinatown. Then Soho. He got on to Canal Street, below a cordoned-off section. He pushed his bike. Every time he looked towards the towers, there was the explicit emptiness left by the South Tower that his eyes and his mind could not compute. The engine of the great powerhouse that is New York was dead. It was silence, only silence and ash.

He wonders, today, what he was doing there, why he made his way into a hell that others were running from. He remembers feeling the need to see for himself if this was real because, framed in his TV screen, it could have been an elaborate hoax live from LA, too outlandish a story to be true. He looked all around and felt what it is to be in the heart of desolation. Then fear took over. Maybe this was it. Maybe now that the whole world was watching, a bomb would whistle through the sky, obliterating all.

After ten minutes of being close enough to the felled buildings to smell the bitter air, he turned back home. He cycled, his brain working as hard as his legs. He felt deep sadness, thinking of all those thousands of workers, innocent people, caught in the crossfire of higher hate, who had gone to the towers that morning to pay their rent or to put food on their children's plates. Everybody understood, as soon as the second tower was struck, that this was a terrorist attack. For Milo, as a Black man, just as for many men and women in Harlem, the sight of the potent symbol that were those pride-of-America tower blocks collapsing, caused complex emotions. Pure patriotism would be the manifestation of some sort of Stockholm syndrome, when you are the descendent of an enslaved people. The loss of lives in such a grotesque and desolating manner was deeply disturbing, and yet.

There was a fatalism in his heart. That same evening, he would feel the shared emotion within Harlem. Outside the barber shop, the one he took his sons to, listening to the little crowd speaking brought a different perspective. It saddened Milo even more. This was when he understood that the level of hope in the Black community had reached the dry bed of the river, numbing it even to an event of such magnitude as this. In every crib, on every street corner, men and women compared their shock that it was possible to strike America in such a way. It sent a feeling through Milo, the same feeling as when you watch *True Crime*, and they catch the killer. Black people had felt so stranded and so helpless, for so long. Imagine how it feels to witness the ascension of a great man or woman within your community, the gratitude and hope that a leader with a powerful mind, a leader who is a great orator, can instil? To believe, yes, yes, this person here could steer us free.

Then they were murdered – Malcolm X, Martin Luther King, Fred Hampton – picked off the wall of life like cut-outs in a shooting alley. The attack on the Twin Towers proved the dollar-shaped heart could take a direct hit. America had bumped up against an enemy who kicked back. It was a thought that began ticking, in parts of the Black community. The master is not invincible. These ideas came and went, unchecked, confusing, along with grief and bewilderment; along with witnessing those who were inconsolable: mothers, fathers, sisters, brothers, husbands, wives, lovers, children, born and unborn, of the victims of 9/11.

It was such a truly fucked up world.

That night, he and Hitomi stayed up until very late. There was a hum through Harlem, like cosmic noise, just energy, echoes, every single human connected to the same thoughts. He and Hitomi sat together in their front room, until the small hours, watching a terrible film unreel, a film they were in.

****

Winter came and went. New York mourned, but got on with life. Freedom was forever dented. People were wary, more so than before, of each other, of the unknown. Milo's life was busy, his sons were growing. He was working hard, harder than ever, so was his wife. Inside the pod that was their life, they were happy. Still happy. He had applied for a Green Card. Then 9/11 happened, and all administrative procedures had been affected. Controls were tightening. He would need to be patient.

Late spring, May.

He was at home, a record turning on the deck. His ringing phone. Juliette crying. Betty had been ill, in hospital. She had got better, they said she was recovered. She was sent home.

Then Betty died, alone.

The day of her death, Milo went to his lawyer, who had a modest office in midtown Manhattan, straight out of *NYPD Blue*. He had barely finished explaining his loss to his lawyer, an old man with a tie knot he wore too low, when the lawyer's hands flew up, "Forget it. You're asking me if you can fly out of the US? Forget it. You'll have to start the process over, the complete shebang. You're looking at a five-year wait. And that's a wait outside the US, you understand? Forget it."

For a day or two, Milo made phone calls, he took notes, drew columns, underlining: one, two, three lines. Trying to find a loophole that would allow him back without the risk of not seeing his sons this side of the Atlantic for years. The truth of his situation settled, there was no way around the fortress of bureaucracy.

Betty's funeral was held in Southampton. Coaches travelled from St Paul's. In the church, people stared at Betty's photograph, so much like Maya Angelou as she aged, Maya Angelou, whom she had admired. Three-hundred mourners were from St Paul's. It was Donovan who had organised and paid for the coaches. It is a tribute to the woman, neighbour and activist Betty was, that so many people made the journey to say farewell – she hadn't lived in St Paul's for decades. She was loved, then. And remembered. Of course, her first-born son was absent. He had been robbed of his mother a second time, now by the hand of fate, come to get her when there was still so much to say. Milo feels that if Betty had lived longer, as he had grown in understanding, he might have been the one to reconcile Betty with herself and they would have helped each other upwards, to the light. He has made the journey to inner peace alone. It is a journey in her name.

How do you mourn a mother like Betty? Do you mourn the mother you had or the mother you did not have? Milo never cried over his mother's death. He thought about her. She remained. He thought about her, over time, over the following two decades. He thought about her, it was like free diving. Going down and down deeper, into stillness. It is an experience of silence, of letting thoughts leave you, emptiness come, new pictures arrive. He knows this: she was proud of him. He had read that in her eyes, along with her pain. He knows this: she was grateful that he had made it through. He had loved his mother, his mother had loved him. She remains, as a wisp of feeling, caught around his soul.

Saint George, Bristol, 2023

Milo is back in Bristol, he has a few gigs. He's staying with Juliette. It's late afternoon, a warm summer's day. A Friday. He's walking down Church Road and there's a good feeling, people are heading to the park to lie in the grass, or are off to the pub. Milo is on his way to the shops, he'll get some food in and eat with Juliette. Arsenal are playing, he might go round and watch the game with Donovan later.

There's a man coming his way, a Black man, middle-aged, like him. He looks right at Milo, smiles. They both stop. Milo has absolutely no idea who this guy is.

"Hi, you're Miles, aren't you?"

"Yeah, that's right."

"Man, I remember you. From the bomb site. You were the only one who could go right the way over on the swing."

Stray is a strikingly honest journey that takes us through the unconventional life of Milo Johnson, a music aficionado and trailblazer He was not only responsible for building the foundations of what would be labelled the Bristol Sound and laying the blueprint for the trip-hop genre, but is also one of the most original DJ/producers and style purveyors to come out of the UK sub-cultural scene of the 80s.

But this is way more than the simple examination of a musical catalyst and his innovative career. This is the story of one young boy's resilience through adversity and uncertainty.

The story starts in 1960s Bristol and takes us on a global journey encompassing London, Tokyo and New York City across decades, making clear the importance of family, in all its forms and permutations. It's a tale of the search for belonging, of loyalty, disappointment and ultimately transformation that brings acceptance and growth.

An emotionally rich testament to the qualities of focus and talent winning through when coupled with principles such as respect and curiosity… and he also has a special skill in the playground that I'll let you discover for yourselves.

Fraser Cooke, Nike Global Energy Relationship Director/DJ

As a founding member and leader of the '80s Bristol soundsystem and music collective Wild Bunch, Milo Johnson was a key figure in helping forge the stylistic and musical innovations which would give the UK its own distinct post hip-hop aesthetic and have global impact via the success of UK acts such as Massive Attack, Soul II Soul and Tricky.

Johnson's musical experimentation as a DJ and producer sowed the seeds for future hybrids such as trip-hop, whilst his stylistic innovations broadened the B-boy look from its American roots to encompass cutting-edge designer elements and Japanese influences more than a decade before the likes of Pharrell Williams and Kanye West would tread a similar path.

Like many trailblazers, a restless soul would lead Johnson onto ever-new horizons, leaving it to others instead to fully capitalise on the innovations he helped ferment.

This book charts Johnson's singular journey: taking readers through the at times harrowing familial and social hardships of Bristol in the '60s and '70s experienced as a Black child and into the sub-cultural spaces provided by fashion, football and music.

The result is a highly personal document but one that also evocatively captures significant moments in the UK's recent social and cultural history.

Tony Farsides, Senior Lecturer in Music, University of Westminster

A gritty and gripping insight into the life of a Bristol legend DJ Milo. A story of hope, vision and one that tells the timeline from dark times to brighter days. A revealing and heart-warming insight.

John Nation, Cultural Historian and Tour Guide, Bristol

*S*tray tells the remarkable life story of Miles Johnson, aka DJ Milo, original chief rocker and founder member of Bristol's mighty Wild Bunch soundsystem.

A singular talent and underground trailblazer, Milo's life experiences from childhood to manhood, and parenthood and perhaps not in that order, are told here in his own words, in vivid and unflinching detail.

Tragically echoing the lives of countless young Black men, forced through the UK's brutal care and prison systems, Johnson's story is one of survival, emerging knowledge of self, heritage and ultimately reconciliation and redemption – of both overcoming trauma and learning to love.

Having been a teenager on the Bristol party scene when Wild Bunch were at the height of their powers, with DJ Milo as their enigmatic 'main man', *Stray* completely consumed me, such is the force of this honest, unapologetic memoir of the most influential UK DJ and producer that you may well not have heard of.

Both evocative of time and place and yet transcendent in its reflective avoidance of nostalgia, Milo Johnson and Laurie Owens have crafted something of unsentimental beauty and heart-rending honesty. *Stray* is a unique and extraordinary book.

**Felix FLX Braun, Author of *Children Of The Can:
Bristol Graffiti And Street Art***

This book is a beautifully-written account of the life arc of a man who is testimony to the power of music, the ever-present curse of racism and the difficulty of living, having relationships and maintaining a sense of belonging in a world divided by inequality and power.

The motivating force of the creative spirit, friendship and music's ability to affect the soul, speak with tangible power in the life story of Miles Johnson.

**Dr Pete Webb, Senior Lecturer in Sociology,
University Of The West Of England**

INDEX

Many of the names in Stray have been changed. Changed names have not been included in the index unless the individual is essential to the narrative.

Bamboo Club 14, 19
Basset, Mr and Mrs 57-64
Bell, The 91, 93, 95, 118
Bomb site 27-28, 33-34, 38, 46-47, 73-74, 80, 113, 138, 225, 247
Bristol City FC (club and fans) 81-83, 86-88, 93-100, 106-108, 114, 117-120, 128
Bristol Rovers FC (club and fans) 81-83, 93, 95-96, 99-100, 117-120
Camden 189, 199, 202
Campbell Street 167, 197
Cherry, Neneh 176
Cotham Grammar School 43-46, 51, 54, 58-61, 64, 74, 77, 80, 85-86, 90, 109, 176
Davis, Miles 17-18
Day-Lewis, Daniel 110, 160-161
Del Naja, Robert (Delge, 3D) 144, 163, 167-170, 172, 179, 189-190, 206, 212, 226
DJ Nature 241-242
DJ's Choice 209, 220
Donovan (Betty's partner) 25-29, 32-37, 44-51, 56, 64-73, 81, 101-103, 120, 135, 138-142, 148, 157, 167-168, 173, 177, 192, 225-226, 246
Dug Out Club 145, 150, 155

Electric City, Tokyo 214
Eric (uncle) 17-22, 51-52, 73, 85
Fujiwara, Hiroshi 177-178, 188, 203, 229
Giro Brothers 187-188
Glastonbury Festival 145-146
Ham Green Hospital 170-172
Harlem High 227-228, 241
Hitomi 201-215, 219-225, 229, 238-239, 242, 245
Hooper, Nellee 114-116, 124, 139-151, 154-156, 161-163, 169-177, 185, 187-190, 198-202, 206, 212, 226
Horfield, HMP 103 123-128, 135
Horfield Probation Centre 103, 108
Humphries, Tony 218-219
Island Records 200-202
Johnson, Betty (mother). 11-31, 34-39, 44-56, 62-66, 111-112, 120, 176, 195-196, 204-205, 223-229, 245-246
Johnson, Juliette (sister) 11-21, 26, 30, 46-52, 56, 73, 111-112, 120, 170, 195, 204-206, 245, 247
K.U.D.O 203
Kensington Market 157, 159-160, 192
Kosta (Special K's) 151, 179, 190, 191-193

Kray House 52-55, 61-64, 170, 176
Lydon, John 112, 200
Mackenzie, Charlie (father) 11-15, 37, 167-168, 191
Major Force 203-204, 209
Marlow 88-90, 97-98, 110, 120, 174, 228,
Marshall, Grantley (Gee, Daddy G) 145, 147-151, 154-163, 158, 167, 172-185, 189-191, 204, 206, 226,
Massive Attack 193, 204
McFarlane, Fred 235-237
Men's Bigi 177, 213,
Moichi 188, 200-202
Mood tapes 192-193, 206
Murison, Duncan 74-75, 78-79, 81-83, 86, 90, 113, 143, 179
Mushroom 206-208
Nature Boy 217, 241
New York 161-163, 178, 201, 204, 206, 207-238, 241, 243-245
Newtrament 156-157, 177, 184-185
Nu Groove 217
Paradise Garage 90, 109-110, 116, 120, 139-140, 143-144, 157-160, 210, 217
Prince, Tony 134, 137, 192
Princess Court Club 91, 100-102
Red House jam 184
Reds, Bunny 11-14, 20
Remi, Salaam 216-217
Santa Pod Raceway 68
Scott-Heron, Gil 233
Soul II Soul 169, 199, 212
Spinner 227-229

St Paul's 14, 17-21, 28, 31, 34, 38-41, 45-47, 53, 62, 66, 73-79, 87, 99, 102, 108, 110, 125, 138, 141, 143, 147-149, 154, 160, 165-167, 174, 183, 191, 197, 203-204, 224, 231, 246
St Paul's carnival 167, 197
Stabbing, Park Street 100-101
Stabbing, Queen's Head 118-121
Stewart, Mark 155-156, 176
Swansea, HMP 131-138
Takagi Kan 203
The Look Of Love 201
Tokyo 177-179, 187-189, 201-204, 208-210, 214-215
Top Of The Pops 44, 124, 200
Toshi 178, 188, 199, 203
Tricky (Adrian Thaws) 89-90, 174, 202, 204-206, 228, 241
Trinity 114
Twin Towers 225, 242, 244
Washington D.C. 237-238
Wheat Sheaf 91, 106, 110, 115, 117, 126
Wild Bunch 150-179, 184-193, 197-206, 217, 225-228, 233-234, 241
Williams, Claude (Willie Wee) 45, 79-80, 114-116, 120, 139, 143, 156, 168-169, 172, 189-190
Wonder, Stevie 221-222
X, Malcolm 133, 143, 204, 235, 244,
Zhigge 215, 227